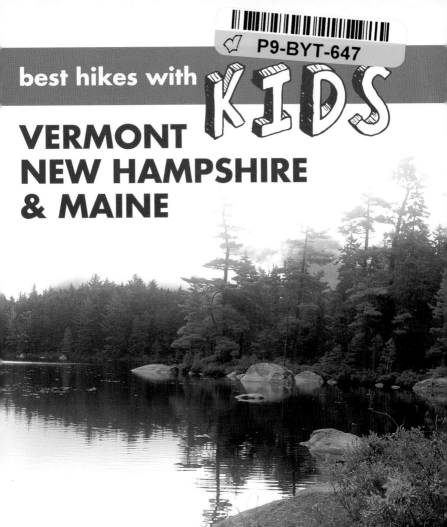

best hikes with **KIDS**

VERMONT
NEW HAMPSHIRE
& MAINE

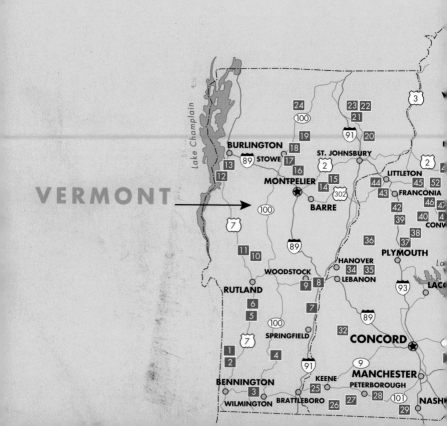

NEW
HAMPSHIRE

VERMONT

Lake Champlain

BURLINGTON
STOWE
MONTPELIER
BARRE
ST. JOHNSBURY
LITTLETON
FRANCONIA
HANOVER
LEBANON
WOODSTOCK
PLYMOUTH
RUTLAND
CONCORD
SPRINGFIELD
MANCHESTER
BENNINGTON
KEENE
PETERBOROUGH
WILMINGTON
BRATTLEBORO
NASH

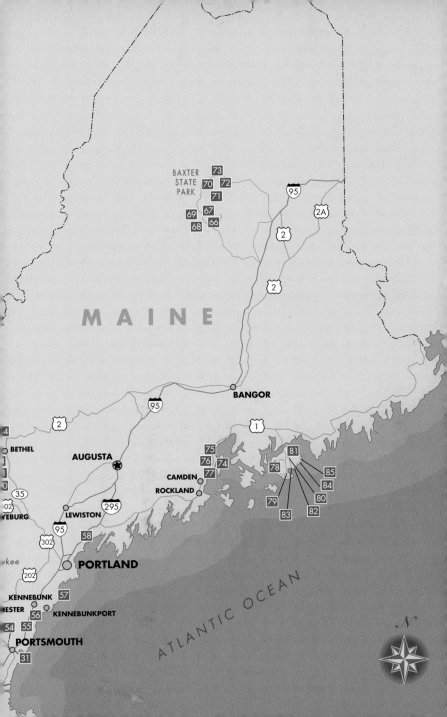

best hikes with KIDS

VERMONT
NEW HAMPSHIRE
& MAINE

**Cynthia Copeland
Thomas J. Lewis
Emily Kerr**

THE MOUNTAINEERS BOOKS

THE MOUNTAINEERS BOOKS
is the nonprofit publishing arm of The Mountaineers Club, an organization founded in 1906 and dedicated to the exploration, preservation, and enjoyment of outdoor and wilderness areas.

1001 SW Klickitat Way, Suite 201, Seattle, WA 98134

Previous edition published as *Best Hikes with Children in Vermont, New Hampshire, & Maine* by Cynthia C. Lewis and Thomas J. Lewis.

Published simultaneously in Great Britain by Cordee, 3a DeMontfort Street, Leicester, England, LE1 7HD

Manufactured in the United States of America

Project Editor: Janet Kimball
Copy editor: Heath Silberfeld/Enough Said
Cartographer: Blue Mammoth Design
Cover and Interior Design: Mayumi Thompson

All photographs are by the authors unless otherwise noted.
Cover photograph: © veer.com/royalty-free
Frontispiece: Emily Kerr

A Cataloging-in-Publication record for this book is on file at the Library of Congress

CONTENTS

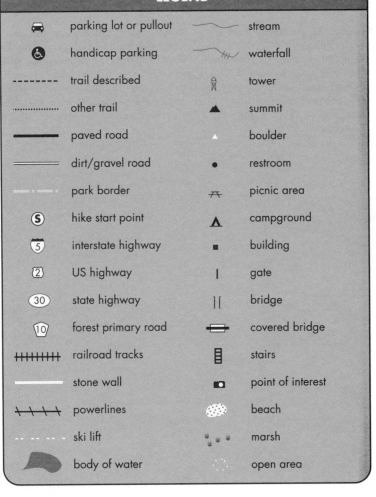

LEGEND

🚗	parking lot or pullout	stream	
♿	handicap parking	waterfall	
- - - - - - - -	trail described	🗼	tower
....	other trail	▲	summit
▬▬▬▬	paved road	△	boulder
═══════	dirt/gravel road	●	restroom
▬ ▬ ▬	park border	🧺	picnic area
Ⓢ	hike start point	◭	campground
5	interstate highway	■	building
2	US highway	I	gate
30	state highway	‖	bridge
10	forest primary road	⬌	covered bridge
++++++++	railroad tracks	🪜	stairs
▬▬▬▬	stone wall	📷	point of interest
┼┼┼┼	powerlines	⬭	beach
- - - - -	ski lift	🌾	marsh
◣	body of water	⋯	open area

ACKNOWLEDGMENTS

I would like to thank Tom for all of his support throughout this project, including help finding places to stay, and loading and unloading the car countless times. Davis and Carter, it is so much fun to explore with you—you make me proud. Thank you to all of my hiking buddies—both big and small—who checked out trails, trudged up hills, got lost, posed for pictures, and ran away from imaginary swordfish with me. And thanks to the Potters for such a memorable and special trip to Baxter State Park.

Emily Kerr

FOREWORD TO THE SECOND EDITION

We've received much positive feedback since the first edition of *Best Hikes with Children® in Vermont, New Hampshire, & Maine* was published nearly a decade ago. Girl Scout and Boy Scout leaders, youth ministers, camp counselors, and parents all have responded enthusiastically to our detailed hike descriptions aimed at keeping kids engaged as well as safe. Many times we've heard readers exclaim, "You included every one of our favorite hikes! How did you know?" We knew because in researching northern New England, we asked people who hiked with kids to reveal their special, out-of-the-way spots, as well as to remind us about the family classics like Mount Monadnock, said to be the second most-climbed mountain in the world. And we have lost count of the number of times we've passed people on the trail who were pausing to refer to our book!

We also found that although most people buy our guidebooks with the intention of hiking with children, they often refer to them when planning a hike with other adults because the very things that make the hikes appealing to children—not too long or too short, frequent points of interest, a satisfying turnaround point—also appeal to adults.

We hope that both avid and occasional hikers, with or without little people, continue to enjoy the trips we've included. As you might expect, we prefer letting our three kids lead the way. Their enthusiasm is contagious!

Cindy and Tom Lewis
October 1999

FOREWORD TO THE THIRD EDITION

When I began working on the new edition of this tried-and-true guide, everyone with whom I spoke was completely enthusiastic, commenting that anything that gets kids into the outdoors and appreciating nature is a great thing. And all were happy to provide their recommendations of great hikes. With this new edition, we've built on the favorite hikes of Cynthia Copeland and Tom Lewis and added hikes recommended by locals and others who work in the outdoors, as well as some of our own family favorites—including a number in Maine's spectacular Baxter State Park.

As in the last edition, there are tips throughout to help experienced and occasional hikers alike. This edition's new sidebars and expanded contact information are useful for anyone who wants to enjoy the gems of these three states. As always, parents, youth leaders, and camp counselors can find helpful hints on hiking with kids.

While working on this book, my children and I got to explore some of Vermont, New Hampshire, and Maine's most gorgeous and out-of-the-way places. My kids now beg me to go hiking—what a great feeling! We hope that this latest edition, with over twenty new hikes and family classics, will keep you exploring for a long time.

Emily Kerr

INTRODUCTION

You have visited a video arcade for the last time, watched your last episode of *Barney*, and taken your final ride on a loop-da-loop roller coaster. Meanwhile, the kids are boycotting art museums, flea markets, and anything that takes place on a stage and requires them to wear a necktie or dress shoes.

Is this the end of family togetherness? No, it's time to take up hiking!

Healthier than television and cheaper than downhill skiing, hiking is within everyone's capabilities and will appeal to toddlers and teenagers, preschoolers and parents. We all love the outdoors, and hiking adds an element of adventure: What will we find around the next bend? A cave? A camping shelter? A waterfall maybe?

Even though hiking with kids requires a good deal more effort than hiking without them, it's worth the extra hassle. Kids notice clouds shaped like hippopotamuses and trees that look like witches; they delight in anthills and spiderwebs. Your daughter will point out everything in the forest that is her favorite color. (She'll also point out everything in the forest that is your favorite color, her cousin's favorite color, and her best friend Rachel's favorite color.) Your son won't remark or observe—he'll squeal, he'll shout, he'll exclaim! Kids react to these adventures the way we'd all like—if only we didn't feel obligated to act so darned grown up. By taking little folks along, we're able to experience nature with renewed enthusiasm.

BUT WILL IT BE FUN?

Keep in mind the one basic rule for family hiking—it's got to be fun. Kids will expect it, and you will have to respond by gearing the trip toward their interests, needs, and capabilities. Try to envision the experience through your children's eyes and plan accordingly. If the first few trips are memorable, they'll be eager to embark on more family adventures.

Here are a few pointers for making hiking with young children enjoyable for everyone:

Bring a Little Buddy. A friend is a distraction from that blister on your kid's big toe and a deterrent to whining—nobody wants to look wimpy in front of a school chum.

Set a Realistic Pace. A child's pace varies tremendously within the course of a walk from ambling along, examining every stone, leaf, and blade of grass, to racing ahead as if the lead runner in the Boston Marathon. By letting children set their own pace (within reason), you will convey the message that a hike's success is not measured in terms of miles covered but rather in the pleasure taken in each step.

Choose an Appropriate Hike. Easier is better than harder, when in doubt, but an athletic twelve-year-old will be bored with the mile-long

ZZZZZZZZZZZZ . . .

amble through the woods that is better suited for a preschooler.

Give Compliments. Nothing means more to a child than his father or mother patting him on the back and telling him he's the best climber around. Such praise makes sore feet suddenly feel a whole lot better.

Make Frequent Stops. A trailside boulder, fallen tree, breezy peninsula. . . . Children may need more frequent rests than adults, but they tend to recover more quickly. Teach them to pace themselves; remind them as they dash out of your vehicle that it will be a long climb to the summit.

Offer Snacks. Granola bars; bananas; cheese cubes; a mixture of nuts, chocolate chips, and dried fruits; boxes of raisins—bring along any favorite that will boost energy. Bring plenty of water, too.

Play Games on the Trail. Have fun! Suggest things for children to listen and look for—frogs croaking, deer tracks, acorns, birds flying south for winter. Don't worry about making proper identifications; if you see something interesting just say, "Look!" Take turns guessing its name. Offer incentives and distractions—"We're halfway there," "The waterfall is just over the hill"—and talk about the day's goals. Have fun—laughter lightens the load.

Encourage Responsibility. Children, like the rest of us, tend to meet the level of expectation. An older child given the responsibility of following the hike on the map, keeping an eye out for a loon through the binoculars, or charting direction with the compass will proudly fulfill his duties and be less likely to engage in horseplay.

Maintain a Good Attitude. Misery is contagious, so even if you're anxious because you think it might rain or your pack has somehow doubled its weight in the last half mile, don't complain in front of your kids. A bad attitude will ruin a good time much faster than a pair of soggy sneakers.

BEST HIKES FOR SEEING A NATURAL WATERFALL

Hamilton Falls, Hike 4
Rattlesnake Point and Falls of Lana, Hike 11
Moss Glen Falls, Hike 18
Devil's Gulch, Hike 24
Walter/Newton Natural Area, Hike 37
Georgiana and Harvard Falls, Hike 39
The Basin and Lonesome Lake, Hike 42
Bridal Veil Falls, Hike 43
Zealand Pond and Zealand Falls, Hike 45

Ripley Falls, Hike 46
Arethusa Falls and Frankenstein Cliff, Hike 47
Dome Rock, Hike 49
Glen Ellis Falls, Hike 50
Step Falls Preserve, Hike 64
Little Abol Falls, Hike 66
Little and Big Niagara Falls, Hike 68
South Branch Falls, Hike 70
Howe Brook Trail, Hike 72

ENVIRONMENTAL CONCERNS

Sometimes the very qualities that make children so much fun to have along on a hike can present the most problems. Adults recognize that what our ancestors referred to as "dismal wilderness" is our most valuable and threatened resource, but to children the outdoors is a vast playground. While the seven-year-old is gleefully stripping a boulder of its moss blanket in search of worms and beetles, his younger sister is stomping among the wildflowers reciting a spontaneous ode to posies. But by springing to the defense of each cluster of ferns, parents may be concerned that they will turn what should be a relaxed family outing into a battle. How can parents creatively direct their children's enthusiasm toward nature-friendly pursuits?

Older children can anticipate the consequences of their actions on the environment. They will learn respect for the wilderness and its inhabitants from their parents' examples. By recycling, buying biodegradable products, and supporting environmental concerns, parents integrate a conservation ethic into the family's daily life so that "clean hiking" and "clean camping" come naturally to their children. Youngsters so raised understand that as hikers and campers they are becoming, for a time, part of the wilderness; they are not seeking to dominate or ruin it. Willingly, they'll "take nothing but pictures, leave nothing but footprints, and kill nothing but time." Children old enough to distinguish "safe" from potentially harmful trash can be encouraged to pick up the litter of previous hikers as well.

Younger children are more likely than older ones to act recklessly and without concern for the environment and its inhabitants. Offering desirable options rather than simply forbidding certain behavior works best with most children. Instead of picking a wildflower, your daughter can smell it, examine the petals under a magnifying glass, or take a photograph. Binoculars, as well, focus attention on soaring birds or far horizons. Such equipment retains its appeal when it is reserved just for special outings. One of the greatest gifts we can give our children is to instill in them a respect for the other living things that share our planet and an understanding of their own importance in determining the future of our natural environment.

Here are some specific ways that hikers can leave the forest without a trace (see also "Important Addresses and Phone Numbers" for additional information):

■ Prepare to take trash out with you by bringing along appropriate bags or containers.

■ Stick to the trails and, when presented with the choice of stepping on delicate vegetation or rocks, pick the rocks.

■ Trails are most vulnerable during "mud season" in March and April; be especially careful then and plan to find lowland hikes that are more suitable for early-season hiking. Additionally, if signs are posted asking you to avoid hiking on trails until a certain date, please respect them.

■ Don't wash in streams.

■ If restroom facilities are not provided, dig a small hole for human waste far from any water source and cover it with soil or pack out waste.

■ Conform to the specific regulations of the state park, wildlife refuge, or other recreational area you are visiting.

BEST HIKES FOR FOLLOWING A STREAM, BROOK, OR RIVER

Little Rock Pond, Hike 5
Quechee Gorge, Hike 8
LaPlatte River Marsh Natural
    Area, Hike 12
Moss Glen Falls, Hike 18
Chesterfield Gorge State
    Wayside, Hike 25
Beaver Brook Association,
    Hike 29
Walter/Newton Natural Area,
    Hike 37

Georgiana and Harvard Falls,
    Hike 39
The Basin and Lonesome Lake,
    Hike 42
Bridal Veil Falls, Hike 43
Vaughan Woods Memorial,
    Hike 54
Bickford Brook Slides and Blue-
    berry Mountain, Hike 61
Step Falls Preserve, Hike 64
Howe Brook Trail, Hike 72

SAFETY

While you cannot altogether eliminate the risks inherent in hiking, you can minimize them by taking proper precautions and by educating yourself and your children. You should carry the supplies necessary to combat the most frequent problems—a well-equipped first-aid kit, flashlight, map, and extra food and clothing (refer to the Ten Essentials in the "What to Take" section). Recognize your own limitations and those of your children: Don't attempt to climb a difficult trail on your first family outing. If you're hiking with very young children, you will probably wind up carrying them, or at least their packs, for some of the way, so choose a hike that is well within your own capabilities.

BEST HIKES FOR BEACH WALKING OR COAST WALKING

Odiorne Point State Park, Hike 31
Wells National Estuarine Re-
    search Reserve at Laudholm
    Farm, Hike 56
East Point Sanctuary, Hike 57

Wonderland, Hike 79
Gorham Mountain, Hike 82
Ocean Trail, Hike 83
Great Head, Hike 84
Bar Island, Hike 85

Getting Lost

Prepare for the possibility of getting lost. Leave your itinerary with a friend or relative (or at the very least leave a visible note on the dashboard of your vehicle). Carry enough extra food and clothing so that if an overnight stay is necessary, you are prepared.

Teach your kids to read maps and pay close attention to trail markers and landmarks. On most marked trails, kids should be able to see two blazes (one ahead of them and one behind them) at all times. (Most trails are marked with paint blazes on trees or rocks. Cairns—small

rock piles—indicate the route when the trail goes above the tree line.)
Kids need to know that double blazes indicate a significant change of
direction and triple blazes usually signal the end of the trail. Instruct
children to look back frequently to see what the route will look like on
the hike out.

You may want to insist on the buddy system or equip everyone with
a whistle and establish a whistle code. Encourage little children to stay
put as soon as they realize they are lost. Older children might be able
to follow a river downstream or retrace their steps looking for particular landmarks. Above all, emphasize the importance of alertness and
remaining calm. If you are unable to attempt a return to your vehicle
because you are lost or injured or both, make a fire using greens that
will smoke and signal anyone looking.

Although trail conditions and routes are described as accurately as
possible, they may be different when you embark on a given hike. Blazes
are painted over, seasonal changes such as erosion or fallen trees cause
a trail to be rerouted, bridges and boardwalks collapse. You'll want to
change your plans if the trail seems too poorly marked to follow or if the
condition of the trail is dangerous.

Bushwhacking

To veteran hikers, even wilderness trails begin to feel civilized. Often,
these adventurous souls take to bushwhacking, which is using topo-
graphical maps to locate trailless peaks or leaving the blazed trail to
make their own way through the forest. Despite the thrill of going where
no one has seemingly gone before, we don't recommend bushwhacking
for families. It's easy to get disoriented and tough to keep everyone together. You're more likely to spot wildlife if you stay on the trails because many animals follow the trails themselves. Crashing through the
underbrush is likely to scare off any animals or birds in the area. You
may also inadvertently trample delicate vegetation or disturb a nesting
site if you leave the path.

Fire Towers

Fire towers that seem dangerous are noted in the hike descriptions, but
you should inspect each one you intend to climb. Many fall quickly into
a state of disrepair, some are sold to private owners, others are in the
process of being torn down. No matter what its condition, never use a
fire tower for overnight camping.

Warm-ups

The colder the weather, the more your muscles will need stretching before the hike. Kids don't need to warm up as much as their parents, but
it won't hurt them. Stretch your calf muscles and hamstrings by leaning
forward against your vehicle or a tree and slowly lowering your heels

until they touch the ground. Hold, rest, and repeat. For your quadriceps (front of the thigh), support yourself with one hand while you grab an ankle behind you with the other and pull it toward your buttocks. Hold the position, then repeat on the other side. (You also will want to repeat these exercises to prevent cramping after your hike.)

Hypothermia

If children are particularly engrossed in what they are doing, they may ignore discomfort or an injury. Watch for signs of fatigue; encourage a rest and food stop. Hypothermia (the most common cause of death for hikers on Mount Washington) may affect a child sooner than an adult exposed to the same conditions. Most cases of hypothermia occur in relatively mild temperatures of between 30 and 50 degrees Fahrenheit, often in windy or wet conditions. If a child seems listless and cranky

An exploration is always more fun with a friend.

(early signs of hypothermia), and certainly once he or she complains of being cold, begins uncontrollable shivering, or exhibits impaired speech, add another layer of warm clothes or change the child into dry clothes, wrap him or her in a sleeping bag, and offer a warm drink or soup.

Weather
Be conscious of weather conditions and do not hesitate to rechart your course due to a potential storm. Even the least challenging trail can pose a hazard in foul weather. And some of the toughest routes—especially those in New Hampshire's White Mountains—are nearly impossible to navigate in a blizzard or severe thunderstorm. The only thing worse than getting caught in bad weather while hiking is getting caught in bad weather while hiking with your children.

The higher the elevation, the colder, windier, and wetter it is likely to be. The summit of Mount Washington in the White Mountains, battered constantly by winds of between 26 and 44 miles per hour, sits in a cloud bank more than half the time. We hiked to Washington's summit on a day when the temperatures in Boston topped a scorching 100°F. On the mountaintop, the temperature hovered around 50°F. The nearby mountains, though not as high as Washington, see similar contrasts between the conditions at their bases and those on their summits.

Ticks
The ticks that spread Lyme disease are known to inhabit much of the area covered by this guide, most notably the coastal sections. In its later stages, Lyme disease can lead to arthritis and heart and neurological problems, but if detected early it can be effectively treated with antibiotics. A red, ringlike rash at the site of the bite is the most common first symptom, often followed by a flulike fever, fatigue, a headache, and stiff, sore joints.

As important as recognizing early symptoms, however, is knowing how to prevent the disease. When hiking in places known to harbor ticks, wear light-colored clothing because the ticks are easier to see on light colors. Opt for a long-sleeved shirt with snug collar and cuffs and tuck long pants into high socks. After the hike, check yourself and your children for the tiny ticks. If you remove a tick with tweezers within 24 hours, the disease is usually not transmitted. Fortunately, not all ticks carry the disease.

Dogs
Dogs can also present a danger to your kids. Locals often use trails to exercise unleashed pets. While the kids probably won't get bitten or attacked, they may get knocked over or frightened by an unexpected encounter with a German shepherd. On trails that allow dogs, you may want to stay close to small children.

BEST HIKES FOR INVESTIGATING A POND OR LAKE

Little Rock Pond, Hike 5
Kettle Pond, Hike 14
Beaver Brook Association,
    Hike 29
Mount Sunapee and Lake
    Solitude, Hike 32
Paradise Point, Hike 35
Three Ponds Trail, Hike 36
Greeley Ponds, Hike 40

The Basin and Lonesome Lake,
    Hike 42
Zealand Pond and Zealand Falls,
    Hike 45
Glen Ellis Falls, Hike 50
Grassy Pond Loop Trail, Hike 67
Daicey Pond Nature Trail, Hike 69
South Bubble, Hike 80
Gorham Mountain, Hike 82

WHAT TO TAKE

The Mountaineers recommends ten items that should be taken on every hike, whether a day trip or an overnight trip. When children are involved and you are particularly intent on making the trip as trouble-free as possible, the following Ten Essentials may avert disaster:

1. **Navigation (map and compass).** Don't assume you'll just "feel" your way to the summit. Teach your children how to read a compass, too.
2. **Sun protection (sunglasses and sunscreen).** Look for sunglasses that screen UV rays and sunscreen with a minimum SPF rating of 15. It is especially important to protect children from the sun. Kids can get sunburned even in wintertime, and their skin will burn faster at higher altitudes.
3. **Insulation (extra clothing).** It may shower, the temperature may drop, or wading may be too tempting to pass up. Be sure to include rain gear, extra shoes and socks (especially a pair of shoes that can be used for wading when bare feet might mean sliced toes), a warm sweater, and hat and mittens.
4. **Illumination (headlamp or flashlight).** Check the batteries before you begin your hike.
5. **First-aid supplies.** Don't forget to include moleskin for blisters, baking soda to apply to stings, and any special medication your child might need for an allergy to bee stings or other insect bites.
6. **Fire (fire starter and matches/lighter).** If you must build a fire, these are indispensable.
7. **Repair kit and tools (including knife).** You never know when you might need to fix a boot, strap, or other piece of equipment. You'll be sorry if you need to and your duct tape and knife are in the drawer at home.
8. **Nutrition (extra food).** Too much food is better than not enough.
9. **Hydration (extra water).** Carry sufficient water in canteens or fanny packs in case no suitable source is available on the trail.

10. **Emergency shelter.** Chances are you won't need it, but it's a necessity if you get stuck on the trail unexpectedly.

In addition to the Ten Essentials, a few other items can come in mighty handy, especially when young children are along.

Until you've hiked or camped during blackfly season (May through mid-June), it's hard to describe how immensely annoying a swarm of these little buggers can be. Insect repellent doesn't deter them all, but it helps (be sure the repellent is appropriate for children). In addition to this protection, dress children in lightweight, long-sleeved shirts and pants. A cap may come in handy as well.

Mosquitoes flourish in low, wet areas like swamps and seem to congregate around little children who haven't perfected their swatting techniques. Repellent and head covers made of mosquito netting (with elastic to gather it at the neck or waist) may save your hike. If you're surrounded and defenseless, try tucking a fern into the back of your shirt collar and give the kids fern "flags" to use to wave away the mosquitos.

Toilet paper may come in handy; a yard or two per person is usually enough for a day hike.

Binoculars, a camera, a magnifying glass, and a bag for collecting treasures are fun to have along and might keep children from trying to push each other into a brook.

Leave your poodle, portable radio, and the kids' toys at home.

BEST HIKES FOR SWIMMING AT A SWIMMING HOLE OR PUBLIC BEACH

Hamilton Falls, Hike 4
Little Rock Pond, Hike 5
Red Rocks Park, Hike 13
Elmore Mountain and Balanced Rock, Hike 19
South Mountain Lookout Tower

Trail, Hike 30
Step Falls Preserve, Hike 64
Maiden Cliff, Hike 77
Beech Cliff and Beech Mountain, Hike 78
Great Head, Hike 84

Footgear

In selecting footwear, make comfort the No. 1 priority. You do not want to find out 2 miles from the car that Mikey's boots, which were a tad small in the store but were half price, have turned his toes purple. Buying shoes that are too small, in fact, is probably the most common mistake new hikers make. Many stores specializing in outdoor equipment have steep ramps that you can stand on to simulate a downhill hike. If your toes press against the tip of the boot when you are standing on the ramp, try a larger size. Be sure to bring the liners and socks that you plan to wear on hikes for a more accurate fit. (In most cases, the sales people in sporting goods stores are very helpful and will be able to guide you to an appropriate pair of boots.) You probably want lightweight, ankle-high leather or fabric-and-leather boots. Be sure they have sturdy soles and provide good ankle support and adequate resistance to moisture. In a few cases, sneakers or running shoes will be adequate, but on most trails, hiking boots are preferable. If you will be doing a lot of hiking, invest in a good pair that will hold up to rugged terrain. (Be sure to wear new boots at home for several days before hitting the trails.)

In winter, insulated boots are a must, and in spring or after a rainstorm, opt for waterproof boots. Snowshoes or cross-country skis also can be used for winter hikes on fairly level terrain, although we do not recommend winter hiking for children because it's not nearly as enjoyable for most kids as hiking in spring, summer, or fall.

Clothing

As with footgear, comfort is top priority for clothing. Think layers—they can be added or taken off as temperature dictates. Often, if you will be visiting a ravine or heading to a summit, factors such as wind and temperature will change noticeably. With layers, the moment you begin to feel warm you can remove an article of clothing to avoid becoming wet. In bug season, long sleeves are best, paired with long pants. Jeans, a perennial favorite among kids, aren't necessarily the most comfortable walking pants. When wet they are very heavy and cold, seem to take forever to dry, and unless well-worn can be stiff as cardboard. A better bet might be sweatpants or cotton slacks or tights. Be sure not to wear clothing that is too loose because it may snag on branches and brush.

If you'll be hiking in cool weather, consider synthetic thermal long underwear. Cotton tends to retain moisture, whereas polypropylene keeps it away from your skin. You don't want to perspire on your climb and then become chilled once you stop for a rest or head back to your vehicle.

Socks should be medium weight and wool (even in warm weather); try the rag-knit type found in most shoe or sporting goods stores. Wear a thin, silken liner under the socks. (Thick over thin will usually prevent blisters.)

A hat will help keep the sun out of your eyes and the blackflies out of your hair. And your head will be somewhat protected if a rain shower takes you by surprise.

A rain poncho with a hood that can be folded into a small pack is essential for every member of the family. Bring a windbreaker if you're heading to a breezy summit.

A few bandanna handkerchiefs are not quite as critical but may prove handy for a multitude of annoyances, such as runny noses, dirty hands and faces, cuts, and sunburned necks.

BEST HIKES FOR INVESTIGATING CAVES, BOULDERS, OR UNIQUE GEOLOGIC FEATURES

White Rocks Overlook and Ice Beds, Hike 6

Quechee Gorge, Hike 8

Elmore Mountain and Balanced Rock, Hike 19

The Basin and Lonesome Lake, Hike 42

Table Rock, Hike 65

South Bubble, Hike 80

Gorham Mountain, Hike 82

Ocean Trail, Hike 83

Packs

Older children will probably want to carry their own packs, while the little ones will want to move unencumbered. Child-size packs can be purchased at stores carrying hiking and camping supplies. Be aware, though, that small packs may quickly become *too* small. Unless you have a number of other little hikers who will be using it, you may want to just fill an adult pack with a light load. Kids like to carry their own liquids and snacks.

Adults should carry as light a load as possible since there will inevitably be times when a child needs or wants to be carried. Backpacks should have a lightweight but sturdy frame, fit comfortably, and have a waist belt to distribute the load.

Child-Related Equipment

Infants can be carried easily in front packs. We took our oldest daughter on a mountain hike when she was just three weeks old. The walking rhythm and closeness to a parent are comforting to the littlest tykes. Older babies and toddlers do well in backpacks. They enjoy gazing around from a high vantage point and are easily carried by an adult. Look for a backpack that also has a large pouch for carrying other hiking essentials. (To keep the "backpacked" toddlers amused, try filling a bottle with juice and several ice cubes—it's a drink and rattle in one!)

You can also use a carrier resembling a hip sling that will accommodate children up to four years old. Some fold into a wallet-size pouch and can be put on when your three-year-old has had enough walking for the day. Look for ideas in outdoor stores, toy stores, and stores specializing in baby furniture and supplies. Ask hiking friends what they have found useful and, whenever possible, try before you buy.

Additional Equipment for Overnight Hikes

You will need additional equipment if you plan to spend the night on the trail. Sleeping bags, foam pads, a small stove, cooking utensils, and a tent or hammocks are obviously needed. Generally, folks who work at stores stocking outdoor supplies are more than willing to help you outfit your family for an overnighter. In some cases, trailside shelters, tent platforms, or lean-tos will be available. Learn everything about the accommodations (including whether you need to reserve or rent space) before your trip.

Food

If you are staying overnight, you may want to buy freeze-dried food made especially for backpackers, although the kids might prefer more familiar nourishment. While a food's nutritional value, weight, and ease of preparation should take precedence over taste, kids—even hungry ones—may turn up their noses at something that just doesn't taste right. You can try one-pot meals, such as chili or beef stew, or try bringing foods that require no cooking at all. Cooking equipment is cumbersome, and it usually takes more time than you expect to prepare and cook a meal.

Day hikers need easy-to-carry, high-energy snack foods. Forget about three filling meals, and eat light snacks as often as you are hungry. The time of year will affect your choices: You won't want to have to peel an orange with fingers frozen by the cold—you're better off with meatballs. Nonsquishable fruit is good—try dried fruit, raisins, papaya sticks, and banana chips. Fig bars, cheese cubes, granola, and nuts are also hiking favorites. Let the kids help you mix chocolate chips, peanuts, raisins, and other "gorp" ingredients because it's cheaper than buying ready-made trail mix. A lot of kids like granola bars, store-bought or homemade. A loaf of your favorite bakery bread, a hunk of mild cheese, and some hard-boiled eggs will appeal to the kids. Let your family's taste buds and your good judgment determine what you bring.

A young hiker gets a lift along Quechee Gorge in Vermont.

Hikers need to drink frequently, and the best way to ensure a safe water supply is to bring it along. The plastic water bottles used by bicyclists are easily packed. It's never a good idea to drink water from an unknown source, even in the wilderness. If you must, use a water-filtration device, boil it for 10 minutes, or treat it with an iodine-based disinfectant to avoid giardiasis, an infection that results from drinking polluted water.

BEST HIKES TO A SUMMIT OR SCENIC VISTA (MANY WITH TOWERS)

Merck Forest and Farmland Center, Hike 1
Mount Equinox, Hike 2
Haystack Mountain, Hike 3
White Rocks Overlook and Ice Beds, Hike 6
Mount Ascutney, Hike 7
Mount Tom, Hike 9
Mount Horrid and the Great Cliff, Hike 10
Rattlesnake Point and Falls of Lana, Hike 11
Owl's Head Mountain, Hike 15
Mount Hunger, Hike 16
Stowe Pinnacle and Hogback Mountain, Hike 17
Elmore Mountain and Balanced Rock, Hike 19
Burke Mountain, Hike 20
Mount Hor, Hike 21
Mount Pisgah, Hike 22
Eagle Cliff on Wheeler Mountain, Hike 23
Little Monadnock and Rhododendron State Park, Hike 26
Mount (Grand) Monadnock, Hike 27
Pack Monadnock and Miller State Park, Hike 28
South Mountain Lookout Tower Trail, Hike 30
Mount Sunapee and Lake Solitude, Hike 32

Blue Job Mountain, Hike 33
Mount Cardigan, Hike 34
West Rattlesnake, Hike 38
Boulder Loop Trail, Hike 41
Artist Bluff, Hike 44
Arethusa Falls and Frankenstein Cliff, Hike 47
North Doublehead, Hike 48
Dome Rock, Hike 49
Imp Face, Hike 51
North Sugarloaf, Hike 52
Pine Mountain and The Ledges, Hike 53
Mount Agamenticus, Hike 55
Burnt Meadow Mountain, Hike 59
Bickford Brook Slides and Blueberry Mountain, Hike 61
East Royce Mountain, Hike 62
The Roost, Hike 63
Table Rock, Hike 65
South Branch Nature Trail, The Ledges, Hike 71
Trout Brook Mountain, Hike 73
Mount Battie, Hike 74
Ocean Lookout on Mount Megunticook, Hike 75
Bald Rock Mountain, Hike 76
Maiden Cliff, Hike 77
Beech Cliff and Beech Mountain, Hike 78
South Bubble, Hike 80
Cadillac Mountain, Hike 81
Gorham Mountain, Hike 82
Great Head, Hike 84

HIKING SEASONS

Although we indicate in each hike's information block the months when the trail is considered hikable (see the "How to Use This Book" section), you can select an optimum time by being aware of certain seasonal hazards and pleasures.

Spring is the best time of the year to visit cascades, waterfalls, or any natural area where a heavy flow of water will add more drama and interest. But watch out for river crossings in spring—August's tiny stream is often May's roaring, swollen river. Waterproof boots may be necessary because the ground is bound to be soggy. Step with care; trails are particularly susceptible to damage in spring.

Mud season is as well-known to New Englanders as hurricane season is to those in the tropics. Many of the mountain access roads are dirt, and these may be tough to navigate (or may be closed) in early and mid-spring. Trails also are easily damaged during this time of year, so try to find areas that aren't as susceptible to mud in early spring.

Because March and April snowstorms are often the fiercest of the year in northern New England, we have often recommended May as the earliest hiking month. Even during the first few weeks in May, you're best off exploring drier trails at lower elevations. The pleasant weather in the lowlands often does not reflect the harsher summit conditions.

One final springtime reminder: Be sure to bring insect repellent and wear long-sleeved shirts and long pants—blackflies and mosquitoes work overtime in May and June.

Summer is a terrific time to hike to cool ravines, breezy mountaintops, or lakeside parks with swimming or cookout facilities. It's also the best time to camp in northern New England because the evenings will not be too chilly for kids. Of course, most folks recognize this and popular spots will be crowded. Whenever possible, hike midweek and avoid holiday weekends. Weekend hikers can get an early start to beat the crowds or head for more remote locations.

New England autumns draw visitors from all over the country. This is the bona fide hiking season, offering hikers pleasant temperatures and colorful views. You'll want to find spots from which to admire the blushing hills as well as to watch the annual hawk migration, a spectacular sight and popular fall pastime.

Late autumn ushers in hunting season, so we have suggested in most cases that you hike just until October. Most children are frightened by the sound of gunshots, and hiking with crying kids is not loads of fun. If you elect to share the woods with the hunters, be sure to dress every member of your family in brightly colored clothing, including the characteristic orange hats worn by hunters. Late fall can also bring an unexpected snowstorm. As is the case in springtime, valley weather conditions do not reflect the conditions on top of the mountains.

Winterlike conditions can descend on the higher elevations (such as in the peaks in the White Mountains) even in midsummer, so be prepared with extra clothing.

Several year-round hikes are included in the hike descriptions, most of them on flat terrain at lower elevations. While some families embark on winter snowshoeing or skiing expeditions along the mountain hiking trails, these are not recommended here for any but the hardiest and most experienced families. Many access roads are closed in the wintertime (lengthening the hike considerably in some cases), and it can be difficult finding trail markers. Often, snow and ice make the route dangerous. Expect a winter trip to take at least twice as long as the time we've allotted, and remember that the daylight hours will be limited. If you do embark on a winter hike, stick to the easy, familiar trails, and follow a leader experienced in such outings.

Weather is likely to undergo abrupt and hazardous changes in winter, especially in the mountainous regions. The exposure and wind-chill factor demand that kids be dressed as warmly and covered as completely as possible.

BEST HIKES FOR VISITING A NATURE CENTER OR VISITOR CENTER

Merck Forest and Farmland
 Center, Hike 1
Odiorne Point State Park,
 Hike 31
Paradise Point, Hike 35

Wells National Estuarine
 Research Reserve at Laudholm
 Farm, Hike 56
Acadia National Park hikes,
 Hikes 74–85

HIKING WITH DOGS

It is fun to bring your canine companion along but not much fun to show up at the trailhead only to find a big "No Dogs Allowed" sign. Check beforehand to make sure dogs are permitted. As a rule, most wildlife refuges, wildlife sanctuaries, and preserves do not allow pets, nor do most beaches. You can take your dog along—on a leash, of course—on many of the trails managed by state parks and forests, but they are usually prohibited from beaches and some campgrounds on these lands. It's always best to call ahead if unsure.

Hiking with dogs requires some extra equipment. Make sure you have food, water, and first-aid supplies for your pet and yourself. Refer to a dog first-aid book to find out what you may need to be prepared for bites, stings, and injuries.

Make sure you have extra bags on hand so you can always, always, always clean up after your pet.

Keeping dogs on leash will prevent them from disturbing wildlife and from getting lost, not to mention that it is respectful to other hikers.

All dogs should be vaccinated against rabies before going on any hike. Some state parks require proof of this, so bring along a rabies vaccine certificate.

BEST LOOP HIKES

Merck Forest and Farmland Center, Hike 1
Mount Equinox, Hike 2
Mount Tom, Hike 9
Red Rocks Park, Hike 13
Kettle Pond, Hike 14
Chesterfield Gorge State Wayside, Hike 25
Pack Monadnock and Miller State Park, Hike 28
Beaver Brook Association, Hike 29
Odiorne Point State Park, Hike 31
Blue Job Mountain, Hike 33
Mount Cardigan, Hike 34
Paradise Point, Hike 35
Three Ponds Trail, Hike 36
Walter/Newton Natural Area, Hike 37
Boulder Loop Trail, Hike 41
Artist Bluff, Hike 44
Arethusa Falls and Frankenstein Cliff, Hike 47
Dome Rock, Hike 49
Imp Face, Hike 51
Vaughan Woods Memorial, Hike 54
Mount Agamenticus, Hike 55
Wells National Estuarine Research Reserve at Laudholm Farm, Hike 56
Sabattus Mountain, Hike 60
Table Rock, Hike 65
Daicey Pond Nature Trail, Hike 69
South Branch Nature Trail, The Ledges, Hike 71
Trout Brook Mountain, Hike 73
Ocean Lookout on Mount Megunticook, Hike 75
South Bubble, Hike 80
Great Head, Hike 84

How tall are the trees?

CAMPING

In the information block for each hike, an "overnight trip" symbol indicates that a designated campsite is located along a trail encompassed by that hike (or a campground is nearby).

Vandalism and overuse of the trails have led to strict regulations regarding backpack camping in all New England states. In cases where an agency or individual has been identified for you to contact for more information, refer to the "Important Addresses and Phone Numbers" section.

BEST HIKES FOR OVERNIGHT CAMPING

Merck Forest and Farmland
  Center, Hike 1
Hamilton Falls, Hike 4
Little Rock Pond, Hike 5
Mount Ascutney, Hike 7
Rattlesnake Point and Falls of
  Lana, Hike 11
Kettle Pond, Hike 14
Elmore Mountain and Balanced
  Rock, Hike 19
Burke Mountain, Hike 20
Devil's Gulch, Hike 24
South Mountain Lookout Tower
  Trail, Hike 30
Three Ponds Trail, Hike 36

The Basin and Lonesome Lake,
  Hike 42
Bridal Veil Falls, Hike 43
Zealand Pond and Zealand Falls,
  Hike 45
North Doublehead, Hike 48
Pine Mountain and The Ledges,
  Hike 53
Baxter State Park hikes,
  Hikes 66–73
Mount Battie, Hike 74
Ocean Lookout on Mount
  Megunticook, Hike 75
Bald Rock Mountain, Hike 76

Vermont

Camping on private property (and trails often cross private property) requires the landowner's permission, while camping on state or locally owned public land in Vermont is limited to those sites designated by proper authorities. Often, trailside shelters or lean-tos, toilet facilities, fireplaces, and a water source are located at these sites. Vermont's primitive-camping guidelines affect state land below the 2500-foot elevation level. For further information on primitive camping on state land, contact the Department of Forests, Parks, and Recreation.

Within the Green Mountain National Forest, campers must practice "clean" camping policies and follow strict fire safety procedures. The restrictions that apply in the national forest recreation areas are posted near these designated areas. Contact the Forest Supervisor of the Green Mountain National Forest or the Vermont Department of Forests, Parks, and Recreation for camping guidelines and information about public and private campgrounds. The reverse side of the Vermont

Official State Map and Touring Guide (available free from local information centers or from the Vermont Travel Division) also lists many of the state's campgrounds.

BEST HIKES WITH LEASHED DOGS IN VERMONT

Haystack Mountain, Hike 3
Hamilton Falls, Hike 4
White Rocks Overlook and Ice
   Beds, Hike 6
Mount Ascutney, Hike 7
Rattlesnake Point and Falls of
   Lana, Hike 11
Red Rocks Park, Hike 13

Kettle Pond, Hike 14
Owl's Head Mountain, Hike 15
Mount Hunger, Hike 16
Stowe Pinnacle and Hogback
   Mountain, Hike 17
Burke Mountain, Hike 20
Mount Hor, Hike 21
Mount Pisgah, Hike 22

(Dogs are typically not allowed on beaches or in campgrounds, even if permitted on trails. Double check regulations before you go, as they can change.)

New Hampshire

In New Hampshire, backpack camping is permitted within the White Mountain National Forest (WMNF) and in other specific locations, such as at campsites along the Appalachian Trail. Camping on private land requires the owner's permission. Campfires built in undesignated areas outside the WMNF require a permit. Camping and campfires are permitted in state parks only in the campgrounds.

The United States Forest Service (USFS) has instituted specific camping regulations for some of the more popular areas in the White Mountains National Forest. These are designated as Restricted Use Areas (RUAs) and have rules that apply within their boundaries. The RUA rules (which

Exploring the rocky shore at Odiorne Point in New Hampshire

are posted at most sites) require that campers be a certain distance (usually 200 feet to 0.25 mile) from roads, trails, streams, lakes, shelters, tent platforms, and other locations. Camping and wood or charcoal fires are not allowed above timberline (where trees are less than 8 feet tall) and in other designated areas—for a complete list, see the regulations posted on the White Mountain National Forest website or contact any of the ranger districts. Portable stoves are preferred to campfires in nearly all locations. For current rules and RUA sites (the sites change based on usage), contact any ranger district office or the USFS in Laconia.

A number of campgrounds managed by the WMNF offer limited facilities for a fee. (Details are available from WMNF offices.) Several state park campgrounds fall within the boundaries of the WMNF; for more information on these, contact the New Hampshire Division of Travel and Tourism.

BEST HIKES WITH LEASHED DOGS IN NEW HAMPSHIRE

Pack Monadnock and Miller State Park, Hike 28
Blue Job Mountain, Hike 33
West Rattlesnake, Hike 38
Georgiana and Harvard Falls, Hike 39
Greeley Ponds, Hike 40
Zealand Pond and Zealand Falls, Hike 45

Ripley Falls, Hike 46
Arethusa Falls and Frankenstein Cliff, Hike 47
Imp Face, Hike 51
North Sugarloaf, Hike 52
Pine Mountain and The Ledges, Hike 53

(Dogs are typically not allowed on beaches or in campgrounds, even if permitted on trails. Double check regulations before you go, as they can change.)

Maine

In the parts of Maine covered in this book, hikers planning to stay overnight on the trail should camp in designated areas or obtain the owner's permission if on private land. Portable stoves are preferred in Maine (as in most areas of New England) because rarely can enough dead or downed wood be found near the campsites for fuel. Fire permits are required if you're outside a designated fire area.

General "clean camping" rules apply: Set up camp well away from streams and trails; avoid clearing a site to pitch a tent; wash dishes and bathe far from ponds, springs, and other sources of water; bury human waste 6 to 8 inches underground and at least 200 feet from water sources; and carry out what you carry in.

Backpack camping is not permitted on Acadia National Park's Mount Desert Island, but it is possible to stay at the Blackwoods and Seawall campgrounds, located within the park boundaries. (Advance reservations are recommended; contact the National Park Service Reservation Center.)

BEST HIKES WITH LEASHED DOGS IN MAINE

Vaughan Woods Memorial, Hike 54

Mount Agamenticus, Hike 55

Wolfe's Neck Woods, Hike 58

Sabattus Mountain, Hike 60

Bickford Brook Slides and Blueberry Mountain, Hike 61

East Royce Mountain, Hike 62

The Roost, Hike 63

Table Rock, Hike 65

Mount Battie, Hike 74

Ocean Lookout on Mount Megunticook, Hike 75

Bald Rock Mountain, Hike 76

(Dogs are typically not allowed on beaches or in campgrounds, even if permitted on trails. Double check regulations before you go, as they can change.)

WHITE MOUNTAIN ADOPT-A-TRAIL PROGRAM

Did you ever wonder who maintains the 1200 miles of hiking trails that crisscross the White Mountains? In many cases, it's people just like you! If you and your family would like to support the efforts of the Appalachian Mountain Club (AMC) and the USFS, you might consider participating in the Adopt-A-Trail Program. (There are also other volunteer opportunities on trail crews, etc.) Trail adopters are responsible for basic maintenance tasks on a specific trail or section of trail that they choose. To find out what is involved and what trails currently need "parents," contact the following:

Trails Program Director, AMC
P.O. Box 298
Gorham, NH 03581
(603) 466-2727

HOW TO USE THIS BOOK

This, the second in a two-volume series, covers northern New England: Vermont, New Hampshire, and Maine. The guide is divided into three sections by state, with state maps that show the locations of the hikes.

Before selecting a hike, read the trip description thoroughly. You will find enough information for you to make an appropriate choice. Each hike description is divided into three general sections: a summary or history of the hike and region, driving and parking instructions, and a complete description of the hike.

A youngster enjoys the sights from a backpack.

Name. This is the name of the mountain, lake, or park as it will appear on most road maps.

Number. Use this to locate the hike on the state map.

Maps. The name of the topographic map published by the United States Geological Survey (USGS) is included for your reference (see the "Important Addresses and Phone Numbers" section). Many outdoor and office supply stores stock USGS maps, which are a good supplement to those in this guide because the contour lines indicate elevations and terrain features. Be aware, however, that trails may have changed since a map was printed (some are quite old), so don't follow any map exclusively. You can pick up maps of specific trails at many visitor or nature centers and can find them online before you go.

Current Conditions. This is the name and phone number of the agency that manages the land or maintains the trails for that hike. You can call the number listed if you have questions before you go, or for further contact information refer to the "Important Addresses and Phone Numbers" section in the back of the book.

Fees. In some cases, a fee is charged for entry or parking. These fees are generally minimal (between $1 and $5), and some, such as those for Audubon properties, do not apply to members. Be aware that fees increase, and some places that only charged in season or didn't charge at all during research for this book may have changed their policies. It's best to come prepared with some cash. Also, many places that don't charge fees will gladly accept donations or have options for membership.

Be generous—many of these areas can use all the financial assistance they can get to maintain their trails.

Over seven million people visit the WMNF in New Hampshire every year. The USFS manages the area, and, until recently, federal money covered the expenses associated with improvements, maintenance, and customer service. Cuts in the USFS budget and an increase in the number of visitors have made it necessary to impose user fees. Fees are collected through the purchase of a parking pass. All the money raised through this program stays in the WMNF and is used for repair and maintenance of trails and facilities such as shelters, wildlife habitat enhancements, resource conservation, interpretation, and signs.

You will need a parking pass in your vehicle when you leave it unattended while visiting the WMNF in a signed area. A pass is not required in areas where site-specific fees are charged, such as at national forest campgrounds. You have four pass options: an annual pass, a household pass (for households with two vehicles), a pass that is valid for one to seven consecutive days, and a daily pass. White Mountain National Forest Use Pass may be purchased from many local merchants and all USFS offices.

Type. *Day hike* means that this hike can easily be completed in a day or part of a day for most families. There is no camping shelter or cabin along the route. *Day hike or overnight* refers to trails along which lean-tos, shelters, or some other accommodations are available for an overnight stay. The overnight location is shown on the trail map. This indication does not necessarily mean that the hike is too long or difficult to be completed in an afternoon.

Difficulty. Hikes are rated for children as easy, moderate, or challenging. Ratings are approximate, taking into consideration the length of the trip, elevation gains, and trail conditions. It's best to gain experience as a family on the easier trails first. Don't reject a hike based on a difficult rating, however, before noting the turnaround point or an optional shortcut.

Season. The months listed are when the trails are hikable. In northern New England, hiking earlier or later may mean that you'll encounter icy terrain or potentially dangerous storms. See the "Hiking Seasons" section to get a better idea of appropriate hiking months.

Distance. This is the loop or round-trip hiking distance. If a side trip to a waterfall or view is included in the text and on the map, it is included in the total distance. An alternate route described within parentheses—whether it increases or decreases the total distance—is not factored into the total.

Hiking Time. Again, this is an estimate, based on length of hike, elevation gain, and trail conditions, and it will vary somewhat from family to family. Short rest stops are factored in; longer lunch stops are not.

High Point/Elevation Gain. The number given reflects the height above sea level of the highest point on the trail. Elevation gain indicates the total number of vertical feet gained during the course of the hike.

When analyzing a hike, this notation will be more significant than the high point in determining difficulty.

Getting There. These directions tell you how to get to the trailhead.

On the Trail. The route is described for your hike in; any potential difficulties you may encounter on the return trip are addressed at the end of each entry. The symbols within the text, in the margins, and on the maps indicate turnaround points, views, campsites, picnic spots, and caution points (see "Key to Symbols").

Happy hiking!

KEY TO SYMBOLS

 Day hikes. These are hikes that can be completed in a single day. There is no camping shelter along the route.

 Overnight trips. These hikes encompass a designated campsite (often with a shelter) or follow a route that leads hikers close to a campground. They are not necessarily too difficult to be completed in one day.

 Easy trails. These are relatively short, smooth, gentle trails suitable for small children or first-time hikers.

 Moderate trails. Most of these are 2 to 4 miles total distance and feature more than 500 feet of elevation gain. The trail may be rough and uneven. Hikers should wear lug-soled boots and carry the Ten Essentials (see "What to Take").

 Challenging trails. These are often rough, with considerable elevation gain or distance to travel. They are suitable for older or experienced children. Lug-soled boots and the Ten Essentials are standard equipment.

 Hikable. The best times of year to hike each trail are indicated by the following symbols: flower—spring; sun—summer; leaf—fall; snowflake—winter.

 Turnarounds. These are places, mostly along moderate trails, where families can cut their hike short yet still have a satisfying outing. Turnarounds usually offer picnic opportunities, views, or special natural attractions.

 Cautions. These mark potential hazards—cliffs, stream crossings, and the like—where close supervision of children is strongly recommended.

A NOTE ABOUT SAFETY

Safety is an important concern in all outdoor activities. No guidebook can alert you to every hazard or anticipate the limitations of every reader. Therefore, the descriptions of roads, trails, routes, and natural features in this book are not representations that a particular place or excursion will be safe for your party. When you follow any of the routes described in this book, you assume responsibility for your own safety. Under normal conditions, such excursions require the usual attention to traffic, road and trail conditions, weather, terrain, the capabilities of your party, and other factors. Keeping informed on current conditions and exercising common sense are the keys to a safe, enjoyable outing.

—The Mountaineers

Opposite: Campers find a secluded swimming hole.

MERCK FOREST AND FARMLAND CENTER

BEFORE YOU GO
Map USGS Pawlet
Current Conditions Merck
Forest and Farmland Center
(802) 394-7836
**No fees for day use;
moderate fee for camping;
donations welcome**

ABOUT THE HIKE
Day hike or overnight with
permit for tent site or cabin
Easy to moderate for children
April–October
**2.1 miles, loop
Hiking time** 1.5 hours
High point/elevation gain
2100 feet, 300 feet

GETTING THERE
- From the junction of VT-30 and VT-315 in East Rupert, travel west on VT-315.
- In 3.0 miles, look for a sign for the Merck Forest and Farmland Center on your left.
- Follow this dirt road to the parking area near the visitor center.

ON THE TRAIL
The animals you see on this hike may not qualify as wildlife, but your kids will enjoy seeing the animals on the farm all the same. The Merck Forest and Farmland Center is a community-supported education organization maintained for the purposes of conservation and learning. Nestled in a picturesque Vermont setting and home to a working farm and sugar house, 28 miles of hiking and cross-country ski trails are available for exploration on the center's 3300 acres. The trail described here takes you up to a viewpoint, but many other hiking trails suit different interests and abilities. Cabins, shelters, and tent sites are available for overnight stays; call or write to get a permit before you go.

Stop by the visitor center to grab a map before you start. To begin, turn left out of the visitor center onto Old Town Road. Follow the road a short distance to the sugarhouse on your right. This houses the second-largest evaporator in the state, and if you visit during maple sugaring season (usually in March), you may get to see the boiling process. Past the sugarhouse, continue straight (now on Stonelot Road) to the barn and livestock. Here you can see poultry, pigs, horses, and sheep, many of them different or rare breeds. When your children are done oinking, baa-ing, and neighing—all quietly, of course, so as not to bother the animals—retrace your steps down Stonelot Road to the junction with Old Town Road. Turn left onto Old Town Road, following the sign pointing to the trails and cabins.

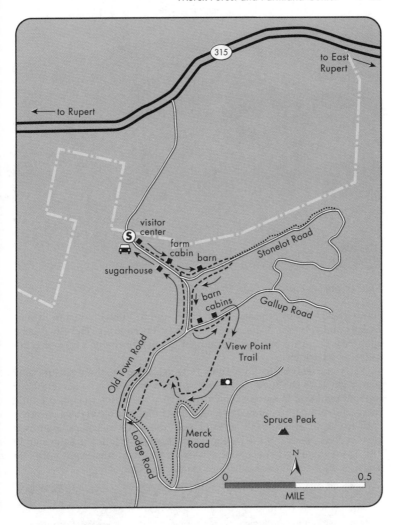

When you reach your next junction, turn left onto Gallup Road toward Spruce Peak. A little over a half mile from your start, you will pass the barn cabins on your left. Shortly beyond the cabins, turn right onto a trail following the sign to the View Point. The trail climbs steadily and steeply through the woods for the next half mile with significant elevation gain. (Younger children will need some encouragement—if they are not up to the challenge, you can always stay on Old Town Road or Stonelot Road to do some wandering and exploring.) After a steady

View of the animals and the farm

climb, reach a trail junction. Follow the sign to View Point (not Spruce Lodge) and in a short distance come to a flat clearing. Here is a good spot for a picnic or snack with views of the mountainous Vermont landscape as a backdrop.

For your descent, look for signs to Lodge Road. At the next junction, turn right onto the View Point Trail while a wide path heads left. Your narrow trail winds steeply down through pine woods and in 0.1 mile turns sharply left to follow the side of the hill. Look for arrows marking trail turns. In another 0.2 mile the trail descends to Lodge Road by a clearing with peaks in the background. Head right following the sign to Old Town Road and the visitor center. In 0.1 mile, turn right onto Old Town Road and follow this 0.7 mile to the start.

MAPLE SYRUP

If you visit at the right time, you may get to witness the process of maple syrup making or "sugaring." In Vermont—the largest producer of maple syrup in the United States—this usually occurs during the beginning of March and lasts four to six weeks. In spring, maple sap contains a small amount of sucrose. The sap is collected from sugar maple trees and boiled down to evaporate the water. It takes approximately forty gallons of sap to create just one gallon of maple syrup. No wonder it's called "liquid gold"!

2 MOUNT EQUINOX

BEFORE YOU GO
Map USGS Manchester
Current Conditions Mount Equinox, the Mountain (802) 362-1114 or (802) 362-1115
Moderate fee

ABOUT THE HIKE
Day hike
Easy for children
May–October
1.2 miles, loop
Hiking time 1 hour
High point/elevation gain 3816 feet, 250 feet
Road to top, picnic areas

GETTING THERE

- From US 7, take exit 3 (Historic VT-7A) to VT-313 West, following signs to Manchester Center and Arlington.

- In 1.9 miles, turn right onto VT-7A North and VT-313 West.
- In 1.4 miles, continue straight on VT-7A as VT-313 turns left.
- At 7.6 miles from the first VT-7A/VT-313 junction, turn left onto Sky Line Drive.
- At the entrance gate, pay a moderate per-car fee and drive 5 miles up the mountain, passing several picnic and parking areas, a monastery, and Little Equinox with its characteristic wind turbines.
- Park in the lot near the Sky Line Inn.

ON THE TRAIL

Think of Mount Equinox as a three-part package: the thrilling (if somewhat hairy) vehicle ride up Sky Line Drive to the highest spot in the Taconic Range; the sensational 360-degree views from the mountaintop; and the foot trail that circles the summit through dense woods. The trail suffers from overuse in some places and neglect in others, but that does not detract from this top-of-the-world experience.

Developed by the late Dr. Joseph C. Davidson, the area has a distinctive character that sets it apart from other mountain trails (for instance, a memorial to Davidson's dog, Mr. Barbo, embellishes the Lookout Rock Trail). This is a terrific choice for a family seeking superb views without a demanding climb. Time your hike so you will return to the parking lot to watch the sun set into the layers of bluish gray mountains.

From the parking area, enjoy the commanding views of Vermont's Green Mountains, New York's Adirondacks, the Berkshires of Massachusetts, New Hampshire's White Mountain Range, and, yes, Canada's Mount Royal! From the Sky Line Inn, walk to the back of the building and drop down a set of stairs to a gravel path. Heading eastward on the Lookout Rock Trail, pass the base of the transmission tower, listening for the deep, resonating hum of the vibrating, windblown tower.

After the Burr and Burton Trail joins from the right in less than 0.1 mile, drop through a tunnel of spruce and hemlock trees along the rocky, eroded path. Though the sheltered trail offers limited views, your other senses will take over. Hear the ceaseless wind howling across the mountaintop, run your fingers over the lush mosses that border the trail, smell Christmas in the evergreens.

The Beartown Trail splits left (north) as you continue straight, reaching Lookout Rock at 0.4 mile. This protected ledge overlooks the Manchester Valley from an altitude of 3700 feet and provides superb views of Mount Ascutney (Hike 7), Mount Monadnock (Hike 27), and the White Mountains. Retrace your steps for 50 feet to a tight Y-intersection that was not evident on the hike in. Here, bear left onto the Yellow Trail (blazed sporadically) and parallel the Lookout Rock Trail for 0.1 mile before curving left to scalp the upper edge of Equinox's eastern ridge.

Dense spruce groves crowd the level trail. Although your distant views are limited once again, look nearby for neon-green mosses and

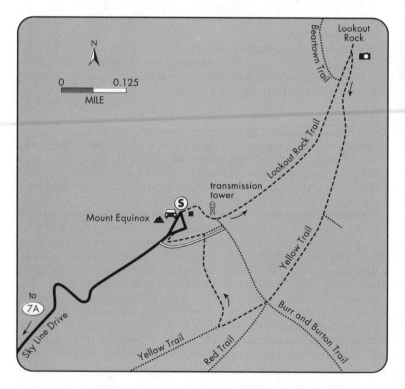

Grand view from atop Mount Equinox

tiny spruce trees straining for sunlight. Shortly, an indistinct side trail splits left as you continue straight (southwest). At 0.5 mile from Lookout Rock, bear right to follow the Yellow Trail as the Red Trail goes straight and the Burr and Burton Trail heads sharply left and right. As you continue to wind below the summit, the path drops gently, still crowded by thickets of spruce.

Shortly beyond the intersection, turn right (north) onto an unmarked trail following a weary sign pointing to the summit. The trail, climbing moderately through more open woods, is not well traveled and you will be forced to push aside encroaching branches and brush. In 0.1 mile, the trail opens onto a woods road. Turn left (west) onto the road and in 0.1 mile, you'll reach Sky Line Drive. A right turn brings you back to the Sky Line Inn parking lot. (The drive down the mountain is even more spectacular than the drive up!)

Note: Sky Line Drive, a toll road, is open from May 1 to November 1 from 8:00 AM to 10:00 PM.

HAYSTACK MOUNTAIN

BEFORE YOU GO
Map USGS Mount Snow
Current Conditions Green
Mountain National Forest,
Manchester Ranger Station
(802) 362-2307 or Main
Office (802) 747-6700

ABOUT THE HIKE
Day hike
Moderate for children
May–October
4 miles, round trip
Hiking time 3.5 hours
High point/elevation gain
3462 feet, 1050 feet

GETTING THERE

- From the junction of VT-9 and VT-100 in Wilmington, travel west on VT-9.
- In 1.1 miles, turn right onto Haystack Road (at a sign for Chimney Hill).
- In another 0.2 mile, turn left onto Chimney Hill Road, following the sign to the clubhouse.
- In 0.2 mile, turn right onto gravel Binney Brook Road.
- Drive 0.8 mile, and turn right onto Upper Dam Road.
- Turn left at an intersection in 0.1 mile, still on Upper Dam Road.
- In another 0.1 mile (2.5 miles from VT-9), look for the Haystack Mountain Trail on the right side of the road.
- Park along the shoulder.

ON THE TRAIL

Attention nervous parents! We've found the perfect mountaintop for you! Haystack's partially treed, conical summit rewards you with the great views you've earned after a 2-mile climb while giving the kids what they want for their efforts: a safe place to explore and roam, romp, and cavort. The climb is steady, but within the abilities of most kids, who will enjoy the walk through pretty forests and alongside babbling creeks. If you've been looking for a worry-free mountain to climb with your own "Dennis the Menace" or with a group of curious little tykes, read on!

Haystack Mountain Trail is a multi-use route, blazed with blue-diamond cross-country ski markers. The washed-out jeep road rises gently, soon reaching a Green Mountain National Forest sign. At 0.1 mile, the trail heading northward passes a metal gate. Amid hemlock and spruce trees, the trail dips into a depression. Who can find something that is perfectly straight?

At 0.25 mile from the start, water spills through a ravine to the left of

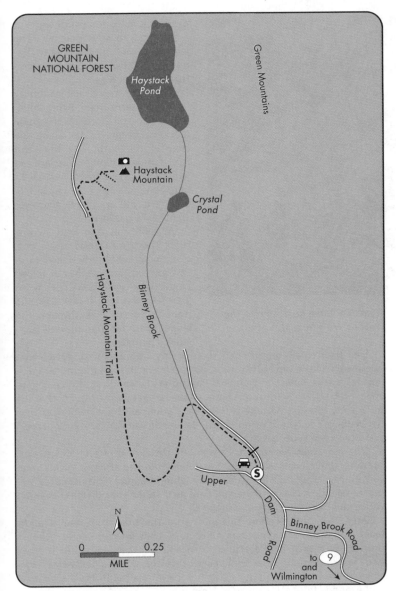

the trail. Tossing twigs and leaves into the hurrying Binney Brook, the kids can experience white-water rafting from a giant's perspective. Cross Binney Brook just under the 0.5-mile mark, following the Haystack Mountain

A garter snake darts across the trail on Haystack Mountain.

Trail as it splits left (southwest) at a sign and an orange arrow. (The jeep road continues straight.) Immediately cross another branch of the brook over logs.

The wide trail drops gradually on soggy terrain following blue-diamond and orange-rectangle markers. Ferns cluster along the edge of the path. The kids can take turns thinking of an animal while the others take guesses. To help the guessers, give clues, like "I have a tail" or "I have poor eyesight" or "I can swim."

At 0.65 mile, the trail sweeps right (northwest) and dries out, climbing gradually, then moderately. Can you find patches of moss? Under what conditions does moss grow? As the trail levels, 0.8 mile from the start, look through the sparse trees for a glimpse of Haystack's pinnacle.

The trail crests on an open shoulder at 1.2 miles with good views northward to the top of Haystack. As you track on level ground through spruce groves, have the youngest child find the smallest spruce tree in the forest. Can the oldest one point to the largest spruce? In another 0.1 mile, soft, wet ground makes for mucky going as the wide path climbs between rock ledges. Play follow-the-leader as you hop from rock to rock, trying to keep your feet dry.

The Haystack Mountain Trail winds through pretty spruce woods, turning right (east) at a sign 1.4 miles from the start; a woods road continues straight. Still guided by blue-diamond cross-country ski markers, follow the gently rising trail as it snakes beside moss-covered rocks and under evergreen canopies.

At a trail intersection 1.6 miles into the hike, continue straight (east) following the blue diamonds as a trail diverges right. Almost immediately, turn left (north) at a second intersection, while another path heads straight. This trail veers eastward, met suddenly by a tree-covered granite outcropping. From here, a number of footpaths wind up and around Haystack's cloistered summit.

For maximum views with minimal effort, turn left and scramble up a rock that affords excellent western views. Work your way southeast toward the open ledges at the height of the summit for superb views to the east, northeast, and southeast. Look for Haystack Pond, Mount Snow, Mount Ascutney (Hike 7) to the north, and Mount Monadnock (Hike 27) on the distant eastern horizon. On a sunny day, tell the kids to touch various objects and compare the surface temperatures. Does a rock feel as warm as a pinecone? Is the top of your head as warm as your backpack? What do you think affects the amount of warmth an object retains?

Let the kids explore freely, playing hide-and-seek among the "Christmas trees," scaling rock outcrops, and peering into crevices and caves. Return the way you came.

 HAMILTON FALLS

BEFORE YOU GO
Map USGS Londonderry
Current Conditions Jamaica State Park (802) 874-4600
Small fee in season

ABOUT THE HIKE
Day hike or overnight
Moderate for children
May–October
6.2 miles, round trip
Hiking time 5 hours
High point/elevation gain
1610 feet, 1050 feet
Accessible restroom in season; West River Rail Trail fully accessible

GETTING THERE
- From VT-30 in Jamaica, turn north onto Depot Street.
- In 0.5 mile, enter the park and pay a small day-use fee.
- Drive 0.1 mile to a parking area on the left above the West River.

ON THE TRAIL
Hamilton Falls lies within Jamaica State Park, an area with as much fascinating history as natural beauty. Because the West River helped to link the Connecticut River and Lake Champlain, it was a significant transportation route for Native Americans. Archaeologists have determined that prehistoric Native American activity centered along the riverbanks for more than 8000 years. When European settlers arrived, they farmed the riverside land and logged the surrounding forests, using the swift-running water to power their sawmills. In the late 1800s, the West River Railroad snaked beside the river, connecting South Londonderry and Brattleboro. Dubbed "36 miles of trouble," the railway was plagued by floods, storms, and other hardships. Today, hikers follow this old railroad bed for much of the way to Hamilton Falls.

If you visit in spring, you'll see Hamilton Falls at its most explosive time of year. Summertime hikers will be able to end the walk with a swim at Salmon Hole, a beach area just west of the parking lot.

At the northern side of the parking area, a sign announces the Railroad Bed Trail, Overlook Trail, Ball Mountain Dam, and Hamilton Falls. The Railroad Bed Trail winds on level terrain along a wide dirt road (the roadbed of the former West River Railroad), sandwiched between the West River and a campground. Soon, the path curls eastward, running about 20 feet above the splashing river.

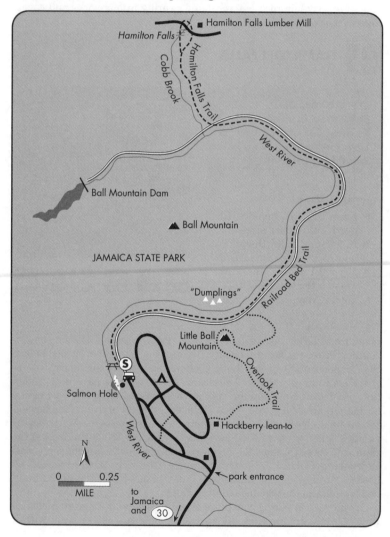

Climbing near the potholes midway up Hamilton Falls

Urge the kids to watch for the huge, rounded glacial erratics rising out of the river that mark the 0.6-mile point. Take turns guessing the name of these boulders ("Dumplings"). Shortly beyond the Dumplings, the Overlook Trail diverges right (east) on blue blazes. (Do not take the Overlook Trail now, but you may want to alter your return route to include this path because it offers lovely views of the West River Valley.) As you continue, trailside benches provide welcome rest stops at river overlooks. If the kids can sit still long enough, they may see a grouse, beaver, or deer.

The trail strays northward, then curls northwestward where a stream joins the river from the right. Depart the Railroad Bed Trail 2.4 miles from the start and turn right (north) onto Hamilton Falls Trail, an old switch road marked in turquoise that leads to the falls. This trail climbs briskly and veers left toward (though up to 125 feet above) Cobb Brook. In 0.6 mile, follow a steep footpath that splits left at a sign for Lower Falls, dropping quickly to the base of the falls.

The dramatic falls are nestled between high ridges with water spilling more than 100 feet in two tiers and crashing onto a smooth, granite base. At the bottom are two pools, the shallow upper pool being the more suitable for exploration by young hikers. (Warn kids that these rocks can be slippery.) Do you think that Native American children played in these pools hundreds of years ago?

If you would like to visit the top of the falls, return to the Hamilton Falls Trail and turn left, following the switch road to its conclusion in 0.1 mile, where you will turn left onto a dirt road. Just past the Hamilton Falls Lumber Mill, turn left onto a trail that leads to the top of the waterfall. Keep the children close as you watch the water cascading 125 feet to the potholes below.

DO NOT climb on any part of the exposed ledges around the falls. It is extremely dangerous, and many have suffered severe injury or even death from doing so.

Return to your vehicle as you came. (If you detour along the Overlook Trail, add 0.3 mile to the total distance.)

5 LITTLE ROCK POND

BEFORE YOU GO
Maps USGS Danby and Wallingford
Current Conditions Green Mountain National Forest, Manchester Ranger District (802) 362-2307 or Green Mountain Club (802) 244-7037
Small fee for camping only

ABOUT THE HIKE
Day hike or overnight
Easy to moderate for children
May–October
4 miles, round trip
High point/elevation gain
1865 feet, 350 feet

GETTING THERE

■ From US 7 in Danby, head east on Brooklyn Road, which becomes Forest Road 10.
■ Drive 3.2 miles to the AT/LT crossing.
■ Park in the lot on the south (right) side of the road.

ON THE TRAIL

You are never far from water on this section of the Appalachian/Long Trail (AT/LT). The trail travels alongside and over Little Black Brook before depositing you on the shores of picturesque Little Rock Pond. Here you can swim, fish, camp, or just take in the scenery. If you want to camp, arrive early—the tent platforms and shelters are on a first-come,

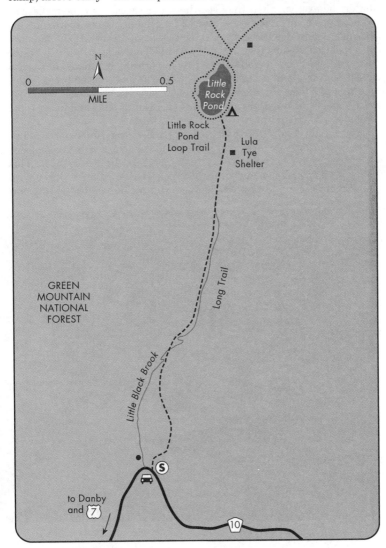

first-served basis. The trail has relatively little incline, so even younger children will enjoy this hike. Just be sure to have sturdy footwear as the trail is rocky in places, and remember to use caution on the stream crossings.

To begin, follow the white blazes of the AT/LT north. Right off the bat, you will be hiking beside Little Black Brook. The kids will immediately be excited when they see the water cascading over rocks. The trail climbs a set of log steps and follows the brook for approximately 0.2 mile before departing from the brook for a stretch. If the kids are disappointed, assure them that it won't be long before they are beside the water once again. You will be traveling through a mixed hardwood forest, and in about a half mile you will hear and see the brook below you as you follow the edge of a ravine. Soon, you will cross the brook over a steel I-beam, dropping down to the water's edge and putting the brook on your right.

Have your children look for little cascading waterfalls as the water courses over moss-covered rocks. As you make your gentle ascent, keep your eyes peeled for a double-white blaze before the 1-mile mark. This indicates a right-hand turn over the brook. Help younger children with the stream crossing—this one is done over rocks. The brook will now

Playing a game on the trail

be close on your left for a long stretch. The trail becomes rockier and requires a little more maneuvering for small feet. The last half of the trail also has a number of footbridges to cross over—these are always fun for kids. Need some distraction? Have the little ones practice their balancing skills by hopping across on one foot or walking on one side of the bridge while pretending they are on a balance beam.

The trail departs the water before reaching a sign at 1.7 miles for the Lula Tye Shelter. Look to your right and you can see the shelter above you. Continue straight another 0.3 mile to Little Rock Pond. If you want to add on to your hike, you can follow the Little Rock Pond Loop around the pond. Otherwise, relax and enjoy before heading back the way you came. If camping, pay your fee to the Green Mountain Club caretaker and claim your spot in the shelter or on one of the platforms on the eastern edge of the pond. Remember to stay on designated trails and to practice Leave No Trace ethics to help protect the fragile environment around the pond.

THE LONG TRAIL

You may be familiar with the Appalachian Trail, but did you know that the Long Trail is the oldest long-distance hiking trail in the United States? In fact, this 272-mile trail (with many more miles of side trails) inspired the creation of the Appalachian Trail. To learn more, or to help protect the Long Trail, contact the Green Mountain Club, whose members began building the Long Trail in 1910 and maintain it to this day.

6 WHITE ROCKS OVERLOOK AND ICE BEDS

BEFORE YOU GO
Map USGS Wallingford
Current Conditions Green Mountain National Forest, Manchester Ranger Station (802) 362-2307 or Main Office (802) 747-6700

ABOUT THE HIKE
Day hike
Easy for children
May–October
2 miles, round trip
Hiking time 1.5 hours
High point/elevation gain
1280 feet, 450 feet

GETTING THERE
- From the junction of US 7 and VT-140 in Wallingford, head east on VT-140.
- Drive 2.1 miles and turn right onto gravel Sugar Hill Road.

- In 0.1 mile, at a sign for Green Mountain National Forest Picnic Area, White Rocks, turn right.
- Drive 0.5 mile to the substantial parking area at the end of the road.

ON THE TRAIL

In junior high school, no one wants to take earth science. Students spend dull hours studying charts of Earth's layers and scratching one rock against another to see which is harder. It's too bad they don't know about White Rocks Overlook and the Ice Beds. They might have a greater appreciation for lessons on the Ice Age and the movement of glaciers and the variety of rocks and how all that affects today's landscape. You can make this your own exciting "field trip."

As you hike along the White Rocks/Ice Beds Trail, you'll pass two overlooks with spectacular views of the cone-shaped slides of White Rocks. Dramatic rivers of boulders tumble down the steep slope. Follow the Ice Beds Trail from the vistas to the valley floor where you can feel the cold air from the ice deep under the rock at the base of one boulder slide. Although parents must protect young children at the precipitous overlooks, this hike is highly recommended for preschoolers, preteens, and in-betweens. (And earth science class will never seem quite so dull again!)

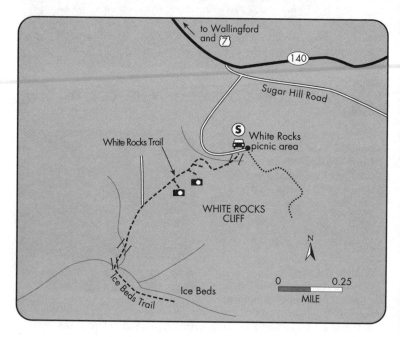

The White Rocks/Ice Beds Trail leads from the southwestern side of the parking area on blue blazes and quickly crosses two streams on footbridges. From here, the first White Rocks overlook is 0.25 mile away and the Ice Beds are 0.75 mile beyond the overlook. The trail snakes along a ridge under a hemlock canopy and past ledge outcroppings, climbing a stiff grade on stone steps. Although hemlock trees grow slowly, they often become very large. Have the kids hug some of the trailside hemlocks. Do their arms reach all the way around?

Five switchbacks in quick succession lead to the top of the ridge and an intersection. For now, disregard the Ice Beds Trail that turns right (west) and bear left, quickly reaching an overlook. Enjoy the tremendous view of White Rocks (elevation 2662 feet) and the two boulder slides that funnel down this sharp peak. Be sure to keep the kids well back from the edge.

Return to the intersection and proceed straight along the Ice Beds Trail. Climb moderately through more hemlocks, approaching the top of a ridge. Swing behind the tallest ledge outcropping. As the trail begins a descent, 0.4 mile from the start, bear left onto a side trail to reach another exposed ledge overlook with similar outstanding views of White Rocks.

Do the rock slides seem to be close by? Put the distance in perspective by watching the tiny climbers scaling the boulders. Pass around the binoculars so that the kids can watch these daring folks up close. Spread out your picnic lunch and drink in the view. If you want to keep younger children away from the edge while you're enjoying your sandwich, bring along a magnifying glass. Ask the kids to sit in one spot and study the ground right in front of them. How many different colors can they spot through the magnifying glass? Can they detect any movement, or is everything still?

Return to the Ice Beds Trail and turn left, dropping quickly down a wooded slope with occasional stone steps to assist you. Are these hemlocks larger than the ones you hugged at the start of the hike? Put your arms around them and see! The grade lessens at 0.55 mile; soon, a woods road joins from the right and the trail follows it southward. As you wind along the valley floor, cross a stream over railroad ties and follow the narrowing path as it twists eastward to cross another stream over a plank.

You'll reach the Ice Beds at the base of the largest rock slide 1 mile from the start. According to a USFS sign, a shattering of Cheshire quartzite rock during the Ice Age probably created the rock slide. Ice and snow that accumulate within the rock crevices during the colder months are preserved throughout the year in this shaded canyon. Straddle the small stream on a hot day and feel the blast of cold air coming off the mountain. Melting ice feeds the stream, maintaining a water temperature of 40°F throughout the summer months. (Big folks will be impressed, too!) Return the way you came.

7 MOUNT ASCUTNEY

BEFORE YOU GO
Map USGS Mount Ascutney
Current Conditions
Ascutney State Park (802)
674-2060
Fee at main park entrance

ABOUT THE HIKE
Day hike or overnight
Challenging for children
May–October
5.6 miles, round trip
Hiking time 5.5 hours
High point/elevation gain
3144 feet; 2600 feet

GETTING THERE

- From I-91 in Ascutney, take exit 8 to US 5, VT-12, and VT-131.

- Follow signs to US 5 North and, in 0.3 mile, turn left onto US 5 North and VT-12 North heading toward Windsor. (Signs indicate that the Mount Ascutney Ski Area is 7 miles away.)
- In 1.1 miles, turn left to head north on VT-44A toward Browns-ville, following a sign to Ascutney State Park.
- At 2.7 miles from US 5, watch for the sign on the right for the Windsor Trail Parking Lot.
- Turn left onto a gravel drive and park in the grassy lot at the bottom of a field.

ON THE TRAIL

It's long, it's tough, it's complicated. But the hike to the Ascutney summit is worth it. In fact, with all the intriguing distractions, the kids will probably notice neither the length of this route nor the steady climb. Numerous stream crossings near miniature waterfalls, water slides, and pools highlight the initial mile, while a series of overlooks with terrific local views characterizes the next mile or so. The frequent trail junctions allow kids to hone their map- and compass-reading skills. A trailside lean-to shelters overnight campers, and the summit lookout tower invites all to survey the landscape from a giant's perspective. An added bonus: Unlike most mountain climbs, as you gain elevation, the slope eases. Your legs will appreciate that!

The Windsor Trail initially follows a farmer's road, heading southward and skirting the left-hand side of a pasture. The road bends right (southwest) shortly, still following the edge of the field, and then veers left into the woods following white blazes. Winding under tall white pines, the road is softened by a carpet of needles. Can you walk without making a sound?

In 0.2 mile, the road rises gently along the northern rim of a deep

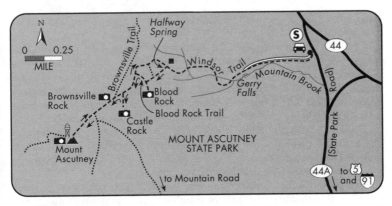

gorge that cradles Mountain Brook. The marked turns are sharp and frequent—let the kids lead the way. As the pine trees surrender to deciduous ones, the pitch gradually steepens so that it is climbing briskly just under the 0.5-mile mark. Here, loose stones underfoot make walking laborious for the little guys.

At 0.7 mile from the start, the trail approaches Mountain Brook, which now rushes through a broad, shallow gulch. Look left to see the miniature twin waterfalls known as Gerry Falls. Between the falls, the water glides over smooth rocks into a peaceful pool.

Here the woods road dissolves into a wide, rocky path. At 0.8 mile, as the brook splits into two branches, the trail crosses the right branch on a moderate ascent. You'll be treading on a ledge now as the path winds between the two streams that are gradually spreading apart. Hugging the left branch, the trail passes another small water slide.

The trail suddenly twists right (northwest) and angles toward the right-hand stream. If it's time for a rest, instruct the children to pick a spot and sit very still for at least five minutes. Tell them to blend in with their natural surroundings as much as possible so that the forest creatures will begin to accept them as part of the environment. Soon, you may see birds landing nearby, squirrels scampering within a few feet of you, or rabbits hopping curiously in your direction.

Just more than 1 mile from the start, the trail reaches the brook's right branch near a pretty water slide that empties into a pool. Cross the brook on stones. Who took the fewest steps? In another 0.2 mile, the trail sweeps left and recrosses the stream. Soon it contemplates another crossing of the left branch but swings right (north) before reaching the bank.

At 1.25 miles, the trail has tracked far away from the brook. What types of plants does this damp soil nourish? (Look for sugar maple, white ash, yellow birch, and beech trees, as well as varieties of mosses and ferns.) The trail narrows and the grade eases as you crest a shoulder. Play a survival game: If you had to live in these woods for a long time, where would you build a shelter? What would you use to build it? What would you eat?

The stiff ascent resumes in a damp area littered with rock outcroppings. At 1.4 miles from the start, the trail divides at a spot known as Halfway Spring; the Windsor Trail to the Blood Rock Trail turns left, and another branch of this trail leads right to a log shelter and running spring. Follow the left path that proceeds southward up a formidable climb. At 1.6 miles, the Windsor Trail meets the blue-blazed Blood Rock Trail.

Bear left onto the Blood Rock Trail as the Windsor Trail departs right. Snake through an evergreen tunnel toward Blood Rock. Soon, a side trail on the left leads, in 250 feet, to the sloping ledge with dramatic views that stretch well into New Hampshire.

Return to the Blood Rock Trail and turn left. This path sweeps right (west) and ends abruptly, 2 miles from the start, as it again meets the white-blazed Windsor Trail. Turn left (southwest). In 0.3 mile, turn left onto the Castle Rock spur (marked in blue) and cut through an area crowded with massive rocks and ledges. Soon, you'll emerge at Castle Rock, a dramatic overlook with eastern views stretching across the Connecticut River Valley. While the older folks rest and enjoy the vistas, let the kids climb and explore (with some supervision) on the rock outcrops farther inland.

Let the kids know that the climbing is over as you return to the Windsor Trail and turn left. The path meanders over wet areas on half-log bridges and arrives, 0.1 mile from Castle Rock, at a junction with the Brownsville Trail. Continue straight (southwest) on the Windsor Trail, crossing more footbridges, and in another 0.1 mile turn right onto the side trail that leads quickly to the Brownsville Rock overlook. Enjoy stunning views over the central and northern Green Mountains. Point out the Killington peaks and Pico Peak to the north and Okemo Ski Area to the west.

Return once more to the Windsor Trail and turn right, dropping into a wet sag with more half-log bridges spanning the soggiest terrain. Avoid a left-going trail that leads to the summit parking area and, 0.3 mile from Brownsville Rock (and 2.8 miles from the start), you'll arrive at the summit.

Here, stunted spruce, birch, and fir trees have adapted to the brutal conditions and cluster around you, limiting the ground views. Climb the tower for spectacular 360-degree panoramas to the Adirondack Mountains of New York, New Hampshire's Presidential Mountains, and even Mount Monadnock (Hike 27), 60 miles away to the southeast.

To complete the hike, retrace your steps to your vehicle.

If you'd like to camp along the trail, return to the junction of the Windsor and Blood Rock Trails and turn left, continuing on the Windsor Trail. Following signs for Log Shelter, hike another 0.3 mile to the lean-to, nestled within a gorge near a brook and a bubbling spring. The rather dilapidated structure will accommodate three campers. In the morning, follow the white blazes of the Windsor Trail down the mountain, arriving at the Halfway Spring intersection in 0.1 mile. Turn left and follow the Windsor Trail back to your vehicle.

 QUECHEE GORGE

BEFORE YOU GO	ABOUT THE HIKE
Map USGS Quechee	Day hike or overnight
Current Conditions	Easy for children
Quechee Recreation Area,	March–November
Vermont Department of Forests,	**1.2 miles, round trip**
Parks and Recreation (802)	**Hiking time** 1.5 hours
295-2990	**High point/elevation gain**
Moderate fee for camping	618 feet, 165 feet
in state park	

GETTING THERE
- From I-89, take exit 1 to US 4.
- Travel 3.0 miles west on US 4.
- Turn right onto Dewey's Mill Road.
- The parking area is 0.1 mile farther on the left.

ON THE TRAIL
Crowded and touristy? Yes. Worth going anyway? Absolutely—especially if you can time your visit to avoid the heaviest crowds. You may not feel like you're in the middle of wilderness, but this natural wonder of Vermont is a sight to behold. The gorge is over a mile long and 165 feet deep. You will have spectacular views hiking on the trail alongside what is sometimes called "Vermont's Little Grand Canyon." Kids can look for water running down the cliff walls on the opposite side of the gorge into the Ottauquechee River below. Camping is available at nearby Quechee State Park.

The trail starts behind the picnic area in a stand of pines and parallels the gorge. A fence runs alongside, so children can safely peer down to the river. In 0.1 mile, the trail heads under the US 4 highway bridge. Who can guess how high up you are? (The depth of the gorge at the bridge is 165 feet.) The wide graveled path travels downhill through a mixture of pine and deciduous trees. Around 0.3 mile, deciduous trees dominate and are surrounded by fields of ostrich ferns. Now closer to the river, you can look back to see the highway bridge in the distance. Soon, a side trail on the left (for the use of campers only) leads to a marshy area. Continue straight on the main trail, but keep your ears alert for the sounds of frogs croaking from the marsh. Also keep your eyes peeled for cascading water on the cliffs on the gorge's far side.

Before reaching the bottom of the gorge, the fence ends, so use caution with children and make sure they stick to the trail. A little over a half mile from the bridge, the path drops to the river's edge where many flat rocks provide good resting spots. As you enjoy the sights and sounds of water rushing over rocky outcroppings, be sure to look back to the

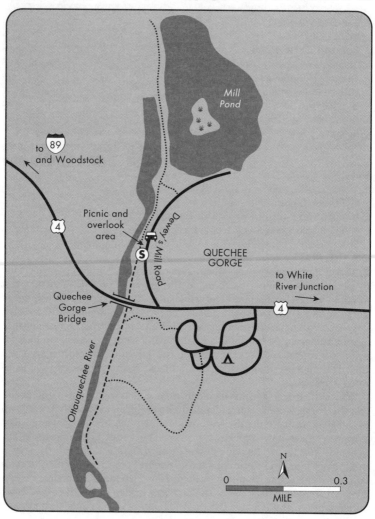

View of Quechee Gorge from the highway bridge

bridge—many photos have been taken from this picturesque vantage point. Look also for people canoeing or fishing for rainbow and brown trout before heading back the way you came. If you still have energy, you can continue north on the trail from the parking area to Mill Pond.

9 MOUNT TOM

BEFORE YOU GO
Maps USGS Woodstock North and South
Current Conditions
Woodstock Area Chamber of Commerce (802) 457-3555 or (888) 496-6378

ABOUT THE HIKE
Day hike
Easy for children
May–October
3.2 miles, loop
Hiking time 2.5 hours
High point/elevation gain 1357 feet, 700 feet

GETTING THERE
- From I-89, take exit 1 to US 4 for "Woodstock, Rutland."
- Head west on US 4 toward Quechee, Woodstock, and Rutland.
- Drive 10.2 miles to the intersection with VT-12 in Woodstock.
- Drive another 0.13 mile on US 4 and, with the Woodstock Green on your left, turn right onto Mountain Avenue.
- Drive through the covered bridge, cross River Street, and, in 0.4 mile, park on the right-hand side of the road next to Faulkner Park.

ON THE TRAIL
The paths that wind over and around Mount Tom are tame by Vermont standards. Reflecting its proximity to Woodstock, the civilized Faulkner Trail switches methodically back and forth up the side of the mountain, passing stone walls, park benches, and a stone bridge. Rather than being intrusive, these subtle human touches are an improvement to the natural landscape. The switchbacks that begin the hike were made for kids, who will delight in this zigzagging route to the summit. More adventurous tykes may prefer the return trip along the slightly wilder North Peak Trail.

Walk toward the northeastern side of Faulkner Park along the paved path. At the edge of the park, turn left onto the gravel, unblazed Faulkner Trail and begin a series of switchbacks. Counting these hairpin turns is a good way for kids to chart their progress. As you begin on an easy grade through tall pines, look straight up to see the kaleidoscope pattern of their branches.

At the third switchback, who will be the first to spot the tree that seems to grow out of a boulder? A sign pointing right, "To River Street," 0.4 mile from the start, marks switchback five as you sweep left. Beyond this turn, the trail squeezes between two boulders (you can count boulder squeezes, too) and passes a stone arch bridge on the right. How many kids can fit underneath at one time?

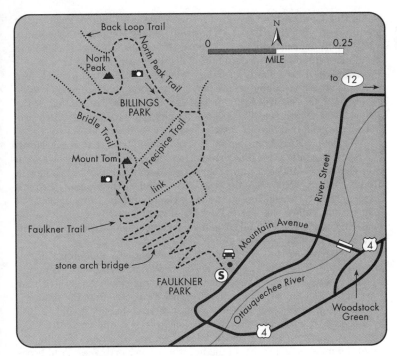

As you round switchback nine at 0.85 mile, drag a stick across the mossy ledges that hug the trail to see if you can make an interesting sound. The first one to reach the huge old oak tree on the right wins a piggyback ride from the one who arrives last. Count another boulder squeeze on the next switchback.

On the eleventh switchback, nearly 1.3 miles from the start, you'll meet the yellow-blazed Upper Link Trail, joining from the right. Can you find any acorns that are still wearing their "hats"? Pass a moss-coated boulder slide on the right, and dodge an overhanging ledge near switchback twelve. Switchback thirteen is quickly followed by two more close turns. As the grade steepens, the switchbacks tighten. Who's counting boulder squeezes? Add one more at switchback number nineteen (you should be up to three).

Pleasant views over Woodstock and the surrounding hills appear through the trees; you'll arrive at an overlook 1.5 miles from the start at switchbacks twenty-two and twenty-three. Beyond the vista, the trail dips into a minor sag and then climbs the route's only stiff grade, winding around the right side of a ledge toward the summit. A wire cable strung along the right side of the trail keeps children safely back from the edge.

Shortly, the trail emerges onto the flat, grassy Mount Tom summit.

Delightful views extend in all directions, with Killington Peak rising prominently on the northwestern horizon, Ludlow Mountain to the south, and the Ottauquechee River to the east. (If you elect to head back now to avoid more climbing, your total hiking distance will be 3.2 miles.)

Follow the Bridle Trail, a carriage road that circles the summit, in a clockwise direction, taking in the panoramas, then plunge into the woods heading northwestward. In 0.3 mile, leave the Bridle Trail to follow the yellow-blazed North Peak Trail right, climbing gently. Heading northward, the narrow, well-blazed trail passes through open, deciduous woods.

As a yellow-blazed trail splits left, continue straight to reach North Peak, just 0.2 mile from the carriage road. The far-reaching views from this peak (over 100 feet taller than the Mount Tom summit) take in Mount Ascutney (Hike 7) to the south. After circling the summit, the path divides: The Back Loop Trail proceeds straight and the North Peak Trail heads right. Follow the North Peak Trail right (north) on a gradual-to-moderate descent. In 0.3 mile, the trail curls southeastward on a descent and drops into a rock-strewn gully.

Warn kids about the cost of whining, grumbling, or complaining: Offenders must tell three riddles or two knock-knock jokes. As you descend the steep mountainside, stone steps facilitate the drop. Leave the gully behind; soon, at 2.4 miles into the hike, the Precipice Trail joins from the right.

Shortly, turn right at another intersection, following a sign to River Street. The trail dives into a wide, deep trench and crosses a baby stream. Catch your breath on the bench beyond the stream crossing.

At 2.6 miles, you'll reach a junction where the North Peak Trail bears left (south) with yellow blazes and the Upper Link Trail bears right (southwest). Follow the Upper Link Trail and the sign for Mountain Avenue. Quickly, at another junction, the Upper Link Trail (marked in yellow) exits right on an ascent as you bear left, dropping gradually on the yellow-blazed Lower Link Trail.

View of Woodstock from the Mount Tom summit

At the next junction (2.8 miles from the start) follow a yellow-marked trail straight (southeast) toward Faulkner Trail and Mountain Avenue. Hop over a second tiny stream and, in 100 yards, join the Faulkner Trail at the fifth switchback. Zigzag down the slope along the familiar path to your vehicle.

OTHER WOODSTOCK HIKES

If you've completed the hike to Mount Tom and don't yet have your fill of hiking, you're in luck. Woodstock has many other hiking opportunities close by. Try Mount Peg, which is accessible from the Village Green, or the trails in nearby Marsh–Billings–Rockefeller National Historical Park. You can also head to Eshqua Bog Natural Area to explore a fen—a low-lying marshy area fed by groundwater. Contact the chamber of commerce for more information.

 MOUNT HORRID AND THE GREAT CLIFF

BEFORE YOU GO
Map USGS Mount Carmel
Current Conditions Green Mountain National Forest, Rochester Ranger District (802) 767-4261 or Green Mountain Club (802) 244-7037

ABOUT THE HIKE
Day hike
Moderate for children
May–October; parts may be closed March 15–August 1 for peregrine falcon nesting
1.4 miles, round trip to the Great Cliff; 2.6 miles, round trip to Mount Horrid Summit
Hiking time 1.5 hours, 3 hours
High point/elevation gain 3216 feet, 1030 feet

GETTING THERE
- From US 7 in Brandon, head east on VT-73 for 8.2 miles.
- Alternatively, from the junctions of VT-73 and VT-100 near Rochester, drive west 9.2 miles on VT-73.
- Parking for the Long Trail is in the lot on the south side of the road.

ON THE TRAIL
The climb to Mount Horrid's Great Cliff is popular for the spectacular views it provides in such a short and achievable distance. From the cliffs you can overlook the surrounding mountains and the marsh and pond below (which you can also observe from the road—it is a good wildlife

watching spot). You will not find south-facing cliff habitat like this in much of New England, which also makes this hike fairly unusual. This cliff provides nesting habitat for peregrine falcons and may be closed from March 15 to August 1 to protect their nests. Please observe these closures as peregrine falcons are still making a comeback after being nearly wiped out in this region in the 1950s. During times of closure, if just the short spur trail to the cliff is closed, you may still be able to

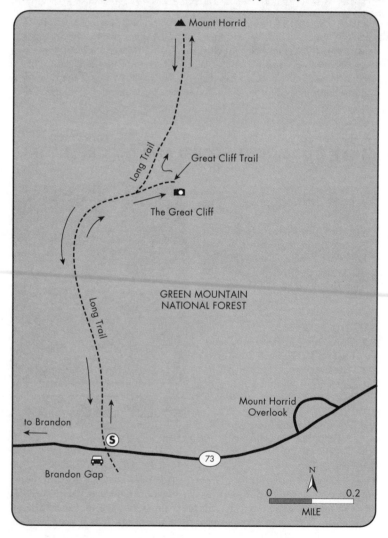

Navigating the boulders near Great Cliff

hike north on the Long Trail to the summit of Mount Horrid. Although views are limited as the summit is fairly treed-in, the accomplishment of climbing a mountain is bound to make kids proud.

From the parking area, cross the road carefully and pick up the Long Trail heading north. The trail quickly turns away from the road and begins winding its way up the mountain at a moderate climb. In 0.1 mile, sign in at the register near the sign indicating that the Great Cliff is 0.6 mile away. Closure orders will be posted here for peregrine falcon nesting. The trail continues climbing up and over rocks with some precipitous drops, but also some good views, to the left. As you wind through a mixed forest that soon becomes predominantly birch, have the kids look for cavelike shelters in the boulders—sharp eyes may spot a couple. In 0.5 mile, you will get a small taste of the sweeping views from the cliff off to your right as the trail flattens in a stand of stunted birch.

Soon, your kids can test their rock scrambling skills as the path heads up a long set of rock stairs. This is a definite highlight for those who like to climb. At the 0.6-mile mark, the short spur trail to the Great Cliff on the south side of Mount Horrid heads off to the right. If this trail is open, follow it to a steep perch high above the ground below. Who can guess why this area makes a good spot for peregrines to nest? Because it is so steep, it is difficult for anything to disturb peregrine nests.

To continue to the summit of Mount Horrid, continue straight on the Long Trail at its junction with the Great Cliff Trail. The trail curves around and heads along the side of the mountain through a grassy wooded area with views through the trees to your left. Soon, pine will start to replace birch as the dominant tree and you will be treated to their fragrant aroma. Although the trail has some steep sections, they are broken up by some less strenuous stretches. Before reaching the summit, a side trail leads to the left to provide some more open views than you will receive on the summit. At 1.3 miles, reach a sign for Mount Horrid announcing that you have arrived on the top. Congratulate your kids for being true mountain climbers and head back the way you came.

 RATTLESNAKE POINT AND FALLS OF LANA

BEFORE YOU GO
Map USGS East Middlebury
Current Conditions Green Mountain National Forest, Rochester Ranger District (802) 767-4261 or main office (802) 747-6700

ABOUT THE HIKE
Day hike or overnight
Moderate for children
May–October; Rattlesnake Cliff Trail closed March 15–August 1 for peregrine falcon nesting
5 miles, round trip
Hiking time 4 hours
High point/elevation gain
1650 feet, 1050 feet

GETTING THERE
- From downtown Middlebury, travel 6.7 miles on US 7 South to the junction with VT-53.
- Turn left (south) onto VT-53.
- In 3.5 miles pass Branbury State Park and the Lake Dunmore camping and swimming areas.
- Drive another 0.3 mile to a sizable parking turnout on the left.
- See a sign that says "Silver Lake, Falls of Lana."

ON THE TRAIL
On this trip, you and your family will wander near the picturesque Falls of Lana (named for an army general, not a beautiful woman named Lana). You'll climb steadily through pleasant woodlands and view Lake Dunmore, the surrounding hills, and far-off New York peaks from cliffs on Rattlesnake Point. Does a 5-mile hike seem too long? Cut the total distance by more than 3 miles by hiking to both sides of the waterfall and then returning to your vehicle.

The trails cross Green Mountain National Forest as well as Branbury State Park property. Be sure to explore the park's swimming area, campground, and playground before you head home.

Near the northern end of the parking turnout, follow the trail that

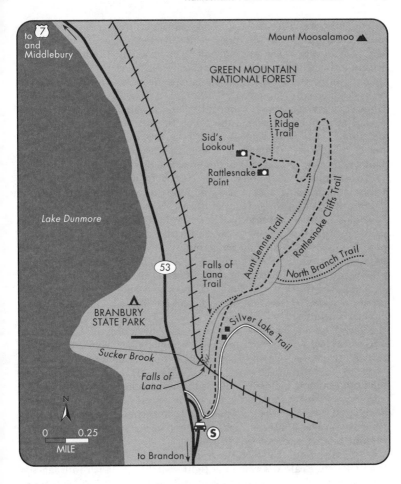

climbs moderately eastward into the woods. (All park trails are blazed in blue.) Shortly, turn right onto a gravel woods road and curl left, passing a sign for the Silver Lake Recreation Area and Falls of Lana. Wander on an easy grade through mature hemlocks and stately white pines. At your first rest stop, have the kids pick out a tree and stand in such a way as to imitate its shape. Several kids can work together to "become" a tree. Notice the distinctive silhouette of each tree.

At 0.3 mile, look to the left across a cleared area crossed by a major water and power line for a pretty view of Lake Dunmore. Beyond the clearing, continue to look left to see massive, moss-covered ledge outcroppings. Soon, follow a side trail on the left to the top of the Falls of

Lana. Here, watch as Sucker Brook explodes through a narrow, deep canyon and spills down the rock face. Return to the gravel road and turn left, with Sucker Brook tumbling along on your left. The brook, cradled within a ravine, widens into several cool pools above the falls.

At a junction 0.1 mile from the falls, near several small structures, a trail splits right (southeast), following a sign to Silver Lake. You continue straight (northeast) toward the Falls of Lana picnic and camping area, Rattlesnake Point, and the North Branch Trail. At 0.6 mile from the start, you'll cross a substantial footbridge over Sucker Brook. (To reach a picnic and camping area and another overlook of the Falls of Lana, follow the left-hand trail just over the bridge.)

To continue to Rattlesnake Point, turn right, now on the Rattlesnake Cliffs Trail, winding northeastward along Sucker Brook's left bank. At 0.7 mile, the Aunt Jennie Trail, a difficult shortcut to Rattlesnake Point, splits left as you continue to follow the Rattlesnake Cliffs Trail. The wide, level path gradually wanders farther away from Sucker Brook, entering an overgrown field at 0.8 mile. Halfway across the field, turn left (north) at an intersection following a sign to Rattlesnake Point (1.5 miles away) as the North Branch Trail heads right (east).

Follow the Rattlesnake Cliffs Trail on a moderate ascent. At 0.9 mile, recross Sucker Brook over a sturdy log bridge with a handrail. The gravel path continues to climb steadily and sidesteps an erratic boulder on the left. What do you think it's shaped like? Look around: Can you find a tree that looks like a witch? A boulder angled like a ship's hull cutting through the water? A cloud shaped like a hippopotamus?

Over a mile from the start, look left through the foliage to see the high ridge leading to Rattlesnake Point. Passing through stands of beech and birch, climb more briskly and begin a series of loose switchbacks, dodging the steepest slope. As the wide path shrinks to a foot trail, work your way over a jumble of rocks and then sweep southwestward. Who can find a leaf that has been chewed?

At 2 miles from the start, the Aunt Jennie Trail rises steeply to join from the left. Scale the ridge via tight switchbacks with railroad ties serving as rustic steps. Can you spot any low-bush blueberries fringing the trail?

As the surrounding forest begins to open up, the trail reaches a junction, 2.3 miles from the start. Follow the trail to the left (southwest), toward Rattlesnake Cliffs, as the Oak Ridge Trail departs right for the summit of Mount Moosalamoo.

This rugged trail trips over roots and protruding ledge as it drops to a junction that forms a brief loop around Rattlesnake Point, a large rock outcrop at the southern end of Mount Moosalamoo. You can loop in either direction. If you continue straight, you'll come upon Sid's Lookout at 2.5 miles, the route's best picnic spot. The waters of Lake Dunmore shimmer far below, reaching westward, it seems, to meet the Adirondack

Mountains of New York. Though the two-tiered ledge provides an element of safety for curious kids, parents should still exercise caution.

Continue to follow the loop trail past a more protected overlook with similar views. Once you've returned to the beginning of the loop, kids may want to explore the various side trails that crisscross the area above the cliffs.

Retrace your steps to your vehicle.

 LAPLATTE RIVER MARSH NATURAL AREA

BEFORE YOU GO
Map USGS Burlington
Current Conditions The Nature Conservancy of Vermont (802) 229-4425

ABOUT THE HIKE
Day hike
Easy for children
May–November
1.4 miles, round trip
Hiking time 1 hour
High point/elevation gain
100 feet/40 feet

GETTING THERE
- From I-89 take exit 13, I-189 and US 7.
- Take I-189 West for 1.3 miles to the junction with US 7.

- Turn left on US 7 South and travel 3 miles to Bay Road.
- Turn right on Bay Road, and in 1.1 miles park in the large fishing access lot on your right.

ON THE TRAIL
Many people flock to nearby Shelburne Farm, a 1400-acre working farm and National Historic Landmark. (This is definitely worth a visit and also has walking trails.) If you are looking for something a little quieter, however, try a trip to the LaPlatte River Marsh Natural Area. This 211-acre preserve offers an interpretive trail along the LaPlatte River, McCabes Brook, and the surrounding marsh. The relatively easy trail—especially great for younger children—follows the water's edge most of the way, providing great views and many opportunities for bird sightings. Over sixty bird species use this area as breeding habitat. Some to look out for are osprey, belted kingfisher, tree swallow, pileated woodpecker, great blue heron, and wood duck. Although you won't get too far from the road and may hear some traffic noise, that will be overshadowed by the chirping of birds, pecking of woodpeckers, and honking of geese.

From the parking area, cross the street carefully and look for The Nature Conservancy sign and information kiosk. Here, trail guides to the interpretive stations and bird checklists may be available along with information about the walk. The trail heads south along the river and in 0.1 mile reaches the first station by the water's edge. This is an ideal place to spot birds in the water. Refer to your checklist to see which ones you can find. See also if you can differentiate between the types of evergreens as you make your way along the trail. White pine, eastern hemlock, red pine, and eastern red cedar all grow here. At the 0.2-mile

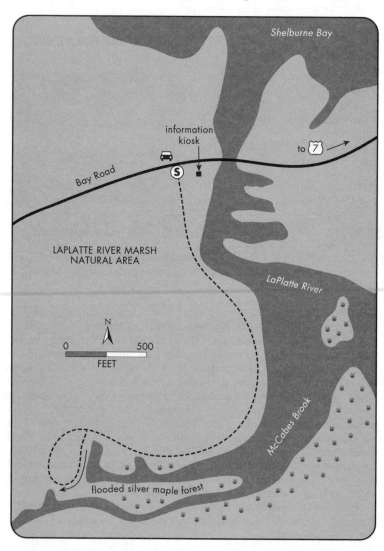

mark, you will have great views of the marsh where the LaPlatte River and McCabes Brook merge with lake water backing up into the marsh. In 0.4 mile you will come to a flooded silver maple forest at station 8 of the interpretive trail. The landscape here looks like something out of mystical tales with a number of large dead trees standing in the middle of the marsh. The not-so-mystical cause of the dead trees, however, is beaver activity that flooded the forest and caused the trees to die.

From this station, the trail curves back into the woods. You will cross some footbridges as the trail makes a miniature loop past station 9 and around a marshy area. To your left you will have views of the flooded silver maple forest that you passed earlier. Halfway around the small loop you will come to a cattail marsh. Look for red-winged blackbirds nesting among the cattails. Continue along the trail—look for arrows to guide you along in confusing spots—to the beginning of the small loop and retrace your steps along the marsh and river to the parking area.

Look for fungus growing on trees.

THE NATURE CONSERVANCY IN VERMONT

In Vermont, The Nature Conservancy has improved twenty of its preserves with trails, boardwalks, or canoe access. As you travel around the state you can also visit the North Pawlet Hills Natural Area near Manchester, the Helen W. Buckner Memorial Preserve at Bald Mountain near Rutland, Williams Woods in Charlotte, Chickering Bog in East Montpelier, Eshqua Bog near Woodstock, and Black Mountain Natural Area near Brattleboro. All these preserves are accessible for families.

RED ROCKS PARK

BEFORE YOU GO
Map USGS Burlington
Current Conditions City of South Burlington Recreation Department (802) 846-4108
Small daily pass fee

ABOUT THE HIKE
Day hike
Easy for children
Year-round
3 miles, loop
Hiking time 2 hours
High point/elevation gain
285 feet, 300 feet
Some paths suitable for strollers

GETTING THERE
- From I-89, take exit 13 to I-189, Burlington and Shelburne.
- In less than 2 miles, I-189 ends at a traffic light; turn left onto US 7 South.
- Almost immediately, turn right onto Queen City Park Drive.
- Cross a narrow bridge over railroad tracks and turn left.
- Continue a short distance to the Red Rocks Park gate.
- Park in the winter parking area outside the gate.

ON THE TRAIL
New England, natives lament, has nine months of winter and three months of darn poor sledding. And, I might add, a rather brief (albeit spectacular!) hiking season. That's what makes Red Rocks Park such a find. A place for

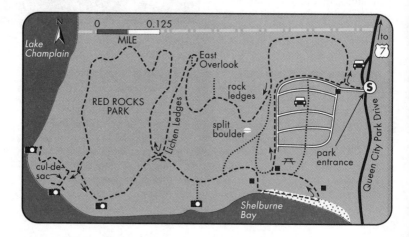

all seasons (and all kids), the park features a dazzling wildflower display in spring, lifeguard-supervised swimming in summer, stunning colors adorning the fifty-plus varieties of trees and shrubs in fall, solitude in winter, and fine bird-watching year-round.

Maintained by the city of South Burlington, the park offers several miles of manicured hiking trails that lead through lovely natural areas and approach a number of cliffs overlooking Lake Champlain and New York's Adirondack Mountains. (A big-wheeled stroller can navigate most of these paths.)

From the park entrance road, turn northward onto a wide path near the ticket house, west of the winter parking lot. Follow the gravel path as it curls left (west) to parallel the fence marking the park's border. How quietly can you walk? Imitate Native Americans hunting for their dinner. Would you catch your prey or scare it off with your noisy footsteps?

At a Y-intersection 0.3 mile from the start, the trail nearly merges with the park road; you

A close-up view of nature at Red Rocks Park

stay to the right, soon passing between a massive split boulder on the left and ledge on the right. Rising gently, the trail reaches an intersection as the ledge ends. Bear left onto the more-traveled path and continue to climb, cresting at 0.5 mile and sidestepping more ledge outcroppings. Follow the right branch of the trail at a junction near the northern edge of the park (the left branch is a shortcut). Pass the East Overlook and curl left (west), rejoining the "shortcut" trail.

Drop beside the Lichen Ledges. Are the children familiar with lichens? These pioneers are often the first plants to establish themselves on a rock's barren surface. They initiate the lengthy process of converting these rocks into soil. Alga and fungus, the two plants that make up a lichen, cooperate to ensure the lichen's survival in its harsh living conditions: The alga shares food with the fungus, which provides a moist environment for the alga.

At 0.7 mile, bear right at an intersection to head northward on a pine needle carpet. Without the noise of traffic and crowds, the forest seems quiet. But is it as silent as it seems? Try this: Begin counting and stop when you hear a noise. With the chattering of squirrels, the rustling of leaves, and the calling of birds, you probably won't count past five! At 0.9 mile, the trail reaches the property boundary and curls left, from north to southwest, still weaving through stands of tall pines.

Who knows what *camouflage* means? (It actually comes from a French word that means "to disguise.") The kids can take turns running ahead and hiding just off the trail, trying to blend in with their surroundings as much as possible. How many creatures can you name that use camouflage to protect themselves from their enemies? (A polar bear's white fur blends in with the snow; the stripes on a zebra make it harder to see it in tall grass; even a soldier's uniform is designed with camouflage in mind.) Can each child find a camouflaged insect?

At 1.2 miles from the start, turn right at a junction and quickly left at another junction to open onto a cul-de-sac and overlook. From here, you have limited views of the vast waters of Lake Champlain. A narrow trail leaves the left (west) side of the cul-de-sac to wind toward the water, soon arriving atop cliffs that loom 30 to 40 feet over the water. Find level ground to enjoy a rest and snack, listening to the soothing rhythm of the waves splashing against the ledges. You may want to follow the trail eastward and westward to explore the cliffs.

Return to the cul-de-sac and turn sharply left at the first junction to wander to another lovely lake overlook at 1.4 miles. Here, parents can relax a bit more because a rail fence provides protection. Venture onto the massive flat rocks at the water's edge and pause, letting the cool lake breeze revive you. The trail loops back and returns to the junction with the first overlook trail. Head straight (east), soon passing another familiar trail that joins from the left. Next the trail skirts another vista of Lake Champlain's Shelburne Bay. Don't the Adirondacks make a lovely backdrop?

At 1.75 miles into the hike, bear right at an intersection with the trail from the Lichen Ledges. Pass a final overlook side trail on the right and, just under 2 miles from the start, turn right at a junction and quickly join a gravel path that cuts through a clearing. Drop down a set of stairs, passing to the left of a pumphouse, to arrive at the shore. Turn left a short distance to the public beach. Swim or stretch out on the sand before following the trail that leads from the bathhouse (with changing and restroom facilities) through the picnic and cookout area to the park road. Follow the park road northward to the parking lot.

 **KETTLE POND**

BEFORE YOU GO
Map USGS Plainfield
Current Conditions Groton
State Forest (802) 426-3042
Moderate fee for camping

ABOUT THE HIKE
Day hike or overnight
Easy for children
May–October
3 miles, loop
Hiking time 2.5 hours
High point/elevation gain
1410 feet, 150 feet

GETTING THERE

- From I-91, take exit 17 to US 302 and US 5.
- Follow US 302 west for 8.2 miles.

- Turn right (north) onto VT-232.
- In 2 miles, enter Groton State Forest.
- At 5.9 miles from US 302, pass a sign for Kettle Pond State Park.
- Turn left into New Discovery State Park to a parking area and the trailhead to Owl's Head.

ON THE TRAIL

Water, so fascinating to children and so soothing to adults, is never far away on this hike around pristine Kettle Pond. The narrow trail winds along the gentle terrain of the pond's northern side with frequent excursions to the water and then tracks over more rugged ground along the less-accessible southern shore. The kids will enjoy a brief visit or an overnight at one of the primitive waterfront shelters (rented for a nominal fee on a first-come, first-served basis at New Discovery State Park in Peacham, just north on VT-232). Bring along a store-bought net or a coat hanger covered with a piece of old nylon stocking to skim the water for aquatic insects. If you would like to view Kettle Pond (and the rest of the expansive Groton State Forest) from above, climb nearby Owl's Head Mountain (Hike 15).

The blue-blazed Kettle Pond hiking loop heads westward from the parking area on level ground. In 150 feet, the trail forks; bear right. Follow the rocky, root-choked path to a clearing at 0.1 mile with a hearth and a lean-to for camping. Beyond the camping area, the trail leads quickly to a small, rocky beach at the water's edge. As you gaze at the unspoiled pond rimmed by high hills, you'll sense the vastness of this Vermont wilderness. Did you bring a net? Skim the top of the water. What did you scoop?

The trail hugs the northern side of the pond, winding amid moss-draped rocks and crowded hemlocks. At 0.3 mile from the start, the

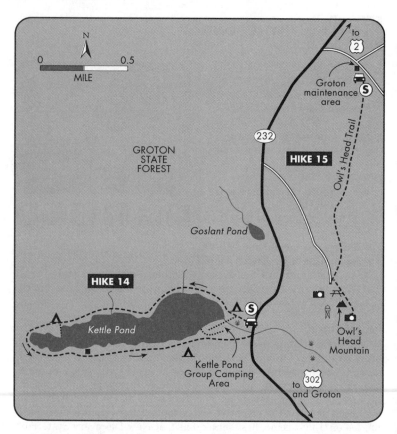

path flirts with the gentle waves that splash the rocky shore, crossing a stream where it empties into the pond. Ask the kids to describe how the plants near the water are different from those inland. Then ask them "What do people have in common with plants?"

Dodge a wet area at 0.35 mile and soon rejoin the water. At the 0.5-mile mark, the trail opens onto a clearing near a large rock that is half-submerged in the water. If the kids have worked up a sweat, you may decide to stop here for a swim.

The trail hops over another stream and passes a second stone hearth at 0.8 mile. In another 0.3 mile, as you near the western tip of the pond, pass a second lean-to with an open hearth. A side trail leads 75 feet from the campsite to the water. Here, the trail begins to curl left (south).

If you notice something of interest along the trail—an insect, a bird, a plant—point it out to your young companions even if you don't know its name. Observing and enjoying nature is more important than identifying it, especially when you are trying to hold a child's attention.

As you round the pond's western side, the trail trudges over rocky terrain (warn the kids to step over rocky crevices that might trap tiny feet), squeezing between large boulders at 1.4 miles. Curling eastward, the path strays to the right of a cabin and avoids the pond's marshy shore.

Who will spot the third lean-to (part of the Kettle Pond Group Camping Area) at 2.3 miles? With the now-distant water shimmering through the trees, the trail finds the main Group Camping Area, strewn with lean-tos, at 2.6 miles. Follow the gravel road that leads from the camping area to the highway. Turn left onto VT-232 and hike 0.1 mile back to your vehicle.

 OWL'S HEAD MOUNTAIN

BEFORE YOU GO
Map USGS Plainfield
Current Conditions Groton State Forest (802) 426-3042
Small fee

ABOUT THE HIKE
Day hike
Easy for children
May–September
2.8 miles, round trip
Hiking time 2 hours
High point/elevation gain
1060 feet, 300 feet

GETTING THERE

- From I-91, take exit 17 to US 302 and US 5.
- Follow US 302 West for 8.2 miles; turn right (north) onto VT-232.

- In 8.1 miles, just past the Groton Maintenance Area, District 4, turn right into New Discovery State Park.
- The trailhead is located 0.5 mile from the contact station at a small parking area
- Alternatively, from the junction of US 2 and VT-232, drive 4.1 miles on VT-232 South to the park entrance on the left.

ON THE TRAIL

Groton State Forest's 25,000 acres encompass mountains and lakes, forests and bogs. The area draws not only hikers but also boaters, fishermen, campers, cross-country skiers, and hunters. It owes much of its current appearance to the work of the Civilian Conservation Corps. Nearly seventy-five years ago, this group reforested areas burned by fires, built forest roads, and erected many of the lean-tos and other structures that still stand today.

Of all the mountaintops within the forest, Owl's Head is the most popular, because of its easy access and magnificent views. Preschoolers, teenagers—even grandparents—will want to be included on this trip.

From the trailhead, follow a level path along an old road, where the Owl's Head Trail ducks into the woods on the left. Who's the best at role-playing? Select an animal that lives within this forest to imitate, perhaps a black bear, deer, moose, mink, beaver, or otter. See who can maintain his or her "role" the longest.

The blue-blazed path winds southward through uncluttered hemlock and spruce woods. Though well maintained, the trail shows a few signs of heavy traffic. Let the kids take turns leading the way, guided by the frequent blue blazes.

At 0.5 mile from the start, the trail trudges up a short hill, swerving left in another 0.2 mile over a squat ledge to avoid a wet area. Hop from stone to stone over another damp section and curl left on an easy ascent. At 1.1 miles, the trail opens onto a gravel turnaround near a picnic shelter. Merge with the gravel road heading westward to reach the picnic shelter shortly.

Pause to take in the delightful views of nearby Kettle Pond (Hike 14) and Vermont's Worcester Mountains. Pass the picnic shelter on the right to climb southward, then eastward, on a rugged trail over exposed granite. (We saw a rabbit family dart into the woods here.) To distract them from the rocky climb, ask the kids to guess whether *hare* is just another name for a rabbit. (No! Hares are larger and are born covered with fur, with their eyes open. Rabbits live with a group in burrows—unlike hares—and are born blind, without hair.)

A CCC stone lookout crowns Owl's Head summit.

The trail skirts the open edge of the summit on smooth, exposed bald-face. Parents can relax as kids explore the low stone tower and romp about the mountaintop—there are no sharp drop-offs. Although spruce trees flourish here, the exposed edges offer views to the west, south, and east. From the summit's southeastern side, look for Groton Lake, Kettle Pond, and New Hampshire's Mount Washington and Franconia-region mountains. To the west, you'll have superb views of Camel's Hump and Mount Mansfield.

Return to your vehicle the way you came.

 MOUNT HUNGER

BEFORE YOU GO
Map USGS Stowe
Current Conditions C. C.
Putnam State Forest (802) 476-0170

ABOUT THE HIKE
Day hike
Challenging for children
May–October
4.3 miles, round trip
Hiking time 4 hours
High point/elevation gain
3554 feet, 2200 feet

GETTING THERE
- From I-89, take exit 10 to VT-100 North.
- In 2.8 miles, near Waterbury Center, turn right (east) onto Howard Avenue.
- In 0.8 mile, turn left onto Maple Street.
- Drive another 0.2 mile and turn left onto Loomis Hill Road.
- Follow Loomis Hill Road (which turns to gravel after 2.1 miles) for 3.6 miles to a parking turnout on the right for Mount Hunger, Waterbury Trail.

ON THE TRAIL
Mount Hunger's open south summit is well-known for its fabulous views of notable Vermont and New Hampshire peaks. The climb is steady and relatively long, but stream crossings, cascades, and ledgy scrambles break up the trip. Inappropriate for most preschoolers, this trip will appeal to older kids who can appreciate the dizzying panoramas.

The Waterbury Trail begins as a wide path heading eastward and soon curls right (southeast) and narrows to rise gently through mature, mixed woods. How about having a scavenger hunt? Tell each child to look for a feather, a seed, a berry, and a smooth rock. In 0.15 mile, the trail bisects mossy granite outcroppings. Do all types of moss feel the same?

Follow sporadic blue blazes along sweeping switchbacks. In fall, the kids will shuffle through layers of leaves as vividly colored as a box of crayons. At 0.4 mile, the moderate climb eases, and in another 0.2 mile the gently rising trail crosses a stream over two 10-foot lengths of halved logs. Beyond the stream, you'll climb easily for a short distance.

Soon, the pace changes and the trail heads eastward into the slope, finding occasional log steps to assist in the moderate-to-steep ascent. At 0.8 mile, the trail curls southward and gradually relaxes its climb, nearly leveling at the 1-mile mark.

Listen for the sound of rushing water. You'll reach a series of cascades 1.1 miles from the start where the water collects in random pools. On a humid day, you'll appreciate the coolness of the poolside perches. What happens to an acorn or a twig tossed into the hurrying water?

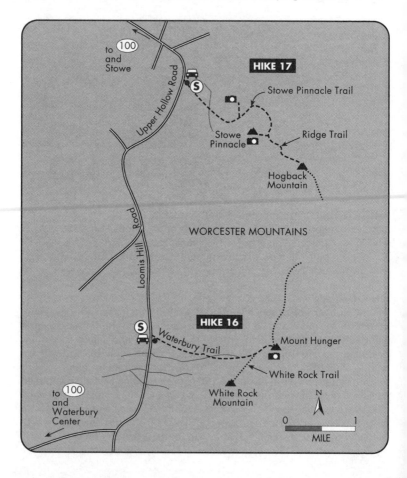

Family hiking on Mount Hunger

The trail climbs along the left bank of the stream, passes the cascades, and quickly turns right to cross the stream over rocks. (Count how many steps it takes you to get across.) Depart the stream on a moderate ascent, then zigzag up a steep slope.

Climb briskly (and sometimes soggily) for the next 0.5 mile. Birch trees fringe the trail at 1.3 miles as the cascading water whispers in the distance. In another 0.2 mile, the trail finds the now meager stream again, crosses to the opposite bank, and crosses back again.

What type of trees first appear at the 1.5-mile mark? (Evergreens.) At 1.6 miles, the trail departs the stream once more, relaxing its climb as it passes through a hemlock and spruce grove 0.1 mile later. Have the children feel the needles of a spruce tree and then a hemlock. How are they different? (Spruces have sharp, square needles; hemlocks have flat, short needles.)

At 1.8 miles, the trail crosses a pair of petite streams on halved logs. In another 0.1 mile, you'll need to help the kids mount a series of steep ledges, squeezing through a crevice along the way. Stay straight (east) at an intersection at 2 miles as the White Rock Trail bears right (south).

On its final surge toward the summit, the trail breaks out onto exposed baldface littered with stunted spruce trees. The pitch eases as you approach the broad, airy mountaintop, safe for exploration by careful kids. (Seek refuge among the ledges if the wind is brisk.)

The superb panoramic views take in nearly every peak in the main range of the Green Mountains, as well as many White Mountain and Adirondack peaks. To the north and south you'll see other mountains in the Worcester Range. Look west to see the distinctive shape of Camel's Hump rising to a height of more than 4000 feet. Focus your binoculars across the valley to the northwest; you'll see the famous Von Trapp Family Lodge.

Reverse direction to return to your vehicle.

STOWE PINNACLE AND HOGBACK MOUNTAIN

BEFORE YOU GO
Map USGS Stowe
Current Conditions C. C. Putnam State Forest (802) 476-0170

ABOUT THE HIKE
Day hike
Challenging for children
May–October
4.5 miles, round trip
Hiking time 4 hours
High point/elevation gain
3300 feet, 2300 feet

GETTING THERE
- From the junction of VT-100 and VT-108 in Stowe, take VT-100 South.
- In 1.7 miles turn left onto Gold Brook Road.
- In 0.3 mile, turn left, still on Gold Brook Road.
- At 2.1 miles from VT-100, turn right onto Upper Hollow Road.
- In 0.5 mile, the road becomes gravel; continue on it another 0.1 mile to a parking area for the Pinnacle Trail on the left.

ON THE TRAIL
Pick your distance: a 2.6-mile "moderate" hike to and from the first overlook, a 3.2-mile "moderate" round-trip hike to Stowe Pinnacle, or a 4.5-mile "challenging" trip to and from the summit of Hogback. Because your best views will come from Stowe Pinnacle, only hardy souls who crave a challenge will push on to the wooded Hogback summit.

With two turnaround points in addition to the final destination, you can be a little generous in assessing your family's abilities. Bring the six- or seven-year-olds who've been begging to climb a "real" mountain and see how they do. Even if they poop out at the initial overlook, you'll all be able to enjoy lovely views of Mount Mansfield and other peaks in the Green Mountains before you head back to your vehicle.

Enjoy the view of your destination—Stowe Pinnacle with Hogback Mountain over its right shoulder—from the parking area. The blue-blazed Stowe Pinnacle Trail leaves the back of the parking area at a sign for the Pinnacle (1.5 miles away) and heads eastward through abandoned (often damp) pasture land. Boards lead over the soggiest sections, but kids will have a hard time avoiding wet feet.

At 0.2 mile, the trail ducks into the woods, still crossing over some damp terrain on planks. How many different types of trees can you identify here? The rugged path climbs briskly at 0.4 mile, with carpets of moss flourishing within the damp, shaded forest. Ask the kids to describe the living conditions of moss. Have they ever seen moss grow in a sunny location? Probably not because coolness and moisture are critical to a moss's reproductive system. The moss plant produces male and female parts on its stem tips, and the sperm must swim to the female part.

At the 0.5-mile mark, the trail cuts left (northeast) and then swings right (east), resuming its moderate ascent through a lovely stand of white birches. Have the kids take turns acting out different forest creatures while the others try to guess the animals being imitated. (No fair using noises!)

The path meets a stream 0.6 mile from the start and wanders along its right bank, crossing to the left side in less than 0.1 mile. Can you find any curls of birch bark along the ground? Toss them into the tumbling water and pretend they are miniature birch-bark canoes.

The trail winds easily through the woods, avoiding the steepest route up the mountain until 0.9 mile from the start, when the pitch intensifies and the trail passes under exposed ledge. Kids may need a hand in another 0.2 mile as the trail picks its way through a chaos of boulders on moderate-to-steep terrain, switching back to alleviate the pitch.

As you crest a shoulder 1.2 miles from the start, the trail splits. The blue blazes lead straight as well as left, to a vista. Follow the spur trail to the left, soon arriving at an overlook on open ledges. With the Stowe Valley spread out before you and Mount Mansfield in the distance, relax and catch your breath. Return to the main trail and continue to head eastward on fairly level ground. Shortly, the trail bends right and drops for about 0.1 mile, curling around the mountain's eastern side and resuming its climb toward the Pinnacle. Pick your way through an area of stones and bony roots with ledge bordering on the right.

At 1.5 miles from the start, you'll reach another shoulder and trail junction. Follow the right-hand trail for 0.1 mile on a gradual ascent through spruce woods to the Pinnacle. There's no need for parents to be overly concerned with roving children because this is a sloping, expansive crown, rather than a summit with sheer drop-offs. The views extend to Camel's Hump, Mount Mansfield, and the Stowe Valley to the west and north, the nearby Hogback Mountain summit to the south, and other Worcester Mountains to the south and east. Gobble down your lunch or just lie on your back and watch the lazy parade of clouds.

If you're up to it, return to the junction and follow the blue-blazed Ridge Trail to the right (south) toward the Hogback Mountain summit. Climb steeply through a spruce forest for 0.5 mile to the wooded peak. Though the views are limited, you'll appreciate the seclusion of this mountaintop hemlock grove. Smell the Christmas scents and peek through the trees for cropped distant views.

Retrace your steps to your vehicle.

 MOSS GLEN FALLS

BEFORE YOU GO
Maps USGS Mount Worcester and Stowe
Current Conditions C. C. Putnam State Forest (802) 476-0170

ABOUT THE HIKE
Day hike
Easy for children
May–October
1 mile, round trip
Hiking time 1 hour
High point/elevation gain
950 feet, 150 feet

GETTING THERE

- From the junction of VT-12, VT-100, and VT-15 in Morrisville, travel south on VT-100.
- In 5.6 miles, turn left onto paved Randolph Road.
- In 0.3 mile, turn right at a fork onto gravel Moss Glen Falls Road.
- Drive another 0.5 mile and, just before the bridge over Moss Glen Brook, park on the left in a large parking area.
- Alternatively, from the junction of VT-100 and VT-108 in Stowe, drive 3 miles north on VT-100 to Randolph Road and turn right. Continue as described above.

ON THE TRAIL

Short and sweet, the hike to Moss Glen Falls is the only one in the book that comes with this guarantee: No one in your hiking party will whine, complain, or grumble. There's just too much to see and do! Even kids who are normally unfazed by nature's marvels will stand in awe of this impressive waterfall and the chasm that carries Moss Glen Brook.

Although most youngsters have the ability to make the trip, parents should be aware of the potential dangers near the waterfall. We recommend at least one adult for every two young children.

Follow the trail southward from the parking area through mixed woods. Let the kids lead the way across a series of boards and logs that span a mucky tract. It may be hard for the children to avoid wet feet because the ribbon of trail soon weaves through a soggy pasture alongside Moss Glen Brook. The shallow brook splashes on a pebble bed, enticing kids to explore its banks and toss in a few stones. Is there any sound more satisfying to a youngster's ears than the *kerplunk* of a rock breaking the surface of the water?

At 0.25 mile from the start, the trail leaves the field and ducks back into the woods. Climbing abruptly up a series of rock steps, the path trudges steadily toward the top of Moss Glen Falls. Partway up, you'll reach an overlook where you can look to the right and see torrents of water spilling through the tight ravine. Only a

Moss Glen Falls

mountain goat (or an extremely agile, experienced hiker and climber) would dare to inch down the gorge wall to the base of the falls. (The view from above is as good as the one from below anyway, and you won't get soaked with the spray.)

Continue to follow the rocky ridge high above the ravine, quickly gaining elevation as well as better views of the falls. You will want to keep young children close to you here. Pause for a look when you reach the top, but don't turn back yet. Follow the trail as it hugs the edge of the impressive 50-foot-deep chasm that cradles the swift brook. Soon, the chasm walls begin to shrink until the canyon is an unassuming riverbed. Now you can drop down the bank to look into the belly of the chasm. Anyone care to return to your vehicle by way of a barrel ride? No? Then return by the familiar route on foot.

ELMORE MOUNTAIN AND BALANCED ROCK

BEFORE YOU GO
Map USGS Morrisville
Current Conditions Elmore
State Park (802) 888-2982
Small fee in season

ABOUT THE HIKE
Day hike or overnight
Moderate for children
May–October
4.5 miles, round trip
Hiking time 4 hours
High point/elevation gain
2608 feet, 1400 feet
Accessible restrooms and
picnic area

GETTING THERE

- From the junction of VT-12 and VT-100 in Morrisville, take VT-12 south.
- In 4.4 miles, just before the village of Lake Elmore, turn right into Elmore State Park.

- At the gate, pay a small per-person fee and drive 0.5 mile along the main park road to the white metal gate that marks the trailhead.
- A picnic pavilion is to the right, and a small parking area is to the left.

ON THE TRAIL

Elmore State Park deserves a weekend rather than an afternoon, offering swimming on the sandy shore of Lake Elmore, picnic facilities, and a camping area at the base of the trail. (In addition to the main trail, a short nature trail loops around near the trailhead.) The mountaintop is easily accessed by most families via an interesting route that winds along a stream and beside moss-covered ledges.

Because Elmore stands alone at the northern end of the Worcester Mountain Range, its views are varied and extensive, taking in the nearby farming valley and faraway mountain ranges. And—surprise—the hike doesn't end at the summit! Continue for another 0.5 mile to Balanced Rock, a huge erratic tipped toward the mountain's steep slope.

The Elmore Mountain Trail passes through the gate, following the gravel road southwestward. The road, lined by hemlocks and birches, curls westward and skirts a beaver pond on the right 0.2 mile from the start. Follow the slow-moving stream that feeds the pond as it meanders alongside the trail for the next 0.1 mile. What does it sound like when a pebble is tossed into the stream? How about a bigger rock? Climb easily along the road with occasional glimpses of Lake Elmore to the east.

When the road ends at 0.5 mile, follow a wide path as it bends right (marked sporadically in blue) into mixed woods heading westward. With no rocks or roots to trip up little feet, your young hikers can dash ahead

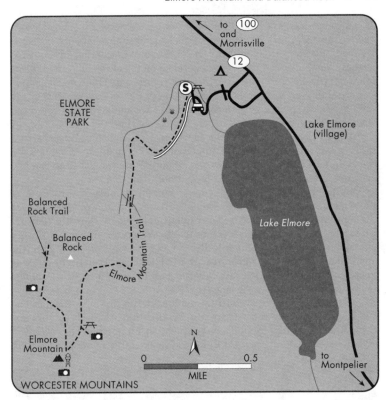

here. The foot trail flirts briefly with the wandering stream just beyond the 0.5-mile mark, then rises gradually until the pitch steepens 0.1 mile later. Climb briefly up this moderate slope and, at 0.7 mile, follow the trail as it bends left (south) and resumes its moderate ascent with occasional rock intrusions.

The trail dodges a moss-covered chunk of ledge and levels 0.8 mile from the start. What does moss feel like? Dry or damp? Soft or rough? Does all moss feel the same? In another 0.1 mile, balance on a half-log bridge over a branch of the stream and begin a gradual-to-moderate ascent, sweeping northward, then southward. At 1 mile, the stream snakes near the sheer, moss-covered walls of a gorge on the right of the trail. Soon after, the trail emerges on the eastern rim of the mountain, with the wooded slope dropping off sharply to the left.

At 1.3 miles, the trail cuts into the mountain on a brief, moderate ascent before curling back to the left (south) on more gradual ground. A picnic table set in a grassy clearing marks the 1.5-mile mark; from here, a short side trail on the left leads on open ground to exposed ledges overlooking the shimmering waters of Lake Elmore, about a mile away. An old cellar hole and a chimney are all that remain of the lookout cabin that once sat here.

From this spot, 1.6 miles from the start, point out to the kids your immediate destination, the fire tower perched on top of the mountain. From the western side of the clearing, the trail resumes its climb up the mountain, trudging up a short, steep ledge. The grade soon eases as the trail rises gradually, twisting on rugged terrain surrounded by spruce groves. How does the end of a spruce needle feel? Sharp or dull?

At 1.7 miles, after traveling southward on a gradual ascent, curl right (west) into the mountain and climb briskly to an intersection with the Balanced Rock Trail. Follow the Elmore Mountain Trail to the left, arriving in less than 0.1 mile at the summit tower.

Climb the tower's sixty-one steps to surround yourself with views of the Green Mountains (notably Camel's Hump and Mount Mansfield) to the west and New Hampshire's Presidential Range to the east. Because Elmore is one of the lowest peaks in the Worcester Range, you'll also look over the pastoral Lamoille River valley at tiny cows roaming the open meadows; patches of striped, planted fields; and red barns clinging to the hillsides. Notice the sun reflecting off the metal roofs so common in central and northern Vermont.

On most hiking trips, the summit marks the final destination and the beginning of the return trip. But on this hike, the kids have something more to anticipate. Return to the junction north of the fire tower and turn left, heading toward Balanced Rock along a narrow trail with

Elmore Mountain and Balanced Rock

ledge underfoot. At 0.1 mile from the summit, the trail opens onto an exposed ledge outcropping with pretty easterly views. At the northern end of the outcropping, the trail turns left into the woods, cresting quickly. Drift through a spruce forest with a moss carpet softening the rocky terrain. Drop easily from east to west across the ridge, reaching a western overlook of Mount Mansfield and the Stowe Valley 0.4 mile from the summit intersection.

Beyond the overlook, the trail cuts back to the eastern side of the ridge and passes to the right of some 20-foot ledges, falling down a gradual-to-moderate slope. After crossing baldface, look eastward for a view of Lake Elmore. As you drop back into spruce woods, let the kids lead the way to Balanced Rock, a cigar-shaped rock teetering precariously on ledge, threatening to plunge down the steep mountain slope. They'll want to examine it up close and offer some opinions as to when the rock might take its final tumble.

Now it's time to head back to your vehicle, looping back over the summit to retrace your steps along the Elmore Mountain Trail.

CIVILIAN CONSERVATION CORPS

Under the leadership of President Roosevelt in 1933, the Civilian Conservation Corps (CCC) was created for unemployment relief and put youths ages eighteen to twenty-five to work in the nation's forests. They planted, pruned, and constructed bridges, buildings, and camping areas. You can see the accomplishments of the CCC in many of Vermont's state parks and forests, including the historic CCC bathhouse at Elmore Mountain State Park.

 BURKE MOUNTAIN

BEFORE YOU GO
Map USGS Burke Mountain
Current Conditions Darling State Park (802) 751-0123

ABOUT THE HIKE
Day hike or overnight
Moderate for children
May–September
6 miles, round trip
Hiking time 5 hours
High point/elevation gain
3267 feet, 1400 feet

GETTING THERE
- From the junction of US 5 and VT-114 in Lyndonville, head north on VT-114.
- In 4.6 miles, turn right following signs to Burke Mountain Ski Resort.

- At 2.1 miles, bear left onto the auto toll road to the summit of Burke Mountain. (Look for the sign for Sugarhouse Store, Camping and Picnic Areas.)
- In 0.1 mile, park before the gate house.

ON THE TRAIL

You've heard that you can't judge a book by its cover, but did you know that the same thing applies to mountains? Indeed, the steep slopes of conical Burke Mountain seem to indicate a formidable trail to the summit. In reality, the grades are surprisingly easy and the walk is a pleasant one. You may even feel a little guilty enjoying such spectacular views from the lookout tower because you didn't have to work very hard to get there.

Burke doesn't cater just to hikers: Downhill and cross-country ski trails crisscross the mountain, camping facilities accommodate overnighters, and a toll road delivers motorists to the summit.

Walk southward for 0.6 mile along the paved summit toll road

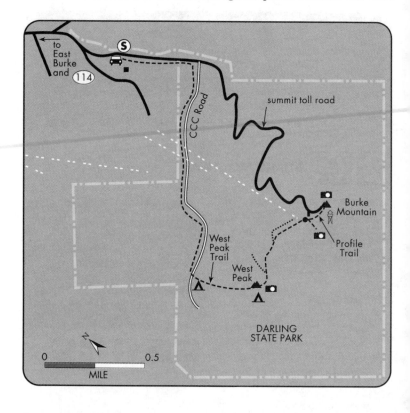

to CCC Road on the right. Turn right (southwest) at the sign onto the level, grassy road, which intersects a number of ski trails within the next 0.4 mile. From the open ski slopes, you'll have good views to the north and west of the characteristic profile of the Lake Willoughby region peaks.

Leaving the ski area behind, climb on a gentle rise, although the slope from left to right drops steeply. Water from hurrying streams spills down the wooded hillside, splashing across (or under) your path several times in the next 0.3 mile. Occasional blue-diamond blazes indicate that cross-country skiers sweep across this snow-covered path in winter. Urge tiring kids to find a sturdy walking stick to help (if only psychologically) on the climb.

At the height of the land, 1.7 miles from the start, follow the blue-blazed West Peak Trail as it splits left (southeast) to skirt a camping shelter and hearth in about 40 yards. Climbing easily, then more briskly, the narrow footpath winds up the mountainside through a birch forest. At 0.2 mile beyond the junction, the slope relaxes and the trail joins a seasonal stream. Who will be the first one to spot a bird's nest?

At 2.1 miles, on a moderate ascent, the trail passes through evergreen stands and dodges moss-covered ledges. Smell the spruce trees as you follow the snaking path through heavy woods. Soon, ledge intrudes underfoot; the lush moss, however, creeps across the path to soften the surface. If you find that your group has scattered with some children lagging behind and others far ahead, consider putting one adult in front with another bringing up the rear.

At 2.5 miles, the trail opens onto exposed baldface with fine views to the west and north of the Passumpsic Valley and Lake Willoughby. At 0.1 mile beyond the baldface, the trail arrives on the wooded summit of Burke's West Peak, where a lean-to camping shelter perches near a rock hearth. Follow the trail to an open area not far from the shelter that offers fine southern and western views. Here, look to the left and you'll see the nearby summit of Burke Mountain.

Drop to an intersection cradled in a sag and turn right (southwest). Track across a level ridge through a thick spruce forest. Shortly, in a col between the West Peak and Burke Mountain summits, bear right at another trail junction.

Shortly, the trail opens onto the parking lot at the end of the auto toll road. The lookout tower looms through the woods to the east. From here, you can follow a paved access road to the summit tower or follow the unblazed Profile Trail. This distinct footpath enters the woods on the southeastern side of the parking lot, leading to the summit in 0.2 mile. You may want to be more adventurous and explore one of the interconnecting paths that splits from the Profile Trail.

More than ninety steps lead to the top of the summit fire tower, as high as a nine-story building. As you might expect, the views into New Hampshire and Canada are unequaled.

Return the way you came or follow the auto road back down. (Remind your weary little hikers that it's all downhill from here!)

 MOUNT HOR

BEFORE YOU GO
Maps USGS Sutton
Current Conditions
Willoughby State Forest (802) 751-0123

ABOUT THE HIKE
Day hike
Moderate for children
May–October
3 miles, round trip
Hiking time 2.5 hours
High point/elevation gain
2660 feet, 1000 feet

GETTING THERE

- From the junction of US 5, VT-122, and VT-114 in Lyndonville, drive 7.2 miles north on US 5 to a junction with VT-5A in West Burke.
- Go straight, now on VT-5A.
- Drive 5.6 miles and turn left (west) onto a gravel road at the parking area for Mount Pisgah.
- Drive through the parking lot and in 1.7 miles, park on the left, at the high point of the land, in a turnout with room for about eight vehicles.

ON THE TRAIL

The three vistas encompassed by this hike take in surprisingly varied scenery. Two offer views of Lake Willoughby and the surrounding mountains, while the third, just below the Mount Hor summit, takes in a mosaic of small ponds with New Hampshire mountains on the horizon. The first section of the hike is the toughest, so let kids know that once they have conquered that initial slope, the rest of the trip is a relative cinch.

Despite the precautions parents must take at the overlooks (where the sheer hillside falls away for up to 1200 feet), this is a terrific hike for youngsters. After all, looking down on things for an afternoon is a nice change for little guys.

Hike along the road in a westerly direction for 50 feet to a sign on the right for the Herbert Hawkes Trail. Head northward into the woods and quickly turn right onto a wide path that climbs easily through thick, young woods. Focus the kids' attention on their surroundings: Have them try to find something sharp, something round, something squishy, and something blue.

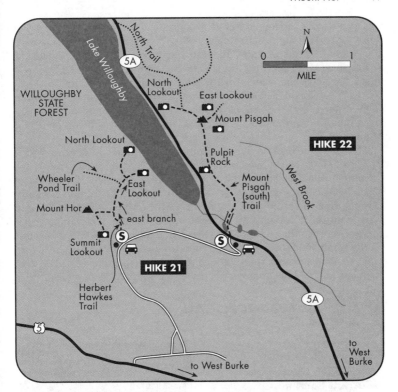

Winding generally northward, the trail climbs more steeply at 0.3 mile as it swings left and cuts into the mountain. In another 0.1 mile, award a granola bar to the first one who reaches the spring that percolates from underground, flooding the trail. Shortly, the trail resumes its northerly course, swinging away from this steep section.

At 0.5 mile into the hike, the trail divides: You turn right onto the east branch as the west branch heads left. Have you found all the items on the first list? Now look for something fuzzy, something that floats, something wet, and something that doesn't belong in the woods (like a gum wrapper). Track along fairly level ground to a wet area at 0.65 mile where you'll have to balance on logs and stones to cross the damp spots. As the trail cuts through hemlock groves, worn rocks and bony roots may trip up tired little legs.

At 0.8 mile from the start, continue straight along the east branch as the Wheeler Pond Trail splits left (northwest). Weave through deciduous woods on rolling terrain to another junction in 0.2 mile. Continue straight toward East Lookout (also called Willoughby Lookout) as the path to North Lookout veers left. (You won't want the kids to precede you here.)

Drop briefly to the sheltered lookout atop precipitous cliffs. From here, Lake Willoughby stretches before you (1200 feet below!) with the cliffs of Mount Pisgah (Hike 22) rising from the water on the opposite shore. Can you pick out tiny boats bobbing on the lake? Enjoy a snack (but save the picnic lunch) before returning to the junction with the path to North Lookout. Turn right and soon descend for 0.1 mile to another dramatic overlook that takes in the lake and peaks along the Canadian border. To the left of Mount Pisgah, you can see Bald Mountain.

Hike 0.7 mile back to the east branch/west branch junction and turn right to follow the seldom-traveled west branch. Climb moderately for 0.1 mile to the wooded summit of Mount Hor. Drop along the trail for a short distance through evergreens to a third overlook, Summit Lookout. Outstanding views unfold to the south of Burke Mountain (Hike 20) and New Hampshire's Mount Moosilauke and Franconia Notch area. Look westward to see the peaks of the Green Mountains. Have the kids count all the small ponds below—among them are Bean, Wheeler, Blake, Duck, and Vail Ponds. Here's the spot to spread out the picnic.

When you're done admiring, retrace your steps to your vehicle.

 MOUNT PISGAH

BEFORE YOU GO
Map USGS Sutton
Current Conditions
Willoughby State Forest (802) 751-0123

ABOUT THE HIKE
Day hike
Challenging for children
May–October; possible closures for peregrine falcon nesting
3.6 miles, round trip
Hiking time 3.5 hours
High point/elevation gain
2692 feet, 1600 feet

GETTING THERE
- From I-91, take exit 23 to US 5 North.
- At the junction of US 5, VT-122, and VT-114 in Lyndonville, continue on US 5 North for 7.2 miles to the junction with VT-5A.
- Bear right onto VT-5A.
- In 5.6 miles, turn left into a substantial parking area.

ON THE TRAIL
Did a climb up Mount Hor (Hike 21) pique your interest in the Pisgah cliffs across the lake? These cliffs, plummeting more than 1000 feet to

View from Pulpit Rock, looking over Lake Willoughby to Mount Hor

the eastern shore of Lake Willoughby, are a National Natural Landmark and offer dramatic views of local spots and distant peaks. Although parents with small children must exercise *extreme caution* at the overlooks (sheer drops of 500 and 1000 feet), older children who are experienced hikers will have no trouble hiking safely. Go for it!

Cross the road to the Mount Pisgah trailhead where a sign announces that the summit is 1.7 miles away. The well-traveled trail, marked in blue, heads northeastward into the woods. Soon, cross a swampy pond outlet over a lengthy log footbridge (with a handrail) and then skirt the base of the pond across a second extended footbridge. (There's nothing like a pair of neat bridges to interest the kids in what lies ahead!)

Climb the bank of the pond and curl left, skirting the pond's eastern side. Quickly, the trail sweeps right, departing the water on an easterly track. Who will be the first to spot the third log crossing at 0.25 mile? In another 0.1 mile, follow the trail on a series of switchbacks leading to the top of the mountain ridge. The trail swings left (north) at 0.45 mile, cresting and then following the ridge, rising gently.

Enjoy your first Lake Willoughby views 0.6 mile from the start, with the cliffs of Mount Hor rising from the opposite shore. Although they'll be tempted, discourage the kids from exploring the left-going side trails. As the main trail ventures northward, the left slope steepens rapidly.

At 0.65 mile, the trail passes high above the southern tip of the lake, Vermont's deepest at more than 300 feet. Trending northwestward with little change in elevation, the path flirts with the edge of the steep, wooded slope that plunges toward the highway and the lake.

At 0.9 mile from the start, follow a side trail that splits left and arrives in 30 feet at Pulpit Rock. (Keep the kids right beside you on this side trip.) The ledge hangs 500 feet over Lake Willoughby and VT-5A, offering magnificent views over the rippling water to Mount Hor. Even folks who are usually immune to acrophobia may feel a few butterflies here. Fall hikers should watch for migrating hawks soaring southward.

Beyond the overlook, the trail climbs moderately through mature woods, wandering away from the edge of the ridge. Here, the kids are free to take the lead. The first one to reach the erratic boulder at 1.1 miles gets to carry the pack. (Most kids consider that an honor, not a drag.) The trail continues to sweep away from the ridge on an abating grade.

After a brief descent at 1.3 miles, the gradual-to-moderate climb resumes. The trail sidesteps another boulder at the 1.5-mile mark and continues its climb to open baldface, where over-the-shoulder views of Burke Mountain (Hike 20) make a lovely backdrop for a picnic.

Turn the pack over to the fellow who's the first to arrive at the sign announcing the upcoming North Trail and Lookouts. As you arrive at the treed summit of Mount Pisgah, 1.7 miles from the start, a side trail leads right to East Lookout. Drop along the side trail for 150 yards to an overlook with excellent easterly views that take in 3300-foot Bald Mountain and southeasterly views extending to the White Mountains. Here, parents can relax and kids can safely enjoy the views.

Return to the junction and continue northward toward North Lookout. In 0.1 mile, follow a side trail to the left, once more taking care to precede the kids. From the ledge that could be called Pulpit Rock II, the world drops away at your feet as you stand 1000 feet above the ice blue water. The dizzying views encompass Jay Peak, local Wheeler Mountain (Hike 23), Mount Hor (Hike 21), and some Canadian peaks. With the forceful winds and tight space on this lofty ledge, you'll want to explore with extreme caution.

Retrace your steps to your vehicle.

23 EAGLE CLIFF ON WHEELER MOUNTAIN

BEFORE YOU GO
Map USGS Sutton
Current Conditions Private land; no contact

ABOUT THE HIKE
Day hike
Moderate for children
May–October
2.3 miles, round trip
Hiking time 2.5 hours
High point/elevation gain
2371 feet, 725 feet

GETTING THERE

- From the junction of US 5 and VT-5A in West Burke, travel north on US 5 for 8.3 miles.
- Turn right onto Wheeler Mountain Road. (Watch for a sign to Wheeler Pond Camp.)
- Follow this gravel road past Wheeler Pond at 0.9 mile.
- In another mile, beyond a pair of private homes, park in the turn-out on the left.
- Alternatively, from I-91 in Barton, take exit 25 to VT-16 North. In 1.3 miles, turn right onto US 5 South. In another 4.8 miles, turn left onto gravel Wheeler Mountain Road, following the sign to Wheeler Pond Camp. Follow the directions above.

ON THE TRAIL

Even though Wheeler Mountain (2371 feet) is one of the lower peaks in the Lake Willoughby area, its Eagle Cliff provides magnificent, long-range views. I know, vistas keep the old folks happy, but what's in it for the kids? They'll delight in the frequent scrambles up rocky outcroppings and alongside massive ledges. And as the trail runs over lengthy, open baldface, even youngsters will appreciate the far-reaching panoramas. You won't have to worry about initial motivation—the view of Wheeler that they'll have from your vehicle will be inspiration enough. You can pick up a map produced by the Westmore Trail Association at Willoughby stores on VT-5A.

From the parking area, drop briefly through the woods to a right turn onto an old jeep road. Follow the trail northward, as it climbs easily along the right-hand side of an overgrown field. Two-thirds of the way across the field, the trail splits: Turn right onto a red-blazed alternate trail (most difficult) as the main white-blazed trail continues straight along the edge of the field (eventually rejoining the red trail).

As you follow the red trail, rising gently through mixed woods, play How Is It Like Me? Pick anything you see—a dead tree, a mushroom, a squirrel—and ask the kids what that object has in common with them.

Does it need water to live? Does it have a family? Does it make any noise?

The pitch steepens and, at 0.25 mile, the trail meets an impressive, smooth ledge that looks like a tidal wave. Cutting beneath the "tidal wave," the trail scales a 10-foot ledge (that will give the kids no trouble) to reach its base. Guided by red blazes, cut left and begin a steep, 150-foot ascent along the left-hand side of the rock slab. Adults may need to lend a hand to

How is a squirrel like me?

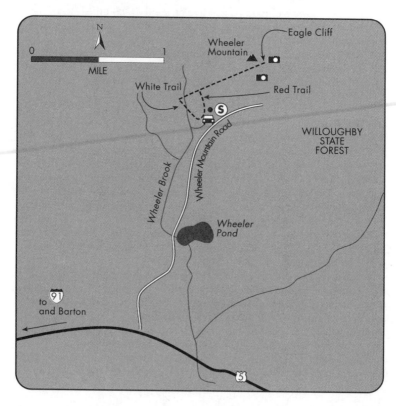

youngsters; kids can repay the favor by watching for the red blazes that stray left and right.

Pause to take in views to the south, west, and east of Norris Mountain and Wheeler Pond. On top of the "tidal wave," 0.4 mile from the start, the white and red trails converge. The trail, now marked in white and red, ducks in and out of woods along the ridge leading to Eagle Cliff, opening onto baldface at 0.6 mile. Expanding views take in Burke Mountain (Hike 20) and Mount Pisgah (Hike 22).

With spruce trees on its left, the trail climbs in the open, about 15 to 20 feet away from the cliffs that drop down Wheeler's southeastern face. As the grade levels, the commanding views extend to Lake Willoughby and Mount Mansfield, Bald Mountain, Jay Peak, and other peaks in the Green Mountains, as well as prominent peaks in the Whites. The trail darts into the woods near the summit and is quickly swallowed by spruce trees.

Follow the rocky path with little change in elevation for 0.15 mile, where it ends abruptly at spectacular Eagle Cliff. This wide ledge, high above Lake Willoughby, offers dizzying views and a choice picnic spot a

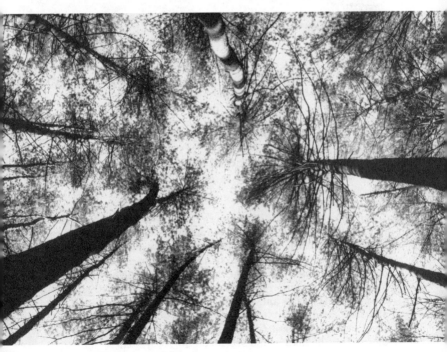

Look up to see the pattern of the pines.

comfortable distance from the edge. A log book is located on a nearby tree. Your comments are welcome.

On the way down, you may want to follow the white-blazed main trail for the entire distance rather than taking the alternate red trail. It's a bit longer, but not as steep.

 Note: Do not hike the Red Trail in wet weather as the granite cliff is slippery when wet. Please be very respectful of the land and the trail. They are privately owned, and use is generously granted by permission of the landowner.

 DEVIL'S GULCH

BEFORE YOU GO
Maps USGS Eden and Hazens Notch
Current Conditions Green Mountain Club (802) 244-7037
Caretaker fee for cabin

ABOUT THE HIKE
Day hike or overnight
Moderate for children
May–October
4.8 miles, round trip
Hiking time 4.5 hours
High point/elevation gain
1670 feet, 1050 feet

GETTING THERE

- From I-91, take exit 26 to VT-58 West and US 5 North.
- In 0.2 mile, turn left onto VT-58 West.
- Travel 12.9 miles to Lowell and turn left (south) onto VT-100.
- After 8.7 miles, in Eden (not Eden Mills), turn right (north) onto VT-118.
- In 4.5 miles, a sign on the left announces the Long Trail; park on the right side of the road.

ON THE TRAIL

When you stand amid the boulders that line the floor of the dark, narrow Devil's Gulch, it's not hard to imagine time turning back a century or even ten centuries. This murky gorge, untouched by modern times, is almost primeval and is sure to be the setting of ghost stories invented on the ride home. But the gulch isn't the only thing for kids to look forward to: Views from Ritterbush Lookout, dozens of stream crossings over stepping stones and log bridges, kid-sized waterfalls and cascades, and the Green Mountain Club's (GMC) Spruce Ledge Camp will keep them excited from start to finish. Unlike most hiking routes, you will descend on the hike in and ascend on the return trip.

If you are planning to break up the hike with an overnight at the

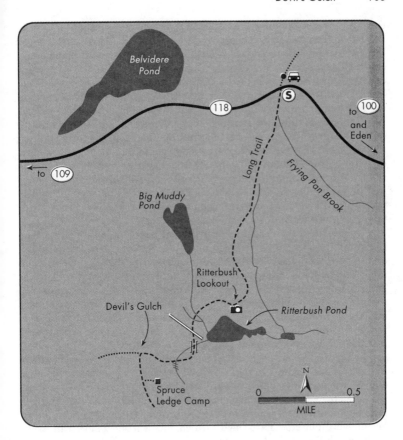

Spruce Ledge Camp structure or at a tent site, bring along a flashlight covered with red cellophane. You can take a midnight stroll to spot wildlife: Animals won't be able to see your red light, but you'll be able to see them!

Cross the road and enter the woods, following the white-blazed Long Trail southwestward. The well-trampled path runs along a ridge that drops off to the left. For the first 0.8 mile, the trail climbs easily through thin, mixed woods sprinkled with birch trees. Do the woods seem quiet and still? Begin counting and stop when you hear a noise—you probably won't get beyond five before a bird whistles or wind rustles the leaves. How quietly can you move through the forest?

At 0.8 mile, the trail embarks on a lengthy descent to the Ritterbush Lookout and Devil's Gulch. (Remind kids to conserve their energy; it will be a long climb back to your vehicle.) Initially, the trail drops through a gully, hopping over frequent wet spots. A stream joins from the left at 1 mile and accompanies you for 0.2 mile. Have a scavenger hunt for sounds: Listen for a birdcall, an airplane, a woodpecker, and a chattering squirrel.

At 1.7 miles, the trail opens onto the safe, narrowly exposed ledge known as Ritterbush Lookout with terrific views of Ritterbush Pond and the surrounding mountain ridges. From the lookout, the trail switches right, then left, tumbling down a rocky hillside. An adult may want to lead the way to choose the best footing. You can see the pond through the trees, but the trail avoids the swampy shoreline.

After a drop of about 100 yards, the trail swings right to circle above the pond from a distance. It drops gently to a pair of stream crossings just under 2 miles from the start. Be patient if the kids stop for a little water play. Beyond the streams, head straight across a woods road, still following the white blazes of the Long Trail.

Over the next 0.2 mile, hop over several trickling streams that feed the pond. Balance on halved logs to cross a wet area, then drop into a cool, moss-covered ravine. At 2.2 miles, cross over a hurrying brook on a log bridge. Remember Pooh Sticks, Winnie the Pooh's favorite water game? Drop twigs off one side of the bridge and look to the other side to see whose stick emerges first. Climb past an overhanging rock mass and along the bank of a racing brook. Water cascades over the jumbles of rocks and spills down miniature waterfalls. If the kids beg to stay here, promise them better things to come.

Navigate a rough section of slippery roots and moss-covered boulders to duck under a rock tunnel into Devil's Gulch. The sides of the dark, damp gorge reach steeply skyward as a maze of boulders twists across the gulch floor. Give the kids plenty of time to explore the caves and hollows before either retracing your steps to your vehicle or continuing on for an overnight stay. Past Devil's Gulch, follow a short side trail to the left to reach Spruce Ledge Camp.

Opposite: Young hikers (with young, limber legs!) have an advantage on steep sections.

25 CHESTERFIELD GORGE STATE WAYSIDE

BEFORE YOU GO
Map USGS Keene
Current Conditions New Hampshire State Parks South Regional Office (603) 485-2034

ABOUT THE HIKE
Day hike
Easy for children
April–November
0.8 mile, loop
Hiking time 45 minutes
High point/elevation gain 850 feet, 125 feet
Accessible pit toilet

GETTING THERE

- From I-91 in Brattleboro, Vermont, take exit 3 for NH-9 East toward Keene, New Hampshire.

- In 9.6 miles, turn left into a large, paved parking lot at a sign for Chesterfield Gorge State Wayside, A Geological Park.

ON THE TRAIL

Pick a sunny, spring day to visit Chesterfield Gorge—you'll want to witness the runoff swelling this narrow ravine. The gorge is a terrific place to evaluate inexperienced hikers—the route is short, easy, and consistently appealing. If kids lose interest or wear out here, it may be a sign that they're not quite ready for family hiking. If they prance around the gorge and beg for more, turn the page!

From the northern side of the parking area, signs direct you to the Gorge Trail or the toilets (where you can also get information about the gorge). The Gorge Trail, wide and well traveled, sweeps left and drops

Peering into the brook that flows through Chesterfield Gorge

on rustic steps along Wilde Brook. In 0.1 mile, the path turns right and spans the stream. Climb the bank of the gorge and head northwest; here, sturdy railings and fences guard the edge. Walk along the level trail for 0.2 mile as the water races through the ravine 20 to 50 feet below.

Soon, the trail sinks gently toward the western end of the gorge where you cross back over the stream on a footbridge without railings—keep an eye on youngsters. Kids may want to take their time here because the bridge offers a great spot from which to examine the tumbling stream up close. The trail switches back to climb the opposite bank and then snakes along the edge of this rim heading eastward. You'll soon return to the first stream crossing; retrace the initial route to the parking area.

WILDE BROOK

Wilde Brook has its beginning in two ponds uphill. After flowing through the gorge, it enters Partridge Brook, which continues on to the Connecticut River. If you see suds floating in the stream, don't be alarmed. This is likely caused by minerals from decomposing wood and roots in the water.

26 LITTLE MONADNOCK AND RHODODENDRON STATE PARK

BEFORE YOU GO
Map USGS Monadnock
Current Conditions
Rhododendron State Park, managed by Monadnock State Park (603) 532-8862
Small fee on weekends and holidays in season

ABOUT THE HIKE
Day hike
Easy for children
April–November
3.3 miles, round trip
Hiking time 2.5 hours
High point/elevation gain
1780 feet, 600 feet
Rhododendron Loop Trail accessible; accessible pit toilet

GETTING THERE

- From the junction of NH-12 and NH-119 in Fitzwilliam, drive 1 mile on NH-119 heading west.

- Turn right onto Rhododendron Road at a sign for Rhododendron State Park.
- In 2 miles, turn right onto the gravel Rockwood Pond Road and into Rhododendron State Park.
- Immediately bear left at a fork and park near the information bulletin board.

ON THE TRAIL

The only Monadnock that exists for most out-of-staters is the "Grand" one, though local hikers have discovered that Little Monadnock in Fitzwilliam has as much to offer—albeit on a smaller scale—as its big brother. Visit in mid- to late July when 16 acres of wild rhododendrons (one of the largest colonies in the Northeast) are in full bloom with generous pink flowers. July is also the month when the mountain's blueberry bushes will be loaded down and ready for picking. Put the kids, camera, and berry buckets in your vehicle and head over!

To the left of the information board, squeeze between two granite posts to head northward (right) on the wide Rhododendron Loop Trail. Soon, as the park name promises, lush rhododendron bushes border the path. The Laurel Trail splits left as you follow the Rhododendron Loop Trail straight to cross a footbridge over a dribbling stream. Can the kids spot any newts or salamanders? (Friends of ours counted more than thirty while hiking this trail after a rainstorm!)

At 0.2 mile, the trail divides again; head right on the white-blazed Little Monadnock Trail, rising gently toward the summit of Little Monadnock. Look for red squirrel *middens:* piles of scales from pine and spruce cones. Squirrels scrape off the scales to get at the cone's small inner seeds.

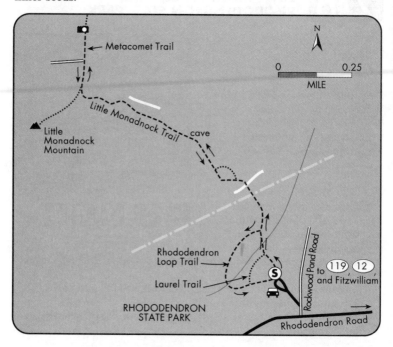

Cresting the summit of Little Monadnock

At 0.6 mile, you'll leave the boundary of Rhododendron State Park and pass through an opening in a stone wall. Soon, climb on all fours up a squat ledge. At the top, the white-blazed trail turns right and a more trodden path veers left. Follow the worn trail on the left, which shortly rejoins the white-blazed trail. Turn left, dipping in and out of a gully. As you work your way up a hillside, look right at 0.8 mile for the kid-size cave formed by a random settling of rocks.

If you've come too early to admire the rhododendrons in bloom, perhaps the wildflowers that edge this section of trail will be showing off their blossoms. The trail climbs briskly to the left of a stone wall through mixed conifers. What will the kids notice first: the signs or the sounds of woodpeckers? (If you see sawdust at the base of a tree, you'll probably see woodpecker holes farther up the trunk. Sawdust may mean gnawing insects, and insects usually attract hungry woodpeckers.)

Near the summit of exposed granite, the Little Monadnock Trail and the white-blazed Metacomet Trail converge. Grand Monadnock (Hike 27) looms on the eastern horizon. Although you could head left (west) to the treed summit of Little Monadnock Mountain, we recommend you bear right (north), now following the Metacomet Trail. The kids can begin to scan the ground for wild blueberry bushes. A logging road branches left in 0.1 mile; you continue straight for another 0.1 mile to an exposed area with superb 180-degree views. To the east, Grand Monadnock broods over southwestern New Hampshire, while Mount Sunapee (Hike 32) and Mount Kearsarge rise over the local hills to the north. The northwestern horizon is consumed by the mountains of Vermont, notably Mount Ascutney (Hike 7).

Relax, snack, and then return along the Metacomet Trail to the Little Monadnock Trail and back to Rhododendron State Park, where you bear right at the first intersection to complete the Rhododendron Loop Trail. From that junction, your vehicle is 0.4 mile away.

NATIONAL NATURAL LANDMARK

In 1982, the rhododendron grove at Rhododendron State Park was designated a National Natural Landmark. This grove is the largest in New England and illustrates the natural diversity that makes up the New England landscape.

 ## MOUNT (GRAND) MONADNOCK

BEFORE YOU GO
Map USGS Monadnock
Current Conditions
Monadnock State Park (603) 532-8862

ABOUT THE HIKE
Day hike
Challenging for children
May–October
4.5 miles, round trip
Hiking time 4 hours
High point/elevation gain
3165 feet, 2000 feet

GETTING THERE
- From the junction of NH-101 and NH-124 in Marlboro, drive 5.1 miles on NH-124.
- Turn left onto Shaker Road (dirt at 0.4 mile becomes much rougher and may be impassable from December to May).
- In under a mile turn left into parking area for the Marlboro Trail.

ON THE TRAIL
Mount Monadnock is to central New England what Mount Washington is to northern New England, and it has the dubious honor of being one of

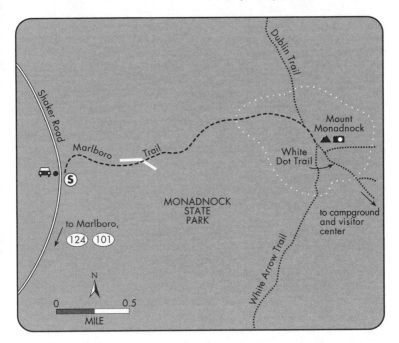

the most visited peaks in the Northeast. Tens of thousands of hikers are drawn to the Grand Monadnock each year for many of the same reasons that Henry David Thoreau and Ralph Waldo Emerson were attracted in the nineteenth century: The sculpted mountain, capped with a barren summit, is the unchallenged ruler of the low, surrounding hills that stretch west to Vermont and east to the Atlantic.

The forty miles of hiking trails within Monadnock State Park include paths that snake to the mountaintop from all sides. The route described here is one of the least traveled, with views emerging early in the route. The mountain is at its best in autumn, but because most people know that, a fall hike feels a lot like standing in line for a movie. To stack the odds for solitude in your favor, visit in early summer. This is a very difficult trail, so be sure your hiking party is experienced and up to the challenge before setting out.

From the parking area, head east across the gravel road to the trail information bulletin board. The wide, white-blazed Marlboro Trail begins to the left (northeast) of the trail sign, initially on level ground. Traveling through hemlocks and hardwoods, the trail begins a gradual climb at 0.15 mile over rocky terrain. (Our preschooler enjoyed jumping from rock to rock here.) Who can find the first rock painted with an M? (Put the youngest hiker in charge of counting M rocks.)

The path hugs and then divides a stone wall at 0.5 mile. A moderate-to-steep ascent up rock steps quickly leads to relatively open baldface. From here to the summit, the trail offers nearly constant views over the southern New Hampshire valley and to the exposed peak ahead. (Be sure to keep a careful eye on the weather because there is little shelter from the elements on this route.) As the trail rises in and out of sturdy evergreen clusters, kids may find a few blueberry bushes amid the low shrubs. Sweeping across more exposed terrain, the trail follows cairns and white blazes on a gradual ascent that conceals the elevation you are gaining. The gentle slope and consistently smooth ledge underfoot mean that kids can quickly and effortlessly cover a significant distance.

Patches of young vegetation and barren slopes testify to the harsh conditions this mountain has withstood in recent history: logging and land clearing in the 1700s and 1800s, the great hurricanes of 1815 and 1938, and several large-scale fires—the most recent one in 1953.

At 1 mile from the start, the trail cuts through a groove between two chunks of ledge and, over the next 0.4 mile, climbs on a moderate-to-steep grade over some formidable ledges (be prepared to lend a hand to young hikers). At 1.8 miles, the trail surmounts another exposed shoulder where hikers have a clear view of the treeless summit. In 0.2 mile, the Dublin Trail merges from the left (north) to join the Marlboro Trail. After scaling several short ledges and rising gently toward the peak, the Marlboro and Dublin Trails meet the White Arrow Trail, which joins from the right. Together the trails lead toward the massive, open summit with weathered ledges that invite kids to climb and explore.

The most devastating of the recent fires was the 1820 blaze that stripped the summit cone of all vegetation and soil; it will be thousands of years before enough soil accumulates to support tree roots again. Farmers reportedly set the mountain on fire in an attempt to kill wolves that had attacked nearby flocks of sheep. The outstanding panoramic view extends westward to Vermont's Green Mountains, northward to the White Mountains, and southwestward to the Berkshires. The Grand Monadnock towers 880 feet over its eastern neighbor, Pack, which also bears the name Monadnock. All Monadnocks have been named after the Grand one, and the word *monadnock* has come to stand for an isolated mountain that has resisted erosion.

After sharing stories with the other hikers gathered at the summit, reverse direction to complete the hike. (*Remember:* The great majority of hiking accidents occur on the descent, so choose your footing carefully and rest whenever you need it.)

Note: Camping and fires are permitted in the state park campground at the base of the White Dot Trail. The visitor center and state park headquarters are located in the same area.

2 8 PACK MONADNOCK AND MILLER STATE PARK

BEFORE YOU GO
Map USGS Peterborough South
Current Conditions Miller State Park (603) 924-3672 May–October; Greenfield State Park (603) 547-3497 November–April
Small fee

ABOUT THE HIKE
Day hike
Moderate for children
April–November
3.2 miles, loop
Hiking time 3 hours
High point/elevation gain
2285 feet, 1000 feet
One accessible pit toilet at base; two accessible viewing areas at summit; auto road to summit

GETTING THERE
- From Milford, travel west on NH-101; from Peterborough, travel east on NH-101.

- The entrance to Pack Monadnock and Miller State Park is on the northern side of NH-101 across from Temple Mountain Ski Area, near the Temple–Peterborough town line.

ON THE TRAIL
Pack (South Pack, to be specific) doesn't attract as many hikers as its formidable neighbor Grand Monadnock (Hike 27), though a steady stream of vehicles chugs up the summit road in season. From the mountaintop on a clear day you can see—if not forever—at least to Boston and to the White Mountains. While you'll share these panoramic views with the tourists, you'll find solitude along the Wapack Trail, which winds for nearly 1.4 miles through heavy woodlands to the summit. This rugged footpath challenges young hikers with just enough rock scrambles and steady climbing to make things interesting but not overwhelming.

Before the hike, you may want to study the trail information board at the northeastern side of the parking lot near the auto road. The foot trail ducks into the woods to the right of the board and toll booth. The yellow-blazed Wapack Trail begins to the left of the hiking board. The blue-blazed Marion Davis Trail, on which you will return, begins to the right. Within 0.1 mile, the trail crosses the paved auto road and reenters the woods, ascending briskly.

For the next 0.3 mile, the trail rises along rocky, rugged terrain with ledges on the right and left; young hikers may need a hand along particularly challenging sections. *Pack* is an American Indian word meaning "little"; at this point in the hike, the kids might consider the name quite inappropriate. As the trail winds along the mountain's western side, it frequently emerges onto open ledge with marvelous views of southwestern New Hampshire, predominantly Temple Mountain to the south and Grand Monadnock to the west.

At 0.6 mile, the trail leaves the rim of the mountain and turns inland to climb at a consistent pace toward the summit. Any grumblers? Get silly: If you were a tree, what kind would you be? Why? Get serious: How do deciduous trees benefit by shedding their leaves each fall? (Once the leaves have fallen off, the tree's interior is sealed off from the frost and snow. Also, less snow accumulates on bare branches, thus fewer branches break off.)

Near the summit, about 1.2 miles from the start, the trail dips into a ravine (saturated though passable in spring). The path struggles out of the gulch to resume its northerly climb through a dense hemlock forest. The trail intersects with the red-blazed Summit Loop Trail. Continue right for a short walk to the summit. At the top you will find a three-sided stone shelter, a lookout tower, pit toilets, a park shed, a drinking fountain, fire rings, and picnic tables.

Dismiss the acrophobia and climb to the top of the lookout tower. The 360-degree view takes in Grand Monadnock to the west and North Pack and Crotched Mountain to the north. Temple Mountain is directly to the south, and beyond it, Wachusett Mountain. The distinctive Boston skyline defines the southeastern horizon, and the peaks of the White Mountains, nearly 100 miles away, outline the northern one.

Leave the auto tourists in the parking lot and follow the red-blazed Summit Loop Trail, which starts near the park shed. This trail runs

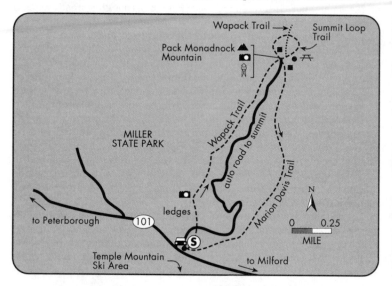

along the northern rim of South Pack, providing stunning views to the north and west, and returns you in 0.4 mile to the summit parking area. Spread out a picnic lunch on one of the tables and savor the spectacular panoramas.

To descend, return to the park shed with the drinking fountain on the corner. Find the sign and blue blazes for the Marion Davis Trail. Head into the woods on this blue-blazed trail. Drop moderately through dense woodlands for 1.4 miles to return to the parking area at the base of the mountain.

 BEAVER BROOK ASSOCIATION

BEFORE YOU GO
Map USGS Pepperell
Current Conditions Beaver Brook Association (603) 465-7787
Donations welcome

ABOUT THE HIKE
Day hike
Easy to moderate for children
Year-round; snowshoes available for rental in winter
3.8 miles, loop
High point/elevation gain
523 feet, 400 feet
Some paths wide enough for jogging strollers

GETTING THERE
- From US 3 in Nashua, take exit 6.
- Turn left onto Broad Street (NH-130).
- Bear right at the split in 6 miles.
- At the next set of lights, turn left onto NH-122 South.
- In 1 mile, take a right onto Ridge Road.
- Look for 117 Ridge Road, on your right in approximately 1 mile.

ON THE TRAIL
Starting with the vision of land stewards Hollis P. Nichols and Jeffrey P. Smith and a meager 18 acres, Beaver Brook now encompasses over 2000 acres of woodlands and wetlands for the public to enjoy. With approximately thirty-five miles of trails, hikers, bikers, birdwatchers, and equestrians have many recreational opportunities. (Some trails are multi-use, and some are designated for hiking, skiing, and snowshoeing only.) The Beaver Brook Association—a private, nonprofit educational corporation dedicated to environmental education and land stewardship—also offers many programs for children and adults to support their mission. This is a great place for kids, as many of the trails pass by ponds and alongside

brooks over fairly easy terrain. The interconnecting trails provide many opportunities for choosing different routes and taking shortcuts when energy wanes. The route described here is just a small sampling of what Beaver Brook has to offer, and you have a good chance of becoming a repeat visitor after your first visit.

During office hours you can pick up a map for a small fee at the Maple Hill Farm and Office Building. To begin, head north of the office on the multi-use trail Cow Lane. (Multi-use trails are marked in blue; hiking, snowshoeing, and skiing are marked only in yellow.) You will see a meadow with bluebird boxes on your right and will travel around this meadow on your return. In a little under 0.2 mile, turn left onto the

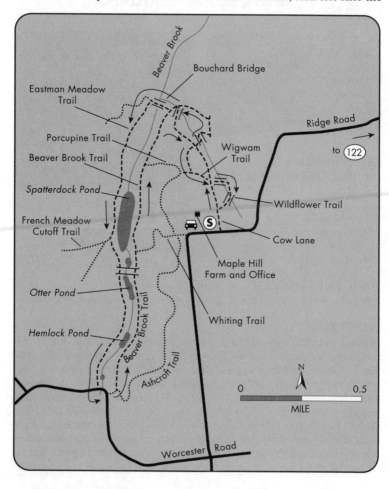

Wigwam Trail, marked in yellow. What is the highlight of this trail? That's right—a wigwam! At the junction with the Porcupine Trail in another 0.1 mile, turn right, following the "To Wigwam" sign. After winding through the woods a short distance, the Wigwam Trail crosses over Cow Lane. Right beyond this crossing, you will spot the wigwam on your left. Who can figure out how it was made? What material was used?

Immediately past the wigwam, cross a bridge over a small stream. At the very next trail junction turn left and left again at the next junction in approximately 300 feet. Cross the stream once more and head back toward Cow Lane where you will find a post with multiple trail signs. Cross over Cow Lane, following signs to the Beaver Brook Trail. In less than 0.1 mile head straight over Beaver Brook on a wooden footbridge, while the Beaver Brook Trail turns left. Who can tiptoe and make the least amount of noise?

Bridge across Beaver Brook

If you are very quiet, you may spot some wood ducks. If you are not so quiet, you may hear the sound of them flying away. At the very least you will see the duck nesting boxes placed here to provide homes for wood ducks, a species protected under the Migratory Bird Treaty Act of 1918. Take a moment to stand on Bouchard Bridge to listen. What sounds does everyone hear? It may feel peaceful, but if you pay attention you will notice it is a noisy place!

At the trail junction on the opposite shore, turn left to pick up the Eastman Meadow Trail. This parallels Beaver Brook and its wetlands before reaching and providing views of Spatterdock Pond. You can tell that beavers live here—who can spot a beaver lodge? Although the trail mainly stays above the water, you will have many pretty views of the pond. The Eastman Meadow Trail meets the French Meadow Cutoff Trail in 0.6 mile; stay left on the Eastman Meadow Trail. In another 0.1 mile you will have an option for a shortcut by turning left and following the bridge back to the Beaver Brook Trail. To continue along Otter and

Hemlock Ponds, follow the Eastman Meadow Trail another 0.4 mile to a small parking area off Worcester Road. Turn left and cross the brook to the Ashcroft Trail on the other side. At the next junction, turn left on the Beaver Brook Trail. In 0.4 mile you will pass the bridge to the Eastman Meadow Trail. (If you took the shortcut, this is where you would be.) Soon after, the Whiting Trail, on the right, another shortcut option, leads back to Maple Hill Farm and the office.

To continue the hike, remain on the Beaver Brook Trail. Another footbridge leads you to a pretty view of Spatterdock Pond, complete with bench for taking in the view leisurely. This could very well be the prettiest spot on the hike. On this side of the pond, the trail hugs the shoreline closely, so water views are constant. (At the next trail junction, another shortcut presents itself. You can turn right on the Porcupine Trail and head straight to Cow Lane.) To finish the entire loop, stay on the Beaver Brook Trail to its meeting with Cow Lane and turn right. Follow Cow Lane 0.3 mile and turn left on the Wildflower Trail. This short trail leads you around the meadow with bluebird boxes you saw at the beginning of the hike. If you visit when the wildflowers are blooming, you can practice your identification. Don't worry if you don't know names, as the gardeners at the center will have many of them labeled for you. Remember—don't pick! This trail drops you off right across from the parking area.

SOUTH MOUNTAIN LOOKOUT TOWER TRAIL

BEFORE YOU GO
Map USGS Mount Pawtuckaway
Current Conditions
Pawtuckaway State Park (603) 895-3031
Small fee at main entrance

ABOUT THE HIKE
Day hike or overnight
Moderate for children
May–October
0.8 mile, round trip
Hiking time 1 hour
High point/elevation gain
908 feet, 370 feet

GETTING THERE
- From NH-101 East or West, take exit 5.
- Head north on NH-107 for 7.6 miles and turn right onto Reservation Road.
- This narrow road soon turns to dirt and forks in 1.2 miles.
- Bear right, following signs to the fire lookout tower.
- Drive another 1.3 miles and turn left onto Tower Road.
- Continue 0.8 mile to parking on the right, at the base of South Mountain.

ON THE TRAIL

Pawtuckaway State Park, located in southeastern New Hampshire, is popular for the many biking, swimming, picnicking, snowmobiling, and hiking opportunities available within its 5500 acres. Although it can be crowded, this short and moderately steep hike is well worth it for young hikers. (More ambitious hikers can follow the entire Mountain Trail from the main entrance of the park to a campground and beach for swimming in Lake Pawtuckaway.) Children will delight in climbing over roots and through boulders to reach the top of South Mountain. At 908 feet, the summit offers breathtaking views of the entire park, as well as the chance to climb to the top of one of New Hampshire's sixteen fire lookout towers.

Taking in the views from the fire tower

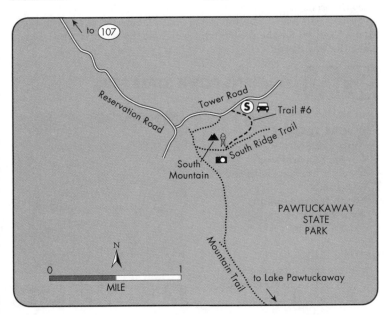

A #6 sign and white blazes guide you to the start of the trail, which begins a gradual ascent through oak, beech, and pine forest. Almost immediately you will come to a trail junction; follow the arrow and turn left. The path continues its climb, and soon you will encounter big rock overhangs and glacial erratics (boulders). These huge rocks deposited by glaciers near the end of the Ice Age will amaze children with their size, many over thirty feet tall.

The trail takes a few twists and turns while heading on a generally southeast course. At around 0.2 mile you will start to get glimpses through the trees of the view that will reward you at the top. See if the kids can peek and find any ponds below. At 0.3 mile, the fire tower is visible and will provide motivation for little legs tired from the climb. Hike one last short stretch through the rocks, and you are at the summit and the tower.

All around are amazing views of the Uncanoonuc Mountains and the many ponds, lakes, and rivers in the area—views that are even more spectacular from the top of the tower. But use caution: Although there are railings, the stairs are very exposed and it can be windy. Small children may want to go only to the first landing and will need assistance at all times. Look for 803-acre Lake Pawtuckaway to the southeast and Mount Pawtuckaway to the northwest, and see if you or the kids can spot any of the turkey vultures that are often seen flying near the summit. The flat rocks surrounding the tower provide ideal picnic spots, so be sure to relax and enjoy the scenery.

Other trails lead to the summit of South Mountain, so be certain you are on Trail #6 for the return trip. A sign at the top and white blazes mark the way down.

31 ODIORNE POINT STATE PARK

BEFORE YOU GO
Map USGS Kittery (Maine)
Current Conditions
Seacoast Science Center (603) 436-8043
Small fee in season; members free

ABOUT THE HIKE
Day hike
Easy for children
Year-round
2.2 miles, loop
Hiking time 2 hours
High point/elevation gain
60 feet, 100 feet
Science center accessible, some paved paths

GETTING THERE
■ From the junction of US 1 and NH-1A in Portsmouth, drive on NH-1A South.

- Pass the Odiorne Point State Park boat launching area on the left at 3.1 miles.
- Drive another 0.75 mile to the Odiorne Point State Park and Seacoast Science Center entrance on the left.
- Turn here and follow the entrance road to the right.

ON THE TRAIL

Odiorne Point State Park's 135 acres include 2 miles of seashore, the largest undeveloped coastal tract in New Hampshire. Extending from Odiorne Point to the Witch Creek salt marsh, the park is an ironic blend of serene, natural beach, once called *Pannaway* by Native Americans, and concrete casements from the long abandoned World War II coastal defense installation of Fort Dearborn.

This land was farmed and fished by ten generations of Odiornes beginning in the 1600s, and it eventually attracted wealthy families who built oceanfront estates with fountains and formal gardens. These turn-of-the-century "summer cottages" and the Sagamore House, a seaside resort, were demolished in the early 1940s to erect the military fortification that was to protect Portsmouth Harbor's naval shipyard in the event of enemy attack. Twenty years later, the state of New Hampshire purchased the parcel for $91,000. Today, the state park offers rugged beach trails, as well as lovely woodland paths that curl gracefully around the ghosts of the seaside mansions.

You'll want to visit at low tide so that the kids can explore Odiorne Point's tide pools and the beach's wrack line, the ribbon of shells, seaweed, driftwood, and smooth stones left by the retreating sea. (Check the Seacoast Science Center's website at *www.seacoastsciencecenter .org* for tide information.) Wear sneakers or rubber-soled shoes, and bring a camera and a picnic lunch to spread out on one of the seaside picnic tables.

Stop in at the Seacoast Science Center, where live animal and interactive exhibits interpret the natural and social history of the park. Programs are offered free with admission, and the nature store carries a variety of books, field guides, and unique nautical gifts. You can also pick up a map to the park. When you are done investigating inside, head toward the southwestern end of the park along a paved sidewalk that brings you to restroom facilities and playground equipment. Promise the kids a return visit to the playground after the hike and follow the path to the edge of a cove known as the Drowned Forest where, at low tide, you may see clusters of stumps. Thousands of years ago, this area was a pine forest.

What causes the sea to rise and retreat twice a day? Explain to the kids that although Earth's gravity holds the water on our planet, the seas are also affected by the weaker gravitational pulls of the moon and sun. These pulls change as Earth rotates, causing the tides. As the

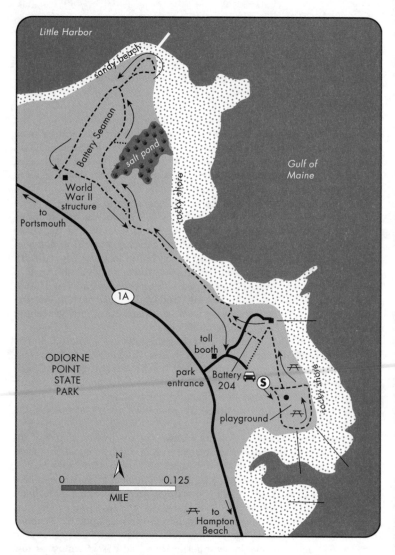

waters recede along one coastline, they advance on a faraway shore, like water sloshing back and forth slowly in a giant bathtub.

Walk along the shore heading eastward toward Odiorne Point, where the kids can join the gulls that prowl the expansive, rocky shore at low tide. (Warn the children that seaweed-covered rocks are slippery.) Look for tide pools teeming with life. You may see a barnacle open the plates of its shell and stick out its feathery feet, trying to kick plankton and other food into its mouth. If the kids try to pull a barnacle off a rock or shell, they'll discover what most ship owners already know: The limestone "cement" that a barnacle makes to anchor itself to another object is stronger than many human-made adhesives.

Can the children find any sponges attached to tide pool rocks? How about green crabs? These creatures, which are actually green and black, are quite common along the New Hampshire and Maine coasts. Advise kids not to pick them up, though, because they have powerful pincers; it's safer to watch them from a distance as they scurry about sideways.

When you're done exploring the rocky tidal area, rejoin the paved path near the Panama Mounts where guns once rested, solemn reminders of this area's diverse history. As the path turns left, you continue straight, stepping down to a grass picnic area surrounded by stone walls. When you reach the Seacoast Science Center again, follow the sidewalk toward the parking area, but before reaching it, turn right and climb the stairs to Battery 204. The earth-covered structure you just scaled houses thirteen rooms and is protected with enough concrete and steel to withstand direct aerial and naval bombardment. Two 6-inch guns placed 210 feet apart had a range of 15 miles. (You can still see their circular concrete bases.)

Exploring the rocky beach of Odiorne Point

Head down the path on the opposite side and cross the driveway to reach the gravel path indicated by a "Trail" sign. This trail leads you along the rocky shore before making its way through shrubs and woodlands. Stay on the main trail as side trails branch off to the left (leading through woods) and right (to the shoreline). About 0.4 mile from Battery 204, reach an obvious fork near large maples; bear right. The trail leads past the Battery Seaman on the left, which housed an underground command center during World War II. This hill and the one behind the visitor center were landscaped to camouflage the military operations. A decaying cement bunker hides among the pines on the knoll and, to the south, a weary turret sits idle.

Approximately 0.2 mile from the fork, a short side trail on the right leads to a salt pond. Continue on the main trail to the other end of the battery and bear right. At the next junction, take the right side of a small loop that leads to the shore. (By the waters of the Gulf of Maine, you can spend time exploring, and if you opt to, you can walk south along the rocky coast for your return trip instead of continuing on the trails.) Follow the grassy path as it heads north along the shore to Frost Point and the jetty that reaches into Little Harbor. From here, the wide trail turns inland as it follows a sandy beach to your right, with stunning views of the harbor and its moored boats. At the trail junction near the northern point of Battery Seaman, follow the trail to the right to walk on the west side of Battery Seaman. Shortly after you pass the battery's southern end, a side trail leads to the right. Ignore this and stay on the main trail. Soon, turn left on a trail by a World War II structure. This leads you back to your fork by the maples. Bear right and retrace your initial footsteps back to the parking area.

Note: Odiorne Point State Park is open seven days a week, 8:00 AM to 8:00 PM. A small park entrance fee is charged seasonally. The Seacoast Science Center charges year-round; it is open from April through October, seven days a week, 10:00 AM to 5:00 PM, and from November through March, Saturday through Monday, 10:00 AM to 5:00 PM.

WHAT CAN YOU FIND?

Along the rocky shore, kids can look for large brown seaweeds known as wracks and kelps that sprawl on the beach, as well as pieces of dead sponges, starfish, gull feathers, and the pincushion-like shells of sea urchins. Most of the sea urchins' spines will be gone, but you'll be able to see the perfect rows of bumps where the spines were attached. You'll probably find signs of human activity, too, such as colorful lobster buoys that have washed up on shore. Did you know that lobster buoys are almost as individual as fingerprints? Each lobsterman has his own special markings for his buoys so that he can identify those that are tied to his traps.

MOUNT SUNAPEE AND LAKE SOLITUDE

BEFORE YOU GO
Map USGS Sunapee
Current Conditions
Sunapee State Park (603) 763-5561
Small fee

ABOUT THE HIKE
Day hike
Challenging for children
May–October
4.8 miles, round trip
Hiking time 4.5 hours
High point/elevation gain
2743 feet, 1510 feet
No special access

GETTING THERE

- From I-89 in Warner, take exit 9 to NH-103 West.
- Travel about 12.5 miles to the junction with NH-103A,

and continue another 2.3 miles on NH-103 to a rotary.
- Circle the rotary and turn right into Sunapee State Park.
- Drive 0.7 mile to the main Mount Sunapee Ski Area parking lot and leave your vehicle near the North Peak Lodge.

ON THE TRAIL

What do you think of when someone mentions Mount Sunapee? Skiing, right? But when the slopes are green and the skiers are sailing or swimming, Sunapee is a wonderful place to bring the family for a smorgasbord-type hike. You'll climb briskly under the dormant chairlift to the Sunapee summit, snake through the woods to the top of the White Cliffs, and drop to the remote, rocky shoreline of Lake Solitude. With something just around the corner at any given moment, kids won't have time to poke each other with sticks or stuff leaves down one another's jackets.

Stretch your calves before you start; you'll feel the muscles working as you hike up the steep slope. (If you visit on a weekend during foliage season, you'll be able to take the chair lift to the summit for a moderate per-person fee; children under six are delivered to the top for free; this cuts 2.5 miles from the total hike and drops it from a challenging to an easy-to-moderate rating.)

Behind North Peak Lodge, begin your climb up the mountain (heading southward) under the Summit Chair ski lift. The "trail" is actually the open, grassy ski slope, a change from the rugged mountain paths hikers usually encounter. To make the steep ascent easier on little legs, follow a route where the grass has been packed down by vehicles or previous hikers.

Distant, over-the-shoulder views emerge immediately and improve with each step. The steady and straight upward climb means that vertical feet are gained quickly but not easily. To prevent complaining, play Follow-the-Leader, sing songs with the word *up* in them, and try to stump each other with silly riddles. When you stop for a breather, kids

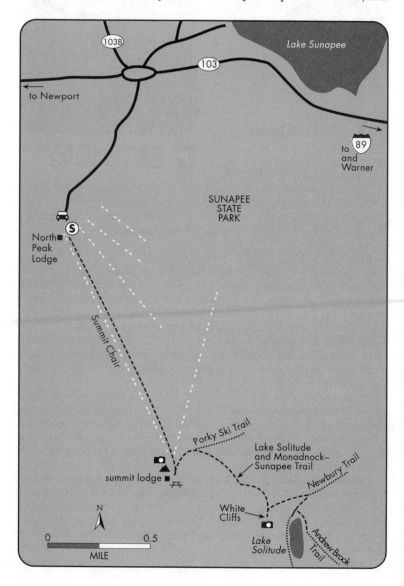

From atop White Cliffs, isolated Lake Solitude seems to live up to its name.

can turn around and imagine what it must be like to plummet down this snowy hill on skis.

Little hikers will need help negotiating two water lines for snow-making as you approach the summit. At the top of the lift, 1.25 miles from the start, look 50 feet to the left (east) for a sign nailed to a birch tree that points toward the orange-blazed Lake Solitude Trail and the white-blazed Monadnock–Sunapee Trail.

Relax (or snack) at the picnic table beyond the summit lodge over-looking impressive Mount Monadnock (Hike 27) before returning to the top of the chair lift. Here, join the white-blazed trail that heads southeastward down the Porky Ski Trail, overlooking Lake Sunapee and Mount Kearsarge. Pass under a chair lift and, about 0.25 mile from the summit, turn right into the woods as the Porky Ski Trail turns left (north) down the mountain.

Guided by orange and white blazes, follow the Lake Solitude and Monadnock–Sunapee Trail through mixed woods dotted with white birch. Sturdy roots spread underfoot.

Soon, 0.4 mile from the summit, the trail twists up a rocky slope to level off 0.2 mile later. Peek through the evergreens for a glimpse of distant Lake Solitude. Just under 1 mile from the summit, a painted arrow points toward a short side trail that leads right (south) to a view of Lake Solitude. Take this trail to the overlook atop the White Cliffs for a lovely view of the aptly named lake. If you decide to stop here for an energy break, you're likely to catch sight of deer, moose, or other creatures visiting the water. Be careful of moose because they will charge.

Return to the main trail and turn right (east) following a sign for Lake Solitude. The trail drops moderately off the White Cliffs along stone steps. Partway down the descent, as the Newbury Trail merges from the left, bend right with the main trail. Shortly, you'll arrive at the northern bank of Lake Solitude. Here, the trail divides: The Andrew Brook Trail heads left on orange blazing and the Monadnock–Sunapee Trail departs right marked with white. Head left on the Andrew Brook Trail, soon emerging on the rocky shore.

If you didn't enjoy a picnic or snack atop Sunapee or the White Cliffs, settle down here. Who can point out the overlook on the White Cliffs from which you just admired the lake? Retrace your steps to your vehicle. (You may be tempted to follow what looks like a surefire shortcut, but trust us when we tell you—from experience—that the fastest way back is the way you came.)

Note: Camping is not permitted at Lake Solitude.

33 BLUE JOB MOUNTAIN

BEFORE YOU GO
Map USGS Baxter Lake
Current Conditions Blue Job Mountain State Forest, Division of Forests and Lands (603) 271-2217

ABOUT THE HIKE
Day hike
Easy for children
April–November
1.4 miles, loop
Hiking time 1.5 hours
High point/elevation gain 1357 feet, 400 feet

GETTING THERE
▪ From the junction of US 202, NH-9, and NH-202A in Northwood, drive east on NH-202A.

- In 10.9 miles, turn left onto First Crown Point Road.
- Turn left at the next stop sign.
- Turn right into the parking area in 5.4 miles.
- Alternatively, from the junction of NH-11 and NH-202A in Rochester, follow NH-202A west for 4.3 miles. Turn right onto Crown Point Road and drive 5.4 miles to the parking area on the right.

ON THE TRAIL

The hike to Blue Job's fire tower is a popular one with local families. An easy, appealing climb leads to an open summit with views that stretch to Boston, the Atlantic, and the White Mountains. What more can you ask of a mountain? Because the views make the hike, save Blue Job for a cloudless, sunny day.

From the northeastern side of the parking lot, head southeast (right) on a wide, well-worn path, following the orange blazes. At first glance, the world of field and forest seems limited to greens and browns. But ask the kids to look for reds, yellows, pinks, and blues, and you'll all be surprised at how colorful nature is.

The initially level path begins a gentle climb at 0.15 mile, stumbling over rocks and roots and gliding across granite. Soon, the chaos

Surveying the central New Hampshire countryside from the Blue Job's fire lookout tower

of boulders submits, forming steps to assist hikers. Cradled by boulders and ledge, the trail continues up the southern side of the mountain. Pause to let the kids flex their rock-climbing muscles. The trail crosses exposed ledge and, at 0.3 mile, bends left (north), squeezing through denser woods.

You'll arrive at the open summit crowned with a fire lookout tower 0.5 mile from the start. Climb the tower and take out your binoculars. Can you spot these landmarks: the former Pease Air Force Base, Boston's Hancock Tower, Mount Washington, the Atlantic Ocean? Although at 1357 feet this is hardly a high peak, the isolated Blue Job soars over the neighboring hills and offers magnificent, long-range views.

From the tower, continue following the orange blazes and begin a gradual, northeasterly descent through sparse pines and across open baldface. The trail soon curves around to offer expansive views to your left. In 0.2 mile, the trail enters the woods and leaves the baldface behind. The moderate descent paralleling a stone wall is carpeted by needles, a marked difference from the rocky terrain of the ascent. Follow this distinct trail as it drops through airy, mature evergreens and crosses a stream over a footbridge. Soon after, the trail turns to the left, cuts through a stone wall and crosses another stream, this time over rocks.

On the ascent, the kids looked for colors. As they descend and hike back to your vehicle, they can survey their surroundings for shapes: A hole in a tree may be shaped like a circle, a leaf like an oval, a rock like a triangle. The trail winds through the trees, leading shortly to the parking area and your vehicle.

 MOUNT CARDIGAN

BEFORE YOU GO
Map USGS Mount Cardigan
Current Conditions
Cardigan State Park (603) 823-7722, ext. 757

ABOUT THE HIKE
Day hike
Challenging for children
April–October
3.2 miles, loop
Hiking time 3 hours
High point/elevation gain
3155 feet, 1800 feet

GETTING THERE
- From I-89, take exit 17 to US 4 East.
- Drive 11.2 miles to the junction with NH-118 in Canaan.

- Turn left (north) on NH-118, following signs to Cardigan State Park.

- In 0.5 mile, turn right onto an unmarked road following another sign to Cardigan State Park.
- At a fork 2.6 miles from NH-118, bear right as the road turns to gravel.
- Drive another 0.7 mile and bear left at a second intersection.
- Continue 0.6 mile to Cardigan State Park's parking and picnic area.

ON THE TRAIL

The *AMC* (Appalachian Mountain Club) *White Mountain Guide* calls Cardigan the "traditional first big mountain climb for children." A well-maintained, easy-to-follow route encompasses sheltered South Peak, where blueberry bushes abound and the dizzying views rival those from Cardigan's exposed summit. Frequent trail signs (despite several conflicting mileages) help kids gauge their progress.

Most of the mountain falls within a 5000-acre state park that is adjacent to the AMC's Cardigan Reservation. The club's Cardigan Lodge includes a main building, cottage, campground, and "Hi-Cabin," where hikers are fed and lodged in summer.

Study the wooden trail map near the parking lot. The red-blazed West Ridge Trail leaves the eastern side of the picnic area and begins a climb through mixed woods dominated by hemlocks and birches. The hard-packed and well-maintained path hops up stone steps at 0.1 mile and crosses a dribbling stream in another 0.1 mile. Tell the children to watch for changes in the vegetation as you climb toward the summit.

Shortly, an unblazed skimobile trail crosses your path, one of many such unmarked trails that crisscross the mountain. At 0.4 mile, a sign marks the intersection with the South Ridge Trail. Here, continue to follow the more heavily traveled West Ridge Trail as it heads left (east). (You'll return along the South Ridge Trail.) At the frequent trail signs that include mileages, test your older children's math skills by asking

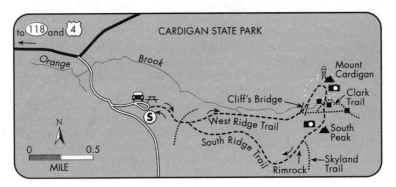

them questions like "How much longer is the hike to the summit on this trail than on the South Ridge Trail?" (0.2 mile).

Rise moderately with rocks and roots underfoot to a stream crossing at 0.75 mile. If the climb is wearing thin on little hikers, play a game: Name all the animals you can think of whose names begin with A, then B, C, and so on. About a mile from the start, you'll scramble over a hemlock-shaded ledge to wind along a cascading brook. Soon, cross the brook over "Cliff's Bridge" as a side trail splits right. (Kids will want to pause on the bridge to examine the tumbling water up close.)

As you continue, the red blazes and stone cairns lead onto baldface, marking your final approach to the windswept Mount Cardigan summit. Western views stretch to Mount Ascutney (Hike 7) and other Vermont peaks while Mount Kearsarge looms to the south. Climb the final 0.1 mile on exposed granite with the fire tower in view. Continue straight at a marked trail junction with the Clark Trail to the rounded peak. Parents can enjoy the 360-degree view while little ones safely explore. You may need to find a cozy nook or cranny to escape the wind if you plan on spending any time here. (South Peak is probably a better choice for a picnic.)

Return to the intersection with the Clark Trail just below the summit and turn left, heading for the South Ridge Trail and the warden's cabins. Follow paint blazes southward, sliding down a barren slope for 0.2 mile. The cabins and outhouse mark the boundary between the stark mountaintop and the edge of the forest. Just before the larger cabin the trail divides: The Clark Trail splits left while you continue straight on the South Ridge Trail. In another 0.1 mile, turn left at a junction (still on the South Ridge Trail) on your way to the Skyland Trail.

Drop through the woods following yellow blazes, heading southward. Continue straight at a four-way intersection with orange- and white-blazed trails, guided by the familiar yellow markings of the South Ridge Trail. After rolling in and out of a damp sag, the trail crests on exposed South Peak, with commanding views that include the Cardigan summit. (You'll have better luck finding a picnic spot here because the winds are less severe than on Cardigan.)

Hike easily for 0.2 mile along the South Peak ridge. Shortly a trail sign at a junction steers you straight, still on the South Ridge Trail, toward the parking area 1.4 miles away. (The Skyland Trail turns left.) Drop moderately down a hemlock-forested slope.

Ledge intrusions define an area known as Rimrock (0.6 mile from the Cardigan summit) and provide the most challenging terrain so far. The kids will most likely need assistance here. Soon, deciduous trees dominate and, 1 mile from South Peak, the rugged South Ridge Trail joins the West Ridge Trail and turns left to arrive in 0.4 mile at the parking area.

 **PARADISE POINT**

BEFORE YOU GO
Map USGS Cardigan
Current Conditions
Newfound Audubon Center,
Paradise Point Nature Center
and Wildlife Sanctuary (603)
744-3516 July 1–September 1
or (603) 224-9909 September
1–July 1

ABOUT THE HIKE
Day hike
Easy for children
Year-round
1 mile, loop
Hiking time 1 hour
High point/elevation gain
600 feet, 75 feet

GETTING THERE

- From I-93 in Plymouth, take exit 26 to NH-25 North/NH-3A (Tenney Mountain Highway).
- Drive 3.6 miles to the rotary in Plymouth, where NH-25 and NH-3A split.
- Head south on NH-3A.
- In 4.8 miles, turn right onto North Shore Road.
- Look for the Audubon Center sign in 1 mile; turn left onto a gravel driveway leading to a parking area.

ON THE TRAIL

The bear may have gone over the mountain, but your four-year-old refuses to do so. Save the high peaks for future years and plan a visit to lovely Paradise Point with its tame, well-marked trails perfectly suited to preschoolers. This 43-acre Audubon-managed natural area supports a nature center with a host of hands-on and live exhibits, as well as a resource library and nature store. Lovely trails wind through marsh areas and forests and follow the rugged shoreline to The Point, where you'll enjoy spectacular views of Newfound Lake. Urge grandparents to guide the little ones on this hike.

From the parking lot, walk southeastward down the gravel road, arriving at the Audubon Paradise Point Nature Center. Here, you can pick up a map or chat with one of the naturalists. From the building, head eastward on a path that leads to the dock area on Newfound Lake. A child-size peninsula reaches into the water to the left of the docks. As kids peer into the water from this promontory, adults will take in the larger picture, looking out over the clear waters of the Newfound Lake inlet.

Follow the yellow-/blue-blazed Ridge/Lakeside Trail southward, winding along the rugged shoreline. Can you hear the call of the common loon?

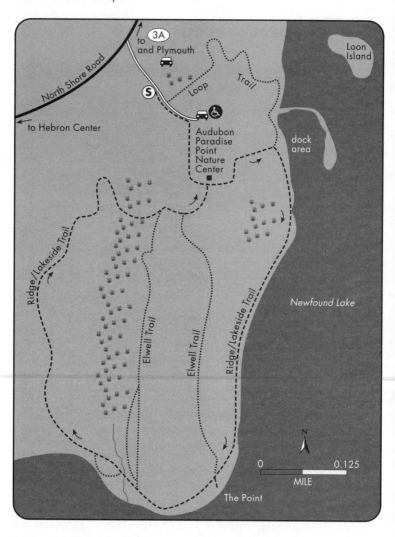

As you approach Paradise Point's southern shore, the trail rises above the lake with the rocky, tree-edged beach thirty feet below. On an open knoll 0.5 mile from the start, the red-blazed Elwell Trail joins from the right.

Turn left (south) onto a red-blazed side trail that leads quickly to a rock ledge, known as The Point, that juts into the water. Newfound Lake stretches before you, melting into the distant mountains. Reaching a depth of 180 feet in some places, the glacial lake is well known for the purity of its water (said to turn over several times a year). Enjoy the delightful concert of the sun's warming rays and the cool breezes sweeping inland.

Return to the knoll and trail junction, turning left (southwest) guided by red and yellow trail markings. Have the kids keep an eye out for tracks of the red fox. Rounding the southern tip of Paradise Point, the red-blazed Elwell Trail branches off to the right as you stay left, now heading northwestward on the yellow-/blue-blazed trail across a rough and rocky tract. Can the kids find any signs of animal homes? A porcupine's boulder den, perhaps? As you leave the water behind, ask your young companions to describe how the inland vegetation differs from the shoreline trees and plants.

Drop moderately eastward through a hardwood forest to a swamp, a little less than a mile from the start. Home to no one's favorite insect,

the mosquito, the swamp also nurtures varieties of frogs and salamanders. (See if the kids can spot the brightly colored red eft salamander.) In spring, the kids can look for frog and salamander eggs floating in the water.

Cross the marsh on a plank walk and emerge from the woods. Follow the blazes to the nature center building. From here, your vehicle is a short walk up the gravel drive.

Note: Paradise Point Nature Center is open from 10:00 AM to 4:00 PM, seven days a week, from late June through Labor Day, as well as some spring and fall weekends. Sanctuary trails are open dawn to dusk year-round. Smoking, swimming, camping, fires, and bicycles are prohibited. Picnicking is allowed with the prior permission of a staff member. Donations are appreciated.

Salamanders abound in pools in early spring.

THREE PONDS TRAIL

BEFORE YOU GO
Map USGS Mount Kineo
Current Conditions White
Mountain National Forest
Pemigewasset/Ammonoosuc
Ranger District (603) 536-1315;
White Mountain National Forest
Supervisor's Office (603) 528-
8721; AMC Pinkham Notch
Visitor Center (603) 466-2721
**White Mountain National
Forest Use Pass required**

ABOUT THE HIKE
Day hike or overnight
Moderate for children
May–October
5.4 miles, loop
Hiking time 4.5 hours
High point/elevation gain
1800 feet, 700 feet

GETTING THERE

- From I-93 in Plymouth, take exit 26 to NH-25 North/NC-3A South (Tenney Mountain Highway).
- Drive 3.6 miles to a rotary in Plymouth where NH-3A and NH-25 split. Continue north on NH-25 for 3.4 miles.
- Turn right onto Main Street in Rumney (at the second blinking light).
- Travel 6.8 miles on Main Street to a gravel driveway and large parking area for hikers on the left. (Look for the "Three Ponds Trail, Mount Kineo Trail, Carr Mountain Trail" sign.)

ON THE TRAIL

You and your family will have a far better time visiting the Three Ponds area than John Stinson did. Nearly 250 years ago, Stinson (for whom the nearby lake and mountain were named) was captured and scalped here by the Native American tribe of St. Francis. Thankfully, your only pursuers will be springtime blackflies. Before the hike, take the kids to the library and study up on the types of vegetation (like hobblebush and marsh fern) that grow in damp, boggy areas. As you hike, see how many of these species you encounter. Notice how the active beavers have affected the vegetation growth by rerouting water. If you enjoyed exploring Lake Solitude (Hike 32), you're sure to appreciate the remote beauty of the Three Ponds (actually, there are four ponds). Waterproof footgear will make the soggy going more fun.

From the northern side of the parking area, the well-worn Three Ponds Trail heads through a damp area in mixed woods. Fun-to-cross plank walks span the wettest terrain. At 0.1 mile, the Mount Kineo

Trail branches right (northeast); follow the yellow-blazed Three Ponds Trail straight (northwest). The trail sweeps easily up a hill, then levels.

At 0.4 mile, cross the first of many streams that trickle through the area. Water always delights children, and water that moves holds a special fascination. In another 0.1 mile, the Carr Mountain Trail splits left

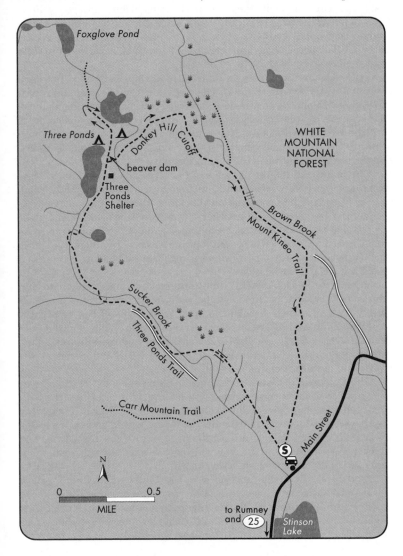

(west) as you continue straight (northwest). Surrounded by a bog (0.7 mile from the start), the Three Ponds Trail weaves across the wettest spots on single logs. At bog's end, cross another stream and drop gently down a wooded slope.

Between the 0.8- and 1-mile marks, cross streams three times, once by way of a footbridge. After the third crossing, the trail meets an overgrown jeep road. Turn right onto the road, still heading in a northwesterly direction, to follow the bank of Sucker Brook. After crossing a tributary, sparse blazes lead uphill as the boisterous brook approaches the trail. At the crest, Sucker Brook turns from right to left and you head straight to cross two shallow sections of the brook on stones.

With Sucker Brook now on its left, the trail rises gradually to hop over the water two more times. The kids can scan the ground for partridgeberry, a plant whose leaves were used by Colonial women to make a pain-relieving tea. At 2 miles, you'll come upon a lovely, remote pond, cradled by forested slopes. Soon a trail diverges right, heading uphill toward the Three Ponds Shelter, a three-sided building that sleeps six. To the shelter's south lies the smallest of the ponds.

The main trail follows the edge of the large pond for 0.2 mile, leaving the water just before a trail junction with the Donkey Hill Cutoff. For now, turn left to continue on the Three Ponds Trail, immediately crossing a beaver dam. In another 0.3 mile, a side trail on the right brings you to a campsite near the upper pond where waterside rocks make a wonderful place to set out a picnic lunch. (From here, the Three Ponds Trail continues northward, passing Foxglove Pond in 0.5 mile and reaching NH-118 in 4.5 miles.)

Return to the Donkey Hill Cutoff intersection and turn left to continue the loop. The trail follows the right (southern) side of a swamp created when beavers flooded the land. What signs of beaver activity can the children find? Tracks? Gnawed tree stumps? Abandoned dams? For the next 0.5 mile, the trail rolls easily through marsh areas, then abruptly changes character as it cuts into a ridge and tracks across rocks and roots for another 0.5 mile.

The Donkey Hill Cutoff ends 3.7 miles from the start of the hike at the junction with the Mount Kineo Trail. Turn right and follow the path (marked occasionally in yellow) along the engaging Brown Brook. Stay on the western side and, in 0.2 mile, you'll pass within 50 feet of a series of cascades that tumbles into a wide pool. Adults can relax while the kids explore. From here, the trail widens to become a woods road, dropping gradually along the splashing brook.

At 0.7 mile from the junction with the Donkey Hill Cutoff, yellow blazes steer you onto a footpath, away from the brook and the woods road. Heading southward, the narrow path snakes through deciduous woods to meet the Three Ponds Trail. Turn left onto the familiar Three Ponds Trail and hike the final 0.1 mile to your vehicle.

3 7 **WALTER/NEWTON NATURAL AREA**

BEFORE YOU GO
Map USGS Plymouth
Current Conditions
Plymouth Conservation
Commission or the Town
of Plymouth Chamber of
Commerce (603) 536-1001

ABOUT THE HIKE
Day hike
Easy for children
March–November
1.4 miles, loop
High point/elevation gain
742 feet, 80 feet

GETTING THERE

- From I-93, take exit 25 and turn right toward Plymouth.
- Turn left at the stop sign onto Main Street (US 3).
- Go around the circle at the town center and continue on US 3.
- In 2 miles, turn right onto Cummings Hill Road.
- Follow this 0.8 mile to a small parking area near a bridge.

ON THE TRAIL

Wetlands, a waterfall, and wildlife make this 163-acre sanctuary an ideal place to explore with children. What could be more fun for kids than traipsing over footbridges alongside a brook on their way to thirty-foot Rainbow Falls? Along the trail, they can also search for signs of wildlife in the bogs—beaver, deer, and even a moose or occasional black bear have been spotted in this natural area, deeded to the town of Plymouth by conservationists Ruth and Henry Walter and Suzanne Newton.

The Ruth Walter Trail to Rainbow Falls starts by Glove Hollow Brook, right past the information board. Cross over a small footbridge and follow the white blazes through a mixed forest of oak, pine, beech, and birch. The flat trail parallels the brook a short distance, providing pretty views of the water before curving away. In 0.3 mile cross another footbridge and soon again get glimpses of the water. Observant hikers will also see signs of the gnawing of beavers on trees. The trail takes a sharp left turn and heads uphill at a slight incline before flattening out and crossing more footbridges to arrive at Rainbow Falls. Here, you will find strategically placed benches for viewing the falls as they cascade over a sheer face of granite, while the kids do some exploring.

To continue the loop, cross a footbridge over the brook, following signs pointing to the Glove Hollow Trail. (A trail to the top of the water-fall splits off to the left for more adventurous hikers.) A short distance after seeing a bench to your right, the trail itself makes a sharp right. Walk over the logs placed on the trail during most of the year to span a

Taking a break from hiking to sit and observe

wet area. Past another bench, the trail climbs steeply before leveling off for the remainder of the hike.

Along the way, you will have views of a bog and the foothills in the distance and can listen for sounds of the brook on your right. This is a fun place to give the kids a compass—see if they can figure out which direction they are heading in and where they were before. They are on the opposite side of the bog from where they started. In the last 0.1 mile, the trail widens as it follows Old Stagecoach Road back to the beginning of the hike.

WEST RATTLESNAKE

BEFORE YOU GO
Map USGS Squam Mountains
Current Conditions Squam Lakes Association (603) 968-7336

ABOUT THE HIKE
Day hike
Easy for children
April–November
1.8 miles, round trip
Hiking time 1.5 hours
High point/elevation gain
1243 feet, 400 feet

GETTING THERE
- From I-93, take exit 24.
- Follow US 3 South for 4.5 miles toward Holderness.
- Turn left onto NH-113 East.
- Drive 5.7 miles to the parking area or roadside parking on the left.

ON THE TRAIL

You will most likely have company on this hike, and for good reason. The views of Squam Lake from the summit of West Rattlesnake are absolutely astounding. With a trip to the top of under 1 mile, it is no wonder that many people flock to this trail to enjoy the sights of this spectacular lake and its many islands. Try to go midweek or off season if you prefer a little more solitude. The flat rock slabs at the top offer

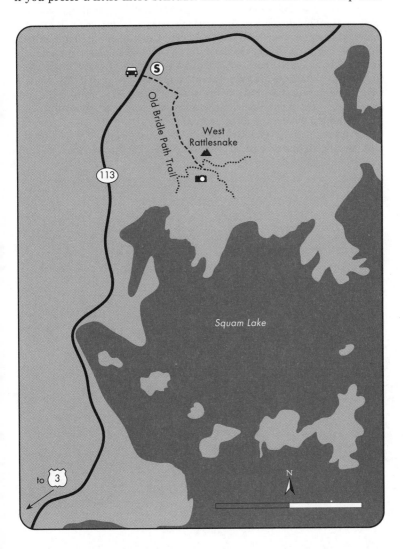

the perfect spot to enjoy a snack or picnic, and the kids will relish climbing around and exploring among the ledges—use caution, however, as there are some precipitous drops.

To begin, cross the street from the parking area and look for signs to the Old Bridle Path Trail. Here, you can look at a map and make a donation toward the trail's upkeep. The trail immediately begins climbing over a path of rock and log steps through a forest of beech, birch, and maple.

There are no blazes to follow, but the trail is so well trod that you will have no trouble following it. In addition to the log steps, you will also see many other signs of the hard work put in by the trail crews that maintain the trail. Point out to your children the logs and rocks placed periodically at an angle along the path with shallow ditches on the uphill side. Can they guess what those are? What would happen to the trail if they weren't there? These water bars help divert water off the trail to prevent the trail from being washed out. Their importance will seem much more obvious if you are hiking during the rainy season.

At approximately 0.2 mile, the trail reaches a short, flat section before curving right and climbing again. A little farther on, look through

A budding photographer looks out over Squam Lake.

the trees to your right—you'll see the elevation you've gained by looking at the mountains across the lake. The last half of the trail becomes less rocky and the forest is dominated by oaks. You will start to get glimpses of the view before climbing a last set of log steps to the summit. Many trails culminate here, so be sure to find the Old Bridle Path sign for your return. (If you want to extend your hike, follow the trail another 0.7 mile to East Rattlesnake before returning the way you came.)

 GEORGIANA AND HARVARD FALLS

BEFORE YOU GO
Map USGS Lincoln
Current Conditions AMC
Pinkham Notch Visitor Center
(603) 466-2721

ABOUT THE HIKE
Day hike
Moderate for children
May–October
2.3 miles, round trip
Hiking time 2 hours
High point/elevation gain
1600 feet, 700 feet

GETTING THERE
- From I-93 in Lincoln, take exit 33 for US 3 North.
- In 0.3 mile turn left onto Hanson Farm Road.
- Drive 0.1 mile to the end of the road and park in the wide gravel area on the right before the barricade.

ON THE TRAIL
There's never a dull moment along the trail to Georgiana and Harvard Falls. Warm up with an easy jaunt on a wide woods road, then hike on a footpath that snakes beside Harvard Brook, and finally scramble up the boulders that fringe cascading Georgiana Falls. Although the last 0.4 mile from Georgiana to Harvard Falls is quite steep and probably not appropriate for preschoolers or adults backpacking small children, youngsters will find the initial 0.8 mile (to the turnaround point) delightful. Bring bathing suits or shoes for wading—nothing but winter weather will keep kids out of the water.

Head westward on a gravel road past the barricade. Walk through a tunnel underneath I-93's northbound lane and immediately turn right with the gravel road as an overgrown path continues straight. Quickly, the road sweeps left and passes under the highway's southbound lane. The noise of rushing vehicles fades as you head into the woods and, 0.2 mile from the start, you'll hear the soothing whispers of the distant Harvard Brook.

The gravel road rises gently to a clearing where it bends right. Follow the bend briefly and then turn left into the woods onto a red-blazed trail that leads to the bank of Harvard Brook. Though not officially maintained (because it crosses private property), the path is distinct, worn down by regular foot traffic. The path heads north, hugging the bank of the wide, shallow brook that spills through a maze of moss-covered boulders. Because a sink full of tap water will keep most kids amused on a rainy afternoon, imagine how many games your young hikers will invent on the banks of this delightful brook!

At 0.7 mile, you'll come upon Georgiana Falls, a spectacular cascade

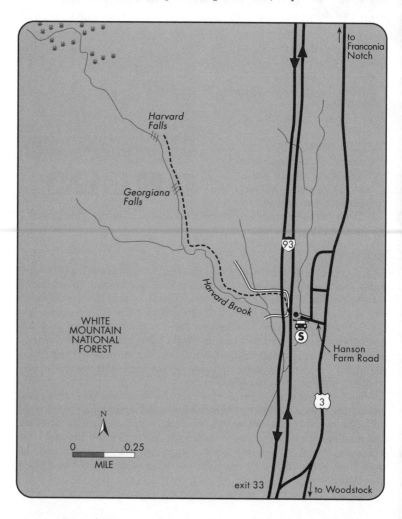

Relaxing on the rocks below Georgiana Falls

that tumbles into a series of deep pools. Daring young hikers will want
to climb the rocks lining the falls, while more conservative youngsters
will probably track through the woods. We recommend that adults with
or backpacking small children end the hike here for a total round-trip
distance of 1.6 miles.

Toward the top of the falls, the trail turns right, away from the water,
to duck under a canopy of hemlocks on a moderate ascent. Soon, as the
pitch steepens, the terrain becomes soft and slippery, forcing hikers to
grasp at trees and sturdy bushes for help. At 1 mile, the trail sweeps
along a ledge 30 feet above the brook and Harvard Falls comes into view.

The trail tapers off to end near the thundering thirty-foot waterfall.
Enjoy the breathtaking view of distant White Mountain peaks and of the
gorge carved by Harvard Brook far below. Set out your picnic lunch on one
of the rocks overlooking the falls, but don't expect to enjoy polite conver-
sation with your meal—you'll have to shout to be heard over the water!

Return to your vehicle the way you came.

40 GREELEY PONDS

BEFORE YOU GO
Map USGS Mount Osceola
Current Conditions White
Mountain National Forest
Saco Ranger District (603)
447-5448; White Mountain
National Forest Supervisor's
Office (603) 528-8721; AMC
Pinkham Notch Visitor Center
(603) 466-2721
**White Mountain National
Forest Use Pass required**

ABOUT THE HIKE
Day hike
Easy to moderate for children
May–October
4 miles, round trip
Hiking time 3 hours
High point/elevation gain
2245 feet, 350 feet

GETTING THERE

- From I-93 in North Woodstock, take exit 32 for North Woodstock, Lincoln, and the Kancamagus Highway (NH-112).
- Travel east on the Kancamagus Highway through Lincoln for 9.7 miles.
- Turn right into a substantial parking area with a sign for Greeley Ponds Trail, White Mountain National Forest.

ON THE TRAIL

It's not panoramic views that excite most kids but plank walks and bridges, frog-filled ponds, and rivers. The 4-mile hike to and from Greeley Ponds includes all these favorites and covers relatively level terrain, making it a great walk for the entire family. Gravelly beaches border the two wilderness ponds and allow ample room for exploring the shore or stretching out under the sun. This is a popular route, so expect to have company.

The worn, yellow-blazed trail leaves the southern side of the parking area to climb gradually through dense woodlands, tripping over exposed roots. Remind children to watch in front of them and to pick up their feet. In 0.1 mile, footbridges carry hikers over damp gullies and dribbling streams and, 0.2 mile later, a pair of long, well-constructed footbridges spans two branches of a brook. (Ignore the side trail that splits left after the first bridge.)

Shortly after crossing a fifth bridge at 0.35 mile, the trail dodges right to avoid a titanic boulder sustaining several trees. Kids, how does a tree grow out of a rock? At 0.5 mile from the start, as you pass through stands of hemlocks, remember Christmas by rolling a few needles between your

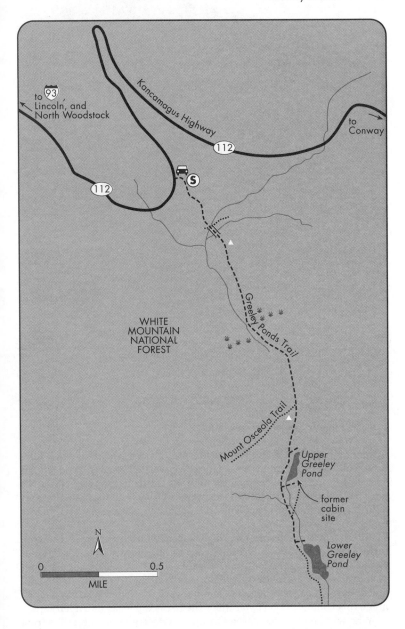

Rest stop beside Lower Greeley Pond

fingers and sniffing. Soon, log trestles and planks stretch about a hundred feet across a marshy area. (Here, we startled a moose who left his spot in the swamp and crashed through the woods to get away!) Over the next 0.5 mile, you'll continue to traverse wetlands and streams by way of footbridges and split logs. The trail bends left (southeast) at 1 mile to begin a mild ascent.

After two more stream crossings, 1.3 miles from the start, the trail divides: The Mount Osceola Trail heads right (southwest) toward Mount Osceola via East Peak. Continue straight (south), still following the infrequent yellow blazing of the Greeley Ponds Trail. At 0.1 mile from the trail junction, you'll pass to the left of another errant boulder. What would you name this boulder? (Don't you think the rock's top looks like a hat?)

Who will be the first to see the upper Greeley Pond, 1.6 miles from the start? The main trail avoids the shore, tracking about fifteen feet above the western side of the pond, but a side trail leads to a sandy beach at the pond's northern end. The jagged cliffs of Mad River Notch rise abruptly out of the water and provide a lovely backdrop for your picnic or energy break. Back on the Greeley Ponds Trail, hike to the pond's southern shore, where a side trail splits left for the site of the former Appalachian Mountain Club (AMC) Greeley Pond Cabin and another natural, sandy beach. (Overuse of this camping area threatened to change the character of the wilderness ponds, so the cabin was dismantled.)

Return to the main trail, descending steadily southward on a less-traveled path toward Lower Greeley Pond. Cross a plank walk to reach the edge of the lower pond, more rugged than the first, with a swampy shore that appeals more to moose and deer than to human visitors. Encourage the children to sit quietly (they probably need a rest) and watch for beavers and swallows, dragonflies, and speckled trout (they'll emerge from the water to gobble up hatching flies).

On the way back, between the upper and lower ponds, you'll notice a trail junction that was not obvious on the hike in (due to the angle at which the path joined the Greeley Ponds Trail). Stay left as this side trail splits right leading to the former camping site on the upper pond. Return along the familiar Greeley Ponds Trail.

 BOULDER LOOP TRAIL

BEFORE YOU GO
Map USGS North Conway West
Current Conditions White Mountain National Forest Saco Ranger District (603) 447-5448; White Mountain National Forest Supervisor's Office (603) 528-8721; AMC Pinkham Notch Visitor Center (603) 466-2721
White Mountain National Forest Use Pass required

ABOUT THE HIKE
Day hike
Moderate for children
May–October
3.1 miles, loop
Hiking time 2.5 hours
High point/elevation gain
1954 feet, 1100 feet

GETTING THERE
- From NH-16 in Conway, head west on the Kancamagus Highway (NH-112).
- In 6.5 miles, turn right onto Dugway Road.
- Pass through the covered bridge and drive 0.1 mile to a parking area on the right.

ON THE TRAIL

As you hike the Boulder Loop, you'll feel as if you have your very own naturalist along. Equipped with a White Mountain National Forest interpretive leaflet (available at the trailhead or at the White Mountain National Forest Information Centers) that is keyed to numbered stops along the route, you will gain a better understanding of such common trailside phenomena as lichens, felled trees, and fallen boulders. Looking for the various stations will keep kids moving and will mark their progress in a way they can understand.

Don't be fooled into thinking that this is just a tame nature walk, though. Halfway through the loop, you'll climb onto a set of sheer cliffs with tremendous views over the Passaconaway Valley. Call it a nature walk with punch.

The yellow trail leaves the northern side of Dugway Road, quickly curves right (east), and splits 0.1 mile from the start. Head left and begin a 1.4-mile climb to the overlooks on the southwestern spur of the Moat Range. As you pass along a sheer 30-foot cliff, you'll come upon the first stop described in the leaflet. Here, lichens, some of the first plants to cover bare earth and rock, flourish on nearby boulders.

Send the kids ahead to find STOP 2, marking the boundary between a deciduous forest and mixed woods that now include conifers. (Explain to children the difference between coniferous and deciduous trees: Conifers, or evergreens, have cones and don't lose their needles all at once while deciduous trees lose their foliage in autumn.) The trail winds moderately up a wooded slope and passes STOP 3, an area hit hard by a nor'easter. What do these toppled trees have in common? (They've all fallen in the same direction, blown by the storm's powerful winds.) At STOP 4, look for young red spruce trees. Red spruces have scaly bark, dark green needles, and pinecone scales with rounded edges.

Before reaching STOP 5, the grade lessens to give hikers a reprieve as they look out over the Swift River and the Kancamagus Highway winding through the Passaconaway Valley hundreds of feet below. Who will be the first to spot STOP 6? Here you'll see sheet joints, fractures near the surface of rocks that result from expansion within the granite mass. If you look to the left (east), you'll see the ledge overlooks, your destination.

STOP 8 features the decaying trunk of an old hemlock. Can the kids guess what might have caused its demise? (The brochure suggests drought, lightning, disease, wind, insects, or a combination of these forces.) Between STOPS 9 and 10, the trail leaves the moist, shady woods and crawls to a dry ledgy area. Hemlock and birch trees flourish in the moister soil, while on the rock outcroppings the red oak has little competition from other varieties of trees.

STOP 11, 1.2 miles into the hike, ushers you toward the overlook. Turn right here onto a side trail that travels for 0.2 mile along the sheer cliffs with dramatic views to the south, east, and west over Mount

Passaconaway, Mount Chocorua, and Middle Sister. Children should be warned to stay far away from the edge. A yellow X marks the end of the ledges (and the best views); return to the trail junction at STOP 11 and turn right to continue the loop.

Dropping steadily, the trail curls westward past STOP 13, 0.4 mile from the ledge overlook. You'll notice that trees have been cut selectively as part of the White Mountain National Forest's timber management program. Descending more steeply after a brief respite, the trail reaches STOP 14 near an impressive hemlock. Hemlocks, capable of surviving under the shaded canopy of the forest, thrive once they are exposed to more direct sunlight. At STOP 15, the boulders that were so frequent at the start of the hike are once again numerous.

Cross a tributary to the Swift River at STOP 16. The Swift River flows into the Saco River in Conway, which eventually feeds into the Atlantic Ocean. Huge boulders seem to block the trail and create a tunnel at STOP 17. These boulders split from the ledges above many years ago. Trees and plants have since grown to accommodate this chaos of rocks. At the final stop, STOP 18, look for stumps that are all that remain of trees felled fifty years ago for timber. Continue to the trail junction marking the end of the loop and go straight (west). Walk the 0.1 mile back to Dugway Road and your vehicle.

A covered bridge spanning the Swift River

4 2 THE BASIN AND LONESOME LAKE

BEFORE YOU GO
Maps USGS Franconia and Lincoln
Current Conditions
Franconia Notch State Park (603) 745-8391; White Mountain National Forest Supervisor's Office (603) 528-8721; Appalachian Mountain Club Pinkham Notch Visitor Center (603) 466-2721
White Mountain National Forest Use Pass required

ABOUT THE HIKE
Day hike or overnight
Challenging for children
June–October
5 miles, round trip
Hiking time 4.5 hours
High point/elevation gain
2760 feet, 1300 feet
Path to The Basin accessible; Flume Gorge Visitor Center accessible

GETTING THERE

- In Lincoln, just north of the 106 mile marker on I-93 North (here, also called the "Franconia Notch Parkway"), exit the highway at a sign that says "The Basin, 0.5 mile."
- Follow signs to The Basin and park in the ample, paved parking area.

ON THE TRAIL

This is one of the most popular White Mountain National Forest (WMNF) hiking routes—and for good reason. The trail departs The Basin, an always crowded tourist attraction, to travel beside Cascade Brook for 2.5 miles to the remote shores of Lonesome Lake. Here, you can spend the night at the Lonesome Lake Hut, which accommodates forty-eight and is open to the public from June to mid-October with full service and mid-October through May with self-service. (Tents are not permitted near the hut or the lake.) For information and schedules, contact the Reservation Secretary by writing to Pinkham Notch Camp, P.O. Box 298, Gorham, NH 03581, or by calling (603) 466-2727.

The trail's *challenging* rating stems from the length and rugged condition of the trail, not the elevation gain. Since the path travels through numerous wet areas, waterproof footgear is recommended.

From the parking area (with restrooms and picnic tables), follow the signs to The Basin that lead under I-93 on the paved bike and footpath.

Beyond the underpass, as directed by the sign to The Basin, cross the Pemigewasset (an Abenaki Indian name meaning "swift") River on a metal bridge. Follow the landscaped gravel path (actually, it is the unmarked Basin–Cascades Trail) for 0.1 mile to The Basin, a magnificent pothole

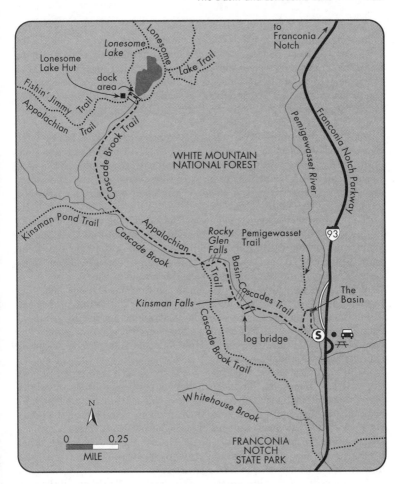

created by the swirling waters of the Pemigewasset River. Adults as well as kids will be mesmerized by this dramatic natural masterpiece.

After admiring The Basin, leave the busloads of tourists behind and follow the Basin–Cascades Trail (unmarked and unblazed) heading westward. Soon, as the Pemigewasset Trail splits right, you bear left, continuing southwestward to a sign for the Basin–Cascades Trail at a junction 0.2 mile from the start. Turn right. The trail heads westward, departing the Pemigewasset River and joining the tumbling Cascade Brook. The worn, root-choked path snakes uphill along the brook's northern bank under lofty hemlocks. Who will notice the national forest boundary at 0.3 mile?

The hurrying brook that rushes alongside the trail for nearly 2 miles is an entertaining, delightfully noisy playmate for the kids. Nearly 0.5 mile into the hike, children will need help (actually, parents will need help, too) crossing the river on a single, springy log several feet above the water. On the southern bank (yea, you made it!), the trail rises above the brook and passes the delightful cascades known as Kinsman Falls. Here, the pitch lessens but the trail may still be tough on little legs because it is very rooty and often soggy.

At the 1-mile mark, granite walls embrace the fierce Rocky Glen Falls, which spills 15 feet through a canyon. The Basin–Cascades Trail ends just beyond the waterfall at a junction with the combined Cascade Brook Trail and Appalachian Trail (AT). Here, you cross from the southern to the northern riverbank over a jumble of boulders as you head westward on the white-blazed AT.

The rugged trail leaves the bank of Cascade Brook and climbs easily in and out of damp sections. Ask the kids to hike with all their senses: What can they see, hear, touch, smell? At 1.6 miles, the Kinsman Pond Trail branches left (southwest) as you continue straight. From here, Lonesome Lake and the hut are just under a mile away.

If you have anything that appeals to the familiar Canada jays, hiking friends tell us, you may entice them to eat right out of your hand. Slippery logs span more damp spots as the trail swings northward away from the brook. On steeper grades, stones create welcome steps. The trail rejoins the brook at 2 miles. How has the character of the brook changed since you last saw it?

Nearly 2.5 miles from the start, you'll arrive at a trail junction near the outlet to Lonesome Lake. Turn left onto the Fishin' Jimmy Trail (which has merged with the AT) and skirt the southern end of the lake over a footbridge. In 0.1 mile, look for the dock area and hut on the lake's western shore that mark the end of your trip in. Here you can go for a swim, enjoy the lovely views of the Franconia Range, chat with other hikers, or prepare for an overnight stay. (By the way, who can figure out how supplies are brought to huts like these?)

On the return trip, kids can race with the Cascade Brook all the way back to The Basin.

FLUME GORGE AND VISITOR CENTER

If you head to Franconia Notch State Park, be sure to stop in at the Flume Gorge and Visitor Center, open early May to mid-October. You can obtain hiking information here for Franconia Notch State Park. For a fee, you can also visit the famous Flume, a spectacular narrow riverbed gorge that extends 800 feet at the base of Mount Liberty. Then head out to some of the other trails in this book for a little more solitude.

43 BRIDAL VEIL FALLS

BEFORE YOU GO
Maps USGS Franconia and Sugar Hill
Current Conditions
Franconia Notch State Park (603) 745-8391; White Mountain National Forest Supervisor's Office (603) 528-8721; Appalachian Mountain Club Pinkham Notch Visitor Center (603) 466-2721
White Mountain National Forest Use Pass required

ABOUT THE HIKE
Day hike or overnight
Moderate for children
May–October
4.8 miles, round trip
Hiking time 4 hours
High point/elevation gain 2100 feet, 1000 feet

GETTING THERE

- From I-93 in Franconia, take exit 38.
- Drive south for 0.1 mile to the junction of NH-18 and NH-116 (Church Street).
- Continue straight on NH-116 and, in 3.4 miles, turn left onto Coppermine Road.
- Park on the road's right-hand shoulder.

ON THE TRAIL

Bridal Veil Falls, one of the more captivating waterfalls in the White Mountain National Forest (WMNF), tumbles down Coppermine Brook in the ravine between Cannon Mountain and the Cannon Balls. The Coppermine Trail leads gradually uphill for 2.4 miles to the falls. With the brook as a delightful companion, the miles will pass quickly for kids. On a steamy summer day, youngsters will be attracted to the frequent wading pools like pigs to mud puddles. Plan to spend the night in the WMNF Coppermine Shelter near the falls.

Begin walking eastward on Coppermine Road. (If you prefer, you can drive along Coppermine Road until it becomes too rough.) In 0.3 mile, the pavement ends and the gravel road divides; bear left at a trail sign following yellow blazes. Can you hear the hollow drumming of the woodpecker? Follow the sound to its source and you'll see a bird climbing up the side of a tree using its claws to grip the bark and its tail feathers for balance. Woodpeckers eat the insects that live under the bark.

At a fork 0.6 mile from the start, continue straight, guided by an arrow for the Coppermine Trail, as an unmarked woods road bears right. Ascend easily along the rugged gravel road. (Who will be the first to hear Coppermine Brook?) At 1 mile from the start, you can listen for the rushing water to the right; in another 0.1 mile you'll be able to see it.

The trail briefly hugs the brook's northern bank at 1.4 miles, departs it on a moderate ascent, and returns to the water's edge. This pattern repeats over the next 0.5 mile as the relatively straight path travels beside the weaving river. Since no one seems to know how Coppermine Brook got its name, take turns making up silly stories. Here's a start: "Legend has it that a hundred years ago, George Copper and Tom Mine went fishing. . . ."

Nearly 2 miles from the start, the trail narrows and rises above the brook on a short, moderate ascent, leaving the riverbank for 0.25 mile. The kids can run ahead and wait for the adults where the trail rejoins the brook near a sturdy footbridge. Have a splashing contest: Drop acorns, pebbles, pinecones, and twigs from the bridge to see what will make the best splash.

After crossing the brook, travel along the southwestern bank for 0.1 mile to the WMNF Coppermine Shelter, nestled between rock ledges and a pool. Travel another 0.1 mile to cascading Bridal Veil Falls, crossing the brook at the base for the best views. Let the kids splash in the pools before retracing your steps to your vehicle or setting up camp.

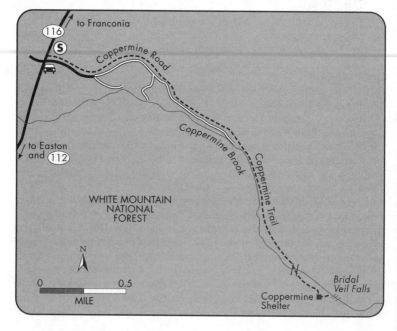

Hikers admire Bridal Veil Falls.

 ARTIST BLUFF

BEFORE YOU GO
Map USGS Franconia
Current Conditions
Franconia Notch State Park
(603) 745-8391; White
Mountain National Forest
Supervisor's Office (603) 528-
8721; Appalachian Mountain
Club Pinkham Notch Visitor
Center (603) 466-2721
**White Mountain National
Forest Use Pass required**

ABOUT THE HIKE
Day hike
Moderate for children
May–October
1.8 miles, loop
Hiking time 1.5 hours
High point/elevation gain
2320 feet, 550 feet

GETTING THERE
- From I-93 (here, also called the Franconia Notch Parkway) in Franconia Notch, take exit 3 to NH-18, Echo Lake Beach and Ski Area.
- Travel 0.8 mile north on NH-18.

■ Just beyond the Cannon Mountain Peabody Slopes parking area, park on the right-hand side of the road near the entrance to a gravel pit at the "Hiker Parking" sign.

ON THE TRAIL

Artist Bluff is not just another pretty face. Although it soars magnificently over NH-18 and I-93 and is dotted on most nice days with dozens of rock climbers, it does more than catch your eye from the highway. It offers you a chance to take in terrific views for very little effort and to escape the tourists that congregate at Profile Lake, The Flume, and The Basin. The trip to Artist Bluff via Bald Mountain will take less than 2 hours, making it a great hike to combine with other local activities.

Cross the expansive gravel pit diagonally left (northeast) of the parking area to the edge of the woods. Put the kids in charge of locating the trailhead (look for the trail sign and the red blazes). As you climb moderately up the rocky path through deciduous woods, play animal charades. Who does the best frog, tiger, elephant, or snake?

At 0.3 mile, the Bald Mountain Trail splits left (west) as the Artist Bluff Trail continues straight (north). For now, head left (still following red) and work your way up the steep, rocky hillside to the open summit of Bald Mountain. You are rewarded for your brief effort with tremendous views of the Franconia area: 5300-foot Mount Lafayette looms to the south, and the ski slopes sweep down the side of Cannon Mountain to the southwest. Look right (west) to see the peaks of Vermont and the tips of the Adirondacks.

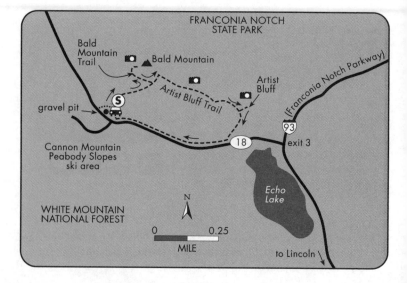

Snack time on top of Artist Bluff

Return to the trail junction and swing left, rejoining the Artist Bluff Trail on an ascent. Can the kids find the trailside spruce trees with trunks scarred by lightning? At 0.2 mile beyond the junction, the trail levels before making a final surge to an overlook with dramatic views of Cannon's crisscrossing ski trails. As we relaxed here for a few minutes, we saw several gliders drifting above the valley.

Hike along gently rolling terrain for the next 0.1 mile to another vista, beyond which the trail slides steeply down the mountainside. Partway down, the trail drops into a gully. At the head of this gully, a side trail branches left and leads quickly to the exposed ledges of Artist Bluff. While there is plenty of room to explore here, the ledges form sheer cliffs and parents should warn kids to stay back from the edge. As you unpack your picnic lunch, you'll be able to watch rock climbers scaling (or clinging to, depending on their capabilities) these cliffs. Look southward across Echo Lake to Eagle Cliff and Mount Lafayette.

After a pleasant rest on the bluff, return to the main trail and bear left (south). The trail falls steeply down the gully for 0.25 mile to NH-18. Turn right (west) and follow the highway for 0.5 mile back to your vehicle.

ZEALAND POND AND ZEALAND FALLS

BEFORE YOU GO
Map USGS Crawford Notch
Current Conditions White
Mountain National Forest
Pemigewasset/Ammonoosuc
Ranger District (603) 536-1315;
White Mountain National Forest
Supervisor's Office (603) 528-
8721; AMC Pinkham Notch
Visitor Center (603) 466-2721;
AMC Highland Center (603)
278-4453
**White Mountain National
Forest Use Pass required**

ABOUT THE HIKE
Day hike or overnight
Moderate for children
May–September
5.4 miles, round trip
Hiking time 4.5 hours
High point/elevation gain
2637 feet, 650 feet

GETTING THERE
- From the junction of US 3 and US 302 in Twin Mountain, travel east on US 302.
- In 2.1 miles, turn right at a sign for Zealand Road, White Mountain National Forest Recreation Area.
- Follow Zealand Road for 3.4 miles to its conclusion at a gate and the start of the Zealand Trail.

ON THE TRAIL
Water, water, water! We know kids love it, so we included this trail on the Twin–Zealand Range, which encompasses a river, bog, pond, and waterfall. Just under 3 miles from the start, you'll come to the Appalachian Mountain Club (AMC) hut near Zealand Falls, at the northern end of Zealand Notch. Here, you can spend the night or just relax for a few hours and trade stories with other hiking families. Since the grade is gradual, this hike is well within the capabilities of most children, especially if you break it up with an overnight. For information about the hut, call the AMC at (603) 466-2727.

The blue-blazed Zealand Trail leaves the southern side of the parking area, initially a wide path lined with young hemlocks. Soon the trail's complexion changes as it scales a knoll over rugged terrain. As you drop off the hill, a solid footbridge carries you over a brook, 0.3 mile from the start. (Although the trail parallels the Zealand River for its length, the two are separated by 100 yards or so for the first 0.7 mile.)

Rising gradually, the wide path now follows a former railroad bed.

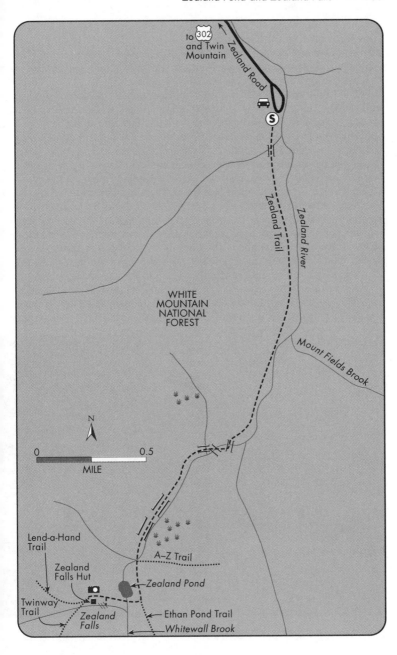

Anyone getting restless? Ask each other some animal trivia questions: How far can an adult kangaroo jump? (27 feet!) How many of its legs does a spider use when it walks? (All eight.) In what two ways might an animal's coat change in preparation for winter? (It may turn white or become thicker.) Do porcupines shoot their quills? (No.)

At 0.7 mile from the start, the trail approaches the Zealand River and weaves along the western bank through mixed woods. At 1.5 miles, cross a series of tributaries over sturdy footbridges and stepping stones. (Because the kids will most likely want to play a few water games, plan to take an extended energy break here.)

As you continue, your first distant mountain views emerge. Skirt a bog on the left and soon cross this soggy swampland over lengthy log bridges. After fording another stream at 2.2 miles, the trail divides: As the A–Z Trail bears left (east) toward Crawford Notch, you continue straight and shortly cross the outlet to Zealand Pond.

This pond is unusual because it has an outlet at each end, as a result of its location at the height of the land in Zealand Notch. Kids, do you realize that if you could turn yourself into a tiny boat and float down the Zealand River, you would eventually end up in the Atlantic Ocean?

As you hike along the eastern shore of Zealand Pond, look right (west) to see the distant falls. The Zealand Trail ends at a junction near the southern tip of the pond (2.5 miles from the start), where the Ethan

Lengthy log bridges span soggy swampland on the way to Zealand Pond.

Pond Trail continues straight. You swing right (west) onto the white-blazed Twinway Trail, skirting the southern end of the pond. Kids, do you see any beaver dams?

After briefly heading northward, the trail again marches westward, nearing the final, steep ascent that leads to the AMC hut. Halfway up the climb, a side trail splits left (south) for Zealand Falls, a cascade that tumbles down a series of square-edged rock steps. The Twinway Trail continues to the hut, 0.2 mile from the end of the Zealand Trail. From here, the views down the valley toward Mount Carrigain are magnificent.

Built in 1932 to accommodate thirty-six guests, the Zealand Falls Hut sits near the bank of Whitewall Brook. It is open to the public with staff during summer and fall and without staff during early spring and winter. Spend the night or just a pleasant afternoon before retracing your steps to your vehicle.

 RIPLEY FALLS

BEFORE YOU GO
Map USGS Crawford Notch
Current Conditions
Crawford Notch State Park
(603) 374-2272; White
Mountain National Forest
Supervisor's Office (603) 528-8721; AMC Pinkham Notch
Visitor Center (603) 466-2721
**White Mountain National
Forest Use Pass encouraged
to support the forest**

ABOUT THE HIKE
Day hike
Easy for children
May–October
1 mile, round trip
Hiking time 1 hour
High point/elevation gain
1750 feet, 300 feet

GETTING THERE
- From the junction of NH-16 and US 302 in Bartlett, travel approximately 17 miles west on US 302.
- At a sign for Ripley Falls, turn left and follow the road 0.3 mile to a parking area at the trailhead.
- Alternatively, from the junction of US 3 and US 302 in Twin Mountain, travel east on US 302 approximately 12 miles to a right-hand turn at the sign for Ripley Falls.

ON THE TRAIL
Want to hike to a waterfall but not quite up for the distance of Arethusa Falls (Hike 47)? Try Ripley Falls! It is short, but the trail is rocky and

rugged, providing youngsters with ample opportunity for a little rock scrambling. At over 100 feet tall, the falls will definitely earn their share of oohs and aahs, especially if you visit during times of high water. You can perch on one of the many boulders along Avalanche Brook to watch as the water cascades over a granite slab. Youngsters will want to explore (carefully!) among the rocks beside the water.

To begin, follow the white blazes from the parking area. The trail you are on for the first stretch is also the Ethan Pond Trail and Appalachian Trail (AT). The path heads up through a birch and maple forest. Almost immediately, a side trail to the left leads to a view of Avalanche Brook as it heads under a railroad trestle. Follow the white blazes of the main trail to cross over the railroad tracks. This is an active railroad, so have the kids practice looking both ways before crossing. Find the sign for the AT and the Ripley Falls Trail on the other side of the tracks and begin a moderate ascent. In 0.1 mile, the trail passes over a jumble of boulders and rocks. At the 0.2 mile mark, the trail forks. Take the left branch marked

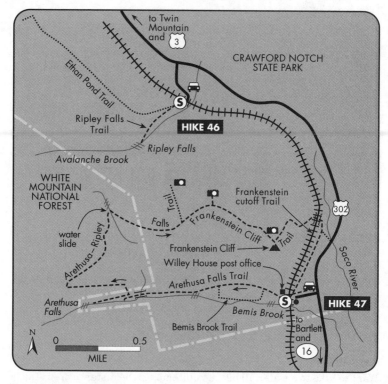

Opposite: Ripley Falls

by blue blazes as the white-blazed Appalachian Trail heads right.

The blue-blazed trail continues high above Avalanche Brook another 0.3 mile, although you can hear and see the water far below as you make your way along a ridge. Right before reaching the falls, carefully descend through a tangle of roots and boulders to arrive at the base of the cascades. When you're done exclaiming and exploring, return the way you came.

Note: It is possible to hike to Arethusa Falls from here via the Arethusa–Ripley Falls Trail. If you are a waterfall lover prepared for a longer hike, bring along a map of the whole area for different trail combinations.

 ## ARETHUSA FALLS AND FRANKENSTEIN CLIFF

BEFORE YOU GO
Maps USGS Stairs Mountain and Crawford Notch
Current Conditions Crawford Notch State Park (603) 374-2272; White Mountain National Forest Supervisor's Office (603) 528-8721; AMC Pinkham Notch Visitor Center (603) 466-2721
White Mountain National Forest Use Pass encouraged to support the forest

ABOUT THE HIKE
Day hike
Challenging for children
May–October
4.7 miles, loop
Hiking time 4 hours
High point/elevation gain 2510 feet, 1500 feet

GETTING THERE

- From the junction of NH-16 and US 302 in Glen, travel west on US 302 for approximately 15 miles.
- After a sign announces nearby Arethusa Falls, turn left onto an access road.
- Park in the lot immediately to your right.
- Alternatively, from the junction of US 3 and US 302 in Twin Mountain, travel east on US 302 for approximately 14 miles to the access road on the right. Park as described.

ON THE TRAIL

Take it to a vote: Who wants to visit the state's highest waterfall? Now, who wants to climb to the top of some 600-foot cliffs? Guess what? On this hike, everyone wins! The trip to Frankenstein Cliff by way of Bemis Brook and Arethusa Falls will satisfy water lovers as well as view lovers.

The 2.4-mile round-trip hike to the spectacular falls, however, may be enough for adults hiking with preschoolers. The continuation of the loop hike to Frankenstein Cliff (named for a local artist, not the fellow with bolts in his neck) is demanding, and the cliffs are not appropriate for unchaperoned exploring. So, alter the route to suit your needs.

Head up the access road, following signs to Arethusa Falls. Cross the railroad tracks near a private residence still known as Willey House Post Office, bearing left toward the Arethusa Falls Trail. The blue-blazed path dives into woods dotted with birch trees, heading southwestward. On the left, Bemis Brook spills raucously down the mountainside through a deep gorge. Soon, the trampled trail veers right, away from the brook. At 0.15 mile, the yellow-blazed Bemis Brook Trail splits left (to visit pools and minor falls), rejoining 0.3 mile later. At all junctions, continue straight on the Arethusa Falls Trail.

Some people believe that the trail and the falls were named for the arethusa orchid that once grew in the area. Can you guess why flowers are so pretty and fragrant? Flowers must attract the insects that will help bring pollen grains and "plant eggs" together to make new plants.

Climb moderately on the rocky trail beside the stately white birch trees. A little over 0.4 mile from the start, where the Arethusa Falls Trail again meets the Bemis Brook Trail, the Arethusa Falls Trail veers right and heads up a set of stone stairs. Soon, the pitch eases as the narrow trail cuts deeper into the ridge. To your left, the hill plummets into the gorge carved by Bemis Brook. At 0.7 mile, you can look down at the water tumbling over the rust-colored stones and spilling into frequent pools.

Around the 1-mile mark, cross a substantial tributary on King's Highway Bridge. Past the bridge, the trail curves again to the right and leads you up a set of log steps. In another 0.1 mile, pass over another bridge and again climb up log steps. Soon you will reach a trail junction, indicating that Arethusa Falls is 0.2 mile away on the left branch of the trail. The trail descends and delivers you to the base of Arethusa Falls, the highest waterfall in New Hampshire. Ribbonlike streams of water plunge more than 200 feet to the rugged rocks below. Here, appropriately, the Arethusa Falls Trail ends. If accompanied by preschoolers, you may want to turn around here and return the way you came for a total hike of 2.4 miles. If you continue, save your picnic lunch for Frankenstein Cliff, where there is more room to spread out.

Return to the previous trail junction and turn left onto the blue-blazed Arethusa–Ripley Falls Trail. The trail cuts across a wooded hillside and shortly switches back to head westward at the top of the ridge. Soon, after curling northward, the trail winds along a fairly level ridge for nearly 1 mile, crossing several streams. (At 1.8 miles, kids will beg for a chance to pause near the stream that splashes down a water slide.)

Just over 1 mile from the falls, the Arethusa–Ripley Falls Trail intersects with the Frankenstein Cliff Trail. Turn right (southeast) onto the

Frankenstein Cliff Trail as the Arethusa–Ripley Falls Trail continues left (north). Follow the trail as it dips and rises; soon, turn left onto a short side trail that leads to an overlook with pretty views of the Crawford Notch area.

The main trail begins a solid descent 0.5 mile from the junction with the Arethusa–Ripley Falls Trail. Dive through thick evergreens for 0.2 mile to the edge of a precipitous drop-off with fine southerly views down into Crawford Notch. You will not want the children to precede you here, because in another 0.1 mile you'll arrive atop the sheer Frankenstein Cliff. The kids can count the tiny vehicles speeding along the highway 600 feet below as adults take in the larger view that includes Moat Mountain and Mounts Paugus, Passaconaway, and Crawford.

After enjoying a picnic lunch with the impressive Notch views as a backdrop, follow the trail as it ducks into the woods, heading northeastward. Ask the kids for their help in following the blue blazes along an initially twisted route. At 0.2 mile beyond the cliffs, the trail switches back right (south) on a steep descent, wrapping around a ledge outcropping. Pick your way through a skimpy boulder field and then approach the base of the cliffs. Kids who like to spin around until they are stumbling and dizzy can achieve a similar feeling by standing close to the cliffs and looking straight up at the rock face.

From here, the blue markings lead hikers across the slope to wind generally eastward to the bottom of the grade. Head under a 70-foot-high railroad trestle and then turn right at a sign to the parking area, still following blue blazes. Enjoy a pleasant 0.5-mile stroll through the woods back to the access road. Turn left and follow the road to your vehicle. The kids have earned a few dozen pats on the back!

48 NORTH DOUBLEHEAD

BEFORE YOU GO
Map USGS Jackson
Current Conditions White Mountain National Forest Saco Ranger District (603) 447-5448; White Mountain National Forest Supervisor's Office (603) 528-8721; AMC Pinkham Notch Visitor Center (603) 466-2721
White Mountain National Forest Use Pass required

ABOUT THE HIKE
Day hike or overnight
Challenging for children
May–October
3.5 miles, round trip
Hiking time 3.5 hours
High point/elevation gain 3053 feet, 1750 feet

GETTING THERE

- From the junction of US 302 and NH-16 in Glen, head north on NH-16.
- In 2 miles, turn right onto NH-16A ("To NH-16B, Jackson Village") and cross a covered bridge.
- In 0.3 mile, bear right onto NH-16B as NH-16A heads left.
- Drive another 1.6 miles to the Black Mountain Ski Area, where you bear right onto Dundee Road as NH-16B bears left.
- Continue 0.7 mile and turn left into a gravel driveway that leads to a parking area for several vehicles. (A sign announces the Doublehead Ski Trail.)

ON THE TRAIL

You've hiked The Roost (Hike 63) and Mount Agamenticus (Hike 55). Now you and the kids are ready to tackle a real mountain (and you're even considering an overnight). North Doublehead is the mountain for you. With a White Mountain National Forest (WMNF) cabin at the summit, you can spend a relaxing evening miles from the nearest television or lawn mower. There's no appropriate turnaround point along this route, so it would be something of a letdown if the group had to head back before reaching the summit. To avoid disappointment, make sure everyone (and everyone's gear) is up to a steep mountain climb. Allow yourselves enough time for frequent rests and energy breaks.

From the parking area, the wide Doublehead Ski Trail heads in an easterly direction toward the summit of Doublehead. At a junction in 100 yards, follow the well-worn cross-country ski trail to the right following blue-diamond blazes as a logging road heads straight.

The trail, rising initially on a gradual grade, steepens at 0.2 mile. A stream briefly visits on the left and, just under 0.5 mile from the start, the trail trudges up a grassy hillside and hops over another stream. At the 0.6-mile mark, follow the narrow Old Path straight (east) as the ski trail veers left. Hike through mature deciduous woods up a

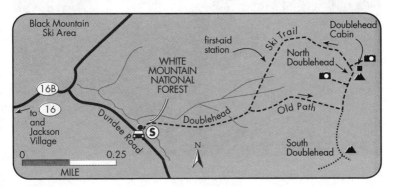

moderate grade that steepens 0.1 mile beyond the junction.

Over the next 0.6 mile, the trail winds steadily up the mountainside on a moderate-to-steep grade. Make sure the kids know the rule: Whiners must walk backward for 30 paces! If fussiness threatens to become contagious, play Simon Says. "Simon says, 'Hop like a bunny!' " "Simon says, 'Wave a leaf in the air like a flag! Gallop like a horse!' " (You're out! I didn't say, "Simon says!")

The trail splits 1.35 miles from the start: As one branch turns right toward South Doublehead, you turn left (northeast) on the path that leads to North Doublehead. A gradual ascent through hemlocks gives everyone a much-needed rest. The respite soon ends as the trail works its way up a steep boulder slide. Play Follow the Leader up the rock steps. (Appoint the pokiest hiker as the leader to spur him or her on.)

At 1.6 miles, a side trail drifts left and drops for 100 yards to high ledges with westerly views over Jackson Village and the White Mountain range. These views are better than those from the sheltered summit, making it the choice spot for an extended rest or picnic.

Back on the main trail, climb steeply under a hemlock canopy to reach the wooded summit and the WMNF Doublehead Cabin 1.7 miles from your start. The cabin, nestled in a spruce grove, has eight bunks, gas lights, and a stove (but no water). Behind the cabin, a short path leads to an overlook with views to the east of the Mountain Pond area, Kezar Lake, the Royces (Hike 62), and North Baldface.

Prepare for dinner and an overnight stay, or follow the blue-diamond

Doublehead cabin at the summit of North Doublehead

cross-country ski trail to the west of the cabin to return to your vehicle. Drop on a moderate-to-steep grade off the mountain with occasional views to the southwest. A WMNF first-aid station (0.85 mile from the summit) offers medical supplies to injured hikers.

At 1 mile from the cabin, the trail crosses a pair of streams (the hike's only reliable water source) and in another 0.2 mile reaches the intersection with Old Path. Bear right to follow the cross-country ski trail back to your vehicle.

 DOME ROCK

BEFORE YOU GO
Maps USGS Pliny Range
Current Conditions White Mountain National Forest Androscoggin Ranger Station (603) 466-2713; White Mountain National Forest Supervisor's Office (603) 528-8721; AMC Pinkham Notch Visitor Center (603) 466-2721
White Mountain National Forest Use Pass encouraged to support the forest

ABOUT THE HIKE
Day hike
Challenging for children
June–September
4 miles, loop
Hiking time 4 hours
High point/elevation gain
2710 feet, 1500 feet

GETTING THERE
- From the junction of US 2 and NH-16 in Gorham, travel west on US 2 for 6.5 miles.
- Turn left on Dolly Copp–Pinkham B Road.
- Parking is on the right in 0.2 mile.
- Alternatively, from the junction of US 2 and NH-115 in Jefferson Highlands, travel 8 miles east on US 2 and turn right onto Dolly Copp–Pinkham B Road to the parking area on the right.

ON THE TRAIL
The hike to Dome Rock is no walk in the park. It is, in fact, one of the more strenuous hikes in the book, with many steep sections. This is best undertaken by experienced hikers and kids up for a challenge. Still reading? Good. This is also a memorable hike, and kids who complete it will be proud and glad that they did. The rewards are numerous, and they will get to practice many of their hiking skills on the route. Each trail junction provides a different point of interest. From babbling brooks,

to summit views and waterfalls, there is much to keep kids enthused, despite the level of difficulty.

From the parking area, head southwest on the Randolph Path. Almost immediately, you will come to a junction with the Howker Ridge Trail. Bear right, continuing on the Randolph Path as it makes its way through a mixed forest lush with ferns, looking for blue blazes to guide you. During wet periods, children will be excited by the number of stream crossings on the trail. Around the half-mile mark, after a short climb up a set of rock steps, the trail breaks out into an open meadow, complete with mountain views. As you head back into the woods, the trail starts climbing more, although the grade is gradual. Look for different wildflowers in bloom or for toads and snakes that cross your path. At a trail junction with Sylvan Way, continue straight on the Randolph Path, again crossing over intermittent streams. Soon, your ears will pick up the sounds of water below you as the narrow, root-covered trail follows Brookbank Brook from above. Around 1.5 miles from the start, you will arrive on the rocky shore of Brookbank Brook. Many rocks along the brook provide excellent resting spots. Take advantage—you will need your energy for the climb ahead! This is a good turnaround point for tired children.

To continue, look for the Inlook Trail on your left. Many trails culminate here, so be sure to find the sign marking the trail. Immediately,

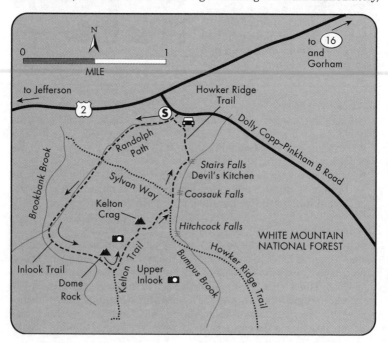

A good resting spot on the way up to Dome Rock

begin a very steep, rocky climb marked by yellow blazes. When the complaints begin, have the kids look behind them to see how far they've climbed. If anyone gets discouraged by the seemingly endless hill climb, play the game I'd Rather Be Hiking Than. . . . Everyone gets to complete the sentence and can make it as silly as they want. "I'd rather be hiking than cleaning my room," or "I'd rather be hiking than eating slimy worms." It's amazing how much more quickly the time goes by when giggles are involved. In 0.4 mile, the trail heads out of the woods onto rock slabs. Follow the rock cairns as you take in the commanding views of the mountains around you. The Inlook Trail still climbs steeply over slabs to arrive at a marker on the top of Dome Rock in 0.7 mile, but the sights and the rocky scrambles will distract the kids from the steepness.

From the marker on Dome Rock, look for the trail to the left of the one you just hiked, marked with a Path sign. In 0.1 mile, upon reaching Upper Inlook and a trail junction, follow the Kelton Trail to the Howker Ridge Trail sign on the left. The Kelton Trail begins a very steep and demanding descent, occasionally helped along by stone steps. Children will need to have their hands free to help navigate and balance as they make their way down. In roughly 0.5 mile, at a sign for Kelton Crag, the trail curves and becomes brushier in spots. Keep your eyes peeled for yellow blazes. The pitch lessens right before reaching a trail junction with the Howker Ridge Trail, a little less than a mile from the start of the Kelton Trail. Bear left on the Howker Ridge Trail as it makes its way along Bumpus Brook. In 0.1 mile, ignore the Sylvan Way Trail on your left, and stay straight on the Howker Ridge Trail to an overlook of Coosauk Falls.

You will once again be following blue blazes as you parallel the brook below. Soon, you will see an interesting gorge, the Devil's Kitchen. Past here, you will be on private property as you pass by Stairs Falls and other smaller cascades, before the trail curves back into the woods. The last stretch leads you on a fairly level path and over a series of wooden footbridges to the junction with the Randolph Path. Bear right and head the last 0.1 mile back to the parking area.

LOOKING FOR AN EASIER HIKE?

If you aren't quite up to the challenge of Dome Rock, you can still hike from this trailhead. Begin on the Randolph Path, but take your first left onto the Howker Ridge Trail. Although the trail doesn't get as close to the water in places as kids might like, this trail will lead you past Stairs Falls, Devil's Kitchen, and Coosauk and Hitchcock Falls. When you reach Hitchcock Falls, retrace your steps to return to your vehicle.

 GLEN ELLIS FALLS

BEFORE YOU GO
Maps USGS Stairs Mountain, Carter Dome, and Mount Washington
Current Conditions White Mountain National Forest Androscoggin Ranger Station (603) 466-2713; White Mountain National Forest Supervisor's Office (603) 528-8721; AMC Pinkham Notch Visitor Center (603) 466-2721
Fee for parking at Glen Ellis trailhead on NH-16

ABOUT THE HIKE
Day hike
Easy for children
June–October
2.2 miles, round trip
Hiking time 2 hours
High point/elevation gain 2050 feet, 150 feet

GETTING THERE
- From the junction of US 302 and NH-16 in Glen, drive north on NH-16.
- In 11.3 miles, turn left into the parking area for the Appalachian Mountain Club (AMC) Pinkham Notch Camp.

ON THE TRAIL

On the hike to Glen Ellis Falls, you will see water at its most peaceful and its most powerful. Follow the hurrying Ellis River to the shores of tranquil Lost Pond. From here, negotiate a boulder maze to rejoin the river and arrive at the waterfall just over a mile from the start. While you'll find solitude along the trail, expect crowds at the impressive falls. This is a terrific hike for the entire family—it's within the capabilities of most preschoolers, yet varied enough to entertain a twelve-year-old. (One rather tricky river crossing makes this a poor choice for springtime or after a heavy rain.)

Cross NH-16 and walk southward on the highway for 50 yards to the Lost Pond trailhead. Heading eastward, cross the Ellis River on log footbridges. Do the kids know where this water comes from and where it is going? The river begins as a trickle on the eastern slope of Mount Washington (6288 feet above sea level), joins the Saco River near Glen, New Hampshire, and winds through Maine to the Atlantic Ocean.

Beyond the bridges, turn right (south) onto the white-blazed Lost Pond Trail and Appalachian Trail (AT). Immediately the Square Ledge Trail heads left as you continue straight (south) on the wide Lost Pond Trail. As you follow along the eastern bank of the Ellis River (soon joined by the Cutler River), the cascading water and the highway traffic compete for your attention. Which little hiker does the best tow truck, motorcycle, or train imitation?

The trail crosses a tributary over a footbridge 0.25 mile from the start and continues to wind southward through an evergreen forest. At 0.4 mile, the trail curls left (southeast) away from the river, shortly crossing a third footbridge over a stream that originates on Wildcat Mountain. Rising gently, the trail hops over wet sections on logs and stones.

You'll arrive at the rugged northern shore of Lost Pond 0.5 mile from the start. Follow the shoreline and, in less than 0.1 mile, rocks offer you front-row seats to a postcard-perfect view of Mount Washington. (On the way back, stop here for a picnic lunch far from the crowds that gather at the falls.)

Departing the shore, the blazes lead hikers through a 0.2-mile boulder maze with overhangs and caves that will entice little explorers. At 0.8 mile, the trail plunges down a rock-strewn hill (you'll have a scramble on the way back) and balances on logs to cross a stream and weave through more boulders.

The Lost Pond Trail ends 0.9 mile from the start at a junction with the blue-blazed Wildcat Ridge Trail. Here, the AT bears left (east) and joins the Wildcat Ridge Trail. You turn right (west) onto the Wildcat Ridge Trail (toward the Ellis River and NH-16). In 0.1 mile, the trail arrives at the bank of the wide, shallow river. Though this stone-to-stone crossing is hairy in spring and after heavy rains, at other times of the year it is not hard to make it across with dry boots.

Follow the western riverbank southward for 75 feet and join the

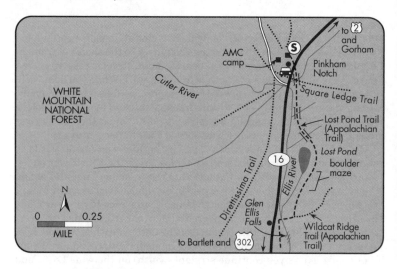

to ② and Gorham

AMC camp

Pinkham Notch

WHITE MOUNTAIN NATIONAL FOREST

Cutler River

Square Ledge Trail

Lost Pond Trail (Appalachian Trail)

Lost Pond boulder maze

N

0   0.25
MILE

Direttissima Trail

Ellis River

16

Glen Ellis Falls

Wildcat Ridge Trail (Appalachian Trail)

to Bartlett and ③⓪②

tourists flocking toward the falls. With stairs and guardrails to assist you, drop to the base of the falls for an impressive view. The water explodes over the cliff and crashes 64 feet to the pool at the base. As placards near the falls explain, within seconds enough water spills over the escarpment to serve a city of 25,000 for a full day.

Retrace your steps along the peaceful Lost Pond Trail to your vehicle.

51 IMP FACE

BEFORE YOU GO
Map USGS Carter Dome
Current Conditions White Mountain National Forest Androscoggin Ranger Station (603) 466-2713; White Mountain National Forest Supervisor's Office (603) 528-8721; AMC Pinkham Notch Visitor Center (603) 466-2721
White Mountain National Forest Use Pass encouraged to support the forest

ABOUT THE HIKE
Day hike
Challenging for children
June–September
6.5 miles, loop
Hiking time 5.5 hours
High point/elevation gain
3200 feet, 2100 feet

GETTING THERE

- From the junction of NH-16 and the Mount Washington Auto Road, drive 1.2 miles north on NH-16.
- Turn right into a parking turnout large enough for four vehicles.

ON THE TRAIL

The trail to Imp Face is a lot like the gangster "Baby Face" Nelson—a cute name belies a tough character. You'll gain more than 2000 feet and cover nearly 6.5 miles as you climb to the Imp Face summit and loop back along an easily followed route. With the only suitable turnaround point at the 2.2-mile mark, you'll want to be sure that you and your family are up to at least four hours' worth of strenuous hiking. Although you'll encounter a number of brooks and streams, the highlight of the trip is the dizzying panorama from atop Imp Face. Gather together a fit group of view lovers and go!

From the parking area, head eastward guided by a sign that tells hikers that the Imp is 2.2 miles away. The Imp Trail, marked in yellow, rises gently through a stand of mature hemlocks, leveling 0.35 mile from the start. To the left of the path, a shallow ravine cradles Imp Brook. Let the kids run ahead, waiting for you beside the giant trailside boulder covered with a web of tree roots 0.5 mile from the start.

At 0.65 mile, the path curls left (northeast), crosses the cascading Imp Brook over stepping stones, and begins a moderate ascent. In another 0.1 mile, the pitch steepens, with stone steps and logs to facilitate the tougher grades. Just under a mile from the start, the trail crests a shoulder and hops over another stream but quickly resumes a moderate ascent. This is a good hike for children to lead: The trail is hard-packed and wide with few rocks or roots.

At 1.25 miles, climb briskly, aided by wooden steps. As you near the 1.4-mile mark, weary kids can look ahead for a cluster of birches bordering the path and marking the easing of the grade.

At 1.75 miles, the trail heads steeply up the slope in a southwesterly direction. Urge kids to imitate rabbits: Because rabbits have longer hindlegs than forelegs, they run faster uphill than downhill. Play Chase the Rabbits: Assign one child to chase the others (the "rabbits") and tell the kids how real rabbits escape. (They crisscross their tracks and take giant leaps to confuse animals following their scent. They also stamp the ground with their hind feet to warn one another of danger.)

As the trail bends southeastward at the 2-mile mark, notice the intrusion of granite, heralding the baldface ahead. On the final approach to the summit, veer eastward and zigzag up the steep slope, arriving at the high, exposed Imp ledges 2.2 miles from the start. Even younger children will be delighted with these panoramas across the Presidentials. The sharp peaks of Adams and Jefferson reach for the clouds beside always impressive Mount Washington. Look southward across the

Imp Brook valley to the adjoining ridge; you will circle the valley and return along this ridge.

After you have admired the layers of impressive mountains, drop off Imp Face through a hemlock grove on a short, steep descent. Continue on rolling terrain with sweeping views across the valley. At 2.5 miles, the trail leads over a stream, the first of many within the next mile. Assign a child to keep count.

The yellow blazes lead generally southward, with cropped views of the Presidentials persisting. Cross a second stream and then a more substantial third at 2.8 miles. The trail rolls through more hemlock stands, leading across streams four and five. (What holiday are you reminded of as you sniff the hemlock trees?)

At 3.1 miles (just under a mile from the summit), the trail arrives at a junction. The North Carter Trail heads left on blue blazes as you turn right (west), heading toward NH-16, 3.1 miles away. Continue to follow

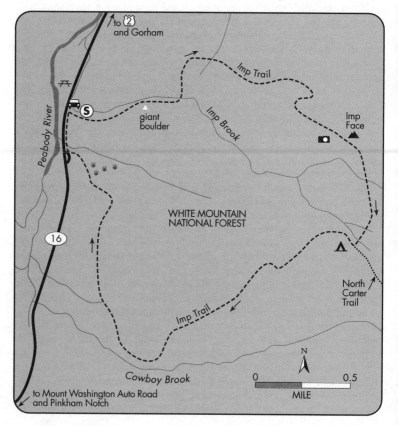

the yellow blazes of the Imp Trail, passing an ideal tent site on the left in 100 yards. The trail leads northward, dropping easily along the bank of the stream you recently crossed, and soon swings westward. At 3.4 miles, balance on a split-log bridge over a wet area and then race with the brook that follows the trail for 0.1 mile.

The now-rocky trail drops first within a dry streambed heading southwestward and then to an old logging road 4 miles from the start. At 5 miles, you'll hear the whispers of water in the distance as the trail tumbles down a series of brief, steep pitches with stone steps. In another 0.5 mile, cut across the left-hand side of an open area that has been seeded by the Forest Service. Cross a swampy section at 5.8 miles on logs as the descent eases and levels.

A final drop at 6 miles leads to the bank of a stream 0.1 mile later. Exit the woods at 6.2 miles and turn right (north) onto NH-16. You'll return to your vehicle in 0.3 mile. Whew! Exchange pats on the back and find an ice cream stand!

A DIFFERENT POINT OF VIEW

After completing this hike, it's fun to reflect upon Imp Face from the west. One of the best places to see the Imp Profile is from Dolly Copp Road off NH-16 in Pinkham Notch. Look up at the profile from the Copp Homestead site (Dolly Copp named Imp Profile, which she could see from her cabin) or Hayes Field in the Dolly Copp Campground.

 NORTH SUGARLOAF

BEFORE YOU GO
Map USGS Whitefield
Current Conditions White Mountain National Forest Pemigewasset/Ammonoosuc Ranger District (603) 536-1315 or White Mountain National Forest Supervisor's Office (603) 528-8721
White Mountain National Forest Use Pass required

ABOUT THE HIKE
Day hike
Moderate for children
May–October
2.6 miles, round trip
Hiking time 2 hours
High point/elevation gain 2310 feet, 700 feet

GETTING THERE
■ From the junction of US 3 and US 302 in Twin Mountain, drive 2.1 miles east on US 302.

- Turn right at a sign for Zealand Pond, White Mountain National Forest Recreation Area.
- Follow Zealand Road for 1 mile and park on the right, just before the bridge over Zealand Brook.

ON THE TRAIL

Volunteers have made major improvements along North Sugarloaf Trail and at the summit. Rustic steps facilitate the ascent and water bars fight the effects of erosion. Mountaintop trees were cut to improve views. These improvements make North Sugarloaf worth another visit.

Follow Zealand Road over Zealand Brook to the Trestle and Sugarloaf trailheads. Turn right (northwest) into the woods following yellow blazes. Wind along the brook for 0.15 mile to a fork. The Trestle Trail continues to hug the riverbank as you turn left (northwest) on the Sugarloaf Trail, departing the river on level terrain. In less than 0.1 mile, cross a grassy road and a ski mobile trail.

As the trail begins to climb 0.25 mile into the hike, it dodges left to avoid a split boulder and then sidesteps a second boulder. (You can pause to let the kids try a little rock climbing.) Now climbing moderately, march past a row of tall white birches that guard the trail. This stiff ascent continues for 0.25 mile, relaxes briefly, then resumes on a slope fitted

Most toddlers are quite content to do their hiking in a backpack.

with log and rock steps. (Can the kids keep a count of the steps?)

Shortly, the trail crests and splits, heading for North and South Sugarloaf. Turn right (north) toward North Sugarloaf and hike on level ground along the top of a ridge. Soon the trail swings left and drops briefly, wrapping around the northern side of the mountain in search of a gentler approach to the summit.

As the trail swerves southeastward, a final surge will bring you to the top, 0.3 mile beyond the North/South Sugarloaf junction. The summit offers patches of trees to escape the wind and large expanses of open baldface to take in views of all the Presidentials, particularly Mount Washington, to the east. Follow the yellow blazes that lead across this expansive summit to take in panoramic views. Did the kids notice the intricate patterns created by logging operations on the adjoining ridge of Mount Oscar? Find a cozy nook for a picnic and then hike back to your vehicle the way you came.

 PINE MOUNTAIN AND THE LEDGES

BEFORE YOU GO
Map USGS Carter Dome
Current Conditions White Mountain National Forest Androscoggin Ranger Station (603) 466-2713; White Mountain National Forest Supervisor's Office (603) 528-8721; AMC Pinkham Notch Visitor Center (603) 466-2721
White Mountain National Forest Use Pass encouraged to support the forest

ABOUT THE HIKE
Day hike or overnight
Easy for children
April–October
4 miles, round trip
Hiking time 3 hours
High point/elevation gain
2405 feet, 600 feet

GETTING THERE
- From US 2 between Jefferson and Gorham, take Pinkham B Road (6.5 miles west from Gorham, 8 miles east from Jefferson).
- In 2.5 miles, park your vehicle in a turnout on the right to access both the Pine Link and Pine Mountain Trails.
- Alternatively, from NH-16 north of the Mount Washington Auto Road and south of Gorham, follow the Pinkham B Road (enter at a sign for White Mountain National Forest, Dolly Copp Campground). Drive approximately 3.5 miles to the parking turnout for the Pine Link and Pine Mountain Trails on the left.

ON THE TRAIL

Pine Mountain rises from the northern tip of the Presidential Range. While not as well-known as its famous neighbors, this 2400-foot peak features a number of open ledges affording hikers commanding views of the Presidentials, including Mounts Madison and Washington, as well as views across to Carter Notch. One ledge can even accommodate a row of sleeping bags for an overnight adventure.

The summit and the ledges can be reached either by a brief, albeit steep, hike up the western flank of the mountain or via a camp access road on a consistent, gradual incline. Families electing to take the road should watch for the occasional vehicle, respect the camp property at road's end, and stay on marked trails.

Cross the Pinkham B Road to the Pine Mountain trailhead where a sign indicates that The Ledges Trail is in 0.9 mile and Pine Mountain Center is in 2 miles. Begin your trip along the gravel access road to Horton Center, a summer camp run by the United Church of Christ. Consider the first mile to be a solid warm-up for everyone in your hiking group. Remind children to walk along the side of the road in case a camp van makes an unexpected appearance. Keep them busy looking for "log hotels" that can be overturned to reveal a variety of "guests."

At the 0.9-mile mark, head right into the woods guided by a sign for The Ledges Trail. (You may opt to follow the road for an additional mile to the trailhead for the Pine Mountain Trail and follow this trail to the top of Pine Mountain where it joins The Ledges Trail.) The Ledges Trail is so named for the breathtaking open ledges at the mountain summit. The trail begins on an easy slope but quickly steepens. Shortly the trail passes through an area of boulders and granite chunks that have fallen from the ledges above. After 0.3 mile of steep, steady climbing, you arrive at the base of Pinkham Ledge. The trail sweeps left across this open, sloping ledge, fringed by wild blueberry bushes.

Pinkham Ledge offers the mountain's most outstanding vistas, as well as some very flat sections if your group has planned to sleep out under the stars. From this vantage point, absorb the imposing view: To the south (left), look for the peak of Mount Madison and the multiple bulges of Mount Washington. Can you spot Mount Adams peeking over the shoulder of Mount Madison? Adams is just to the right of Madison and can look like a shoulder to Madison. Here are other ways to identify the peaks: The top of Mount Madison forms a slightly skewed M while the summit of Mount Washington, appropriately enough, forms a lopsided W.

The children will enjoy the intrigue along the next section of trail. As you continue, you'll need to look hard to find the next ledge, aptly

Opposite: A young hiker nears the Pine Mountain summit. Mount Washington is in the background.

named Mystery Ledge. As the least visited of the mountain's ledges, Mystery Ledge hides at the end of an overgrown access. If you arrive at the fire tower abutments at the crest of the mountain, you have missed the access path.

Just before the summit, the Fire Tower Ledge offers comparable views but is more isolated than Pinkham Ledge from the trail. At the fire tower abutments, The Ledges Trail becomes the Pine Mountain Trail. As you follow the Pine Mountain Trail, two more short side trails open onto ledges with widespread vistas. One ledge features a small shelter. From either of these ledges, look southeast across the valley to the Carter Range. Can you see the sleeping monkey that makes up a substantial portion of the mountain range across the valley? On Pine Mountain, look for the Horton Center Camp and the rock climbing ledges.

Continue to follow the Pine Mountain Trail and, in 0.1 mile, join the camp access road. Reverse your direction or turn left onto the road and walk the 2 miles to your vehicle. (The Pine Mountain Trail continues to Gorham. The hike described here starts from the trailhead, rather than in town.)

Opposite: Hiking is easier with a hiking stick.

MAINE

VAUGHAN WOODS MEMORIAL

BEFORE YOU GO
Map USGS Dover East (New Hampshire)
Current Conditions Maine Bureau of Parks and Lands, Vaughan Woods Memorial State Park (207) 384-5160 in season or (207) 624-6080 off season
Small fee

ABOUT THE HIKE
Day hike
Easy for children
Year-round
1.5 miles, loop
Hiking time 1 hour
High point/elevation gain 160 feet, 200 feet
Some paths suitable for strollers

GETTING THERE

- From the junction of ME-236 and ME-4 in South Berwick, travel south on ME-236 for 0.5 mile.
- Turn right onto Vine Street.
- In 1 mile turn left on Old Fields Road.
- Follow this 0.3 mile to a parking area on the right.

ON THE TRAIL

Take this easy jaunt along the east bank of the Salmon Falls River almost anytime. Even when the gate is closed during the colder months, you can park along Old Fields Road and hike 0.25 mile to the trailhead. The generally level path follows the riverbank for just under a mile, then loops back to the parking area through airy woodlands. At least one major trail is suitable for strollers.

The Shady Stroll Trail, originating at the southeast corner of the parking and picnic area (end closest to the road), starts as a dirt path heading downward. In about 150 yards it comes to a bridge crossing a stream that flows into the Salmon Falls River a little farther downstream. Soon, you will come to a Y-junction in the trail. The Bridle Path (suitable for wheelchairs and strollers) bears to the left and the River Run to the right. Mobile kids will prefer River Run, which wanders through a hemlock and spruce forest along the sloping riverbank. Along the 0.75-mile River Run Trail, ignore the numerous side trails (with cheerful names like Porcupine Path, Windy Walk, and Nubble Knoll) that split left (east) away from the river.

Immediately after heading out on the River Run Trail, another trail heads sharply to the right. This trail exits the park and leads to the Hamilton House, a historical home owned and operated by the Society for the Protection of New England Antiquities. (Touring the grounds is free; there is a small fee to tour the house.) In another 200 yards, adults can relax on a bench overlooking the river and the Hamilton House while kids explore the water's edge. Ask the youngest hikers how squirrels help to propagate oak forests. (They bury acorns in fall to retrieve in winter, but sometimes their memory or sense of smell fails them and they miss some of their caches. With warm spring weather, some of the forgotten acorns begin to grow into oak trees!) Beyond a second bench at a river overlook is a huge white birch surrounded by hemlocks. Can the kids guess what the Native Americans made from birch trees? (Give them a hint: The tree is also called "canoe birch.")

As the trail continues, it crosses a number of bridges over gullies that form intermittent streams during rainy seasons. Just before the Old Gate Trail branches left, the kids can imitate Winnie the Pooh in search of honey. By looking for the large white pine on the left side of the trail with a hole 3 inches in diameter and about 15 feet from the ground, they will find a bee tree that would make Pooh Bear sigh. Perhaps they'll spot the bees entering or exiting their hive through the opening.

More footbridges will bring you to the head of Cow's Cove less than a mile from the start, so named because the first cows to arrive in this part of Maine landed here in 1634. The trail continues another 0.25 mile before coming to Trail's End, where another bench overlooks the river. Head left on the Bridle Path, passing through stands of spruce

A cold weather hiker peeks out from behind a tree.

and hemlock. The trail gradually curls north and passes the site of the 1656 Warren homestead, reduced to a cellar hole and some crumbling gravestones. Warren, a Scottish prisoner of war to the British who came to America as an indentured servant, homesteaded here in 1656 after fulfilling his period of indenture. Once again, disregard the side trails that depart left from Bridle Path (shortcuts to River Run). At the Y-junction near the start, continue over the bridge and up the road to the parking lot.

> ### SALMON FALLS RIVER
>
> This river got its name from the salmon that were plentiful at the falls during this fish's annual migration. The Salmon Falls River provided transportation to early settlers harvesting timber and also powered the first sawmill built in America.

 MOUNT AGAMENTICUS

BEFORE YOU GO
Map USGS York Harbor
Current Conditions
York Parks and Recreation Department, Mount Agamenticus Conservation (207) 363-1040

ABOUT THE HIKE
Day hike
Easy for children
April–October
1.5 miles, loop
Hiking time 1.5 hours
High point/elevation gain 691 feet, 350 feet

GETTING THERE
- Take exit 7 on I-95 in York, heading west (left) on Chases Pond Road.
- Soon the road swings sharply right to head north.
- In 3.8 miles, Chases Pond Road merges with Mountain Road.
- Bear left to travel west on Mountain Road for 2.6 miles to the gravel parking area on the right-hand side of the road (just before a right-hand turn onto the summit road).

ON THE TRAIL
At nearly 700 feet above sea level, Mount Agamenticus looms over the seacoast of southern York County. For the younger ones who can't handle a lengthy climb up a mountainside, this route offers a 0.7-mile

ascent to a broad, grassy summit with impressive views. The nonhikers in the family can drive to the summit via the auto road and enjoy the same panoramas.

From the parking lot, enter the logged woods at a tree farm sign, heading north on a woods road that parallels the auto road. Soon you will reach a junction marked by signs for the Ring Trail. Bear right and follow the Ring Trail as it heads north toward the summit. Can the kids imitate or recognize some of the bird calls they are hearing? Did you know that birds have "accents" just like people do? Even though a bird's ability to sing is instinctive (as opposed to learned), a bird living in one part of the world sounds different from the same kind of bird living in another part, just like a person from Georgia might speak differently than a person from Boston.

Soon, the trail widens as it climbs briskly northward over granite. (Warn the kids that the granite underfoot is slippery after a rainstorm.)

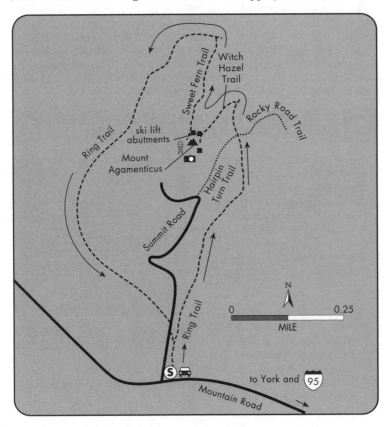

Continue moderately uphill on a rocky, wide trail in mixed woods dotted with small white pines, hemlocks, and oaks. Ask young hikers to feel the bark on different trees and guess what uses people have for bark. Any child who guesses that some spices (like cinnamon), certain medicines, and commercial cork come from bark wins a piggyback ride for 30 paces. Head past the junction with Hairpin Turn and Rocky Road Trails, and take your next left onto Witch Hazel Trail up to the top.

The broad, grassy summit is a terrific place for kids to run and to explore the remains of the defunct ski operation; on the northeast side of the mountaintop are abutments that once supported the ski lift mechanism. A ski lodge and other summit buildings are closed to the public. Climb the viewing platform for expansive views. Mountains interrupt the northern and western horizons; on a clear day, you'll spot Mount Washington and other major peaks in the White Mountains.

To return to your vehicle, look for signs for the Sweet Fern Trail and follow this path over rocky slabs alongside an old ski lift. At the next junction, turn left onto the Ring Trail and enter thick woods. Continue on the Ring Trail as it meets up with other trails along the way. Upon reaching the summit road, turn right and in 100 yards reenter the woods on the left, heading downhill on the familiar woods road near the base of the mountain. In 0.1 mile, you'll see your vehicle.

 ## WELLS NATIONAL ESTUARINE RESEARCH RESERVE AT LAUDHOLM FARM

BEFORE YOU GO
Map USGS Wells
Current Conditions Wells National Estuarine Research Reserve (207) 646-1555
Small fee Memorial Day weekend through Columbus Day

ABOUT THE HIKE
Day hike
Easy for children
Year-round
1.7 miles, loop
Hiking time 1.5 hours
High point/elevation gain
62 feet, 62 feet
Partially accessible Visitor Center and Ecology Center

GETTING THERE
- From the south, take exit 19 off the Maine Turnpike.
- Turn left on combined ME-9 East/ME-109 South and follow 1.5 miles to US 1/ME-9.
- Turn left on US 1, and in 1.5 miles go right onto Laudholm Farm Road, where ME-9 heads to the right.
- In 0.5 mile, take a left on Skinner Mill Road to the entrance.

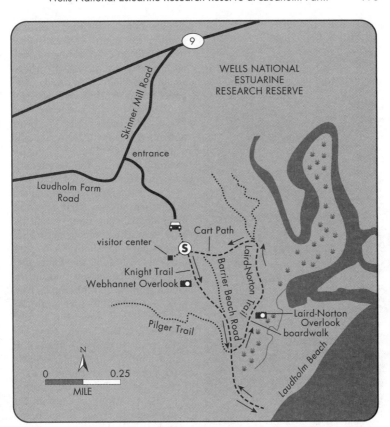

- *Alternatively*, from the north take exit 25 off the Maine Turnpike to US 1. On US 1 travel south 3.3 miles to a left turn onto Laudholm Farm Road and follow the directions above.

ON THE TRAIL

Seven miles of trails wind through fields, woods, wetlands, salt marsh, estuary, and barrier beach on this historic former farm, now part of the National Estuarine Research Reserve System. Do your kids know what an estuary is? It's where salty sea waters meet fresh land waters. Estuaries provide important habitat for a number of birds, fish, and other animals, including some rare species that can be found here. At the Wells Reserve, you can observe where the currents of the Little and Webhannet Rivers meet the salty waters of the Atlantic Ocean along the coast of Maine. Before hitting the trails, pick up a trail map, visit

A young hiker reads a sign.

the exhibits, and browse the gift shop at the visitor center, housed in the restored farmhouse. Located in another building, the Maine Coastal Ecology Center also has educational exhibits and research and teaching laboratories. Call ahead for current hours. The route described here will take you past a salt marsh, through a maple swamp, down to the beach, and over an extensive boardwalk.

Find the signs pointing to the trails behind the visitor center. Take the Knight Trail, which begins near the flagpole as a wide grassy path paralleling a wooden fence. In 0.1 mile, the fields give way to shrubs as you take in the views from the Webhannet Overlook. In 0.3 mile, turn right on Barrier Beach Road at a sign pointing to the beach. Now the path travels through woodlands and a maple swamp before reaching a junction with the Pilger and Laird-Norton Trails in another 0.1 mile. Continue straight on the beach road to travel through salt marsh to a lookout over water in 0.1 mile. Here you can look for herons, egrets, ibises, and other long-legged birds. Does anyone know why they have such long legs? It's so they can walk in shallow water to find and catch frogs, insects, and other animals that serve as their food source. In 0.2 mile cross the wooden walkway to the beach and ocean waters.

After frolicking on the beach, head back to Barrier Beach Road. At the intersection with the Laird-Norton Trail, turn right and follow the Laird-Norton Trail over an extensive boardwalk—always a highlight for kids—through woodlands along the edge of a marsh. At the halfway point of this approximately 0.5-mile trail, the Laird-Norton Overlook provides you with stunning views of the Little River Inlet and surrounding marsh. Continue along this trail and turn left onto the Cart Path back to the visitor center.

EARLY INHABITANTS

The first people to make their homes here were Native Americans. From fall through early spring, they hunted beaver, moose, bear, otter, and other animals. Through spring and summer, they caught fish and shellfish off the coast. When Europeans settled here, they established farms and harvested salt hay from the marshes to sustain cattle through the winters. Only four families lived on this farm before it was preserved and protected in the surrounding natural habitat.

 EAST POINT SANCTUARY

BEFORE YOU GO
Map USGS Biddeford Pool
Current Conditions Maine Audubon Society (207) 781-2330

ABOUT THE HIKE
Day hike
Easy for children
Year-round
0.8 mile, round trip
Hiking time 45 minutes
High point/elevation gain
43 feet, 20 feet

GETTING THERE
- From Biddeford, head south on ME-9/ME-208.
- In 5 miles, head left onto ME-208.

- Bear left at the T-intersection at 0.6 mile.
- In another mile, turn right onto Lester B. Orcutt Boulevard.
- Follow this road 0.6 mile to its point and the gate entrance on the left.
- Park in the widened area along the street.

ON THE TRAIL
Although this Audubon Sanctuary is relatively small at a mere 30 acres, the views it offers are big and sweeping. The trail passes by rocky cliffs and pebble beaches as it wraps around the tip of East Point at the very tip of Biddeford Pool. Along the way you will be serenaded by the sounds of waves crashing and birds calling. The wide path is easily navigated by young children who are sure to be awed by the sights and sounds along the way. And what would a hike along Maine's coast be without a lighthouse? On the northern side of the trail, you will have unobstructed views of Wood Island Lighthouse, which has a fascinating history and is even said to be haunted.

To begin, pass through the chain-link fence by the road posted with

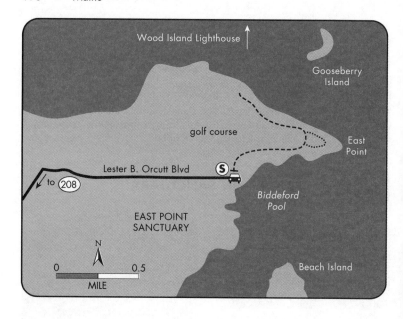

Washed up lobster traps with a view of Wood Island Lighthouse in the distance

Maine Audubon signs. The trail passes between a residence on your right and a golf course on your left as it heads east. Soon it leaves the golf course behind and presents you with stunning views of the ocean. In a little less than 0.2 mile, the path turns north by a flat open area. Although there is a path around the tip of East Point, be sure to follow the designated trail signs more inland so as not to damage fragile plants or further erode the cliffs.

In less than another 0.1 mile, the trail curves west around the opposite shore above a rocky beach. Across the water you will see the Wood Island Lighthouse. This lighthouse was built in 1808 and boasts an interesting past of shipwrecks, rescues, a murder/suicide, and possibly ghosts. (For more information, contact The Friends of Wood Island Lighthouse at *www.woodislandlighthouse.org*.) The trail continues along the northern perimeter and heads through shrubs and bushes. Depending on when you visit, bushes may be flowering or in bloom. Have your kids look for washed-up lobster traps near the shore and look and listen for seabirds such as black back gulls, herring gulls, and common eiders. Be sure to stay on the trail so as not to come in contact with poison ivy. In a little under 0.5 mile, the Audubon property ends. Please respect the boundary with private property and head back the way you came.

Note: No pets or bicycles allowed.

 WOLFE'S NECK WOODS

BEFORE YOU GO
Map USGS Freeport
Current Conditions Wolfe's Neck Woods State Park (207) 865-4465
Small fee

ABOUT THE HIKE
Day hike
Easy for children
Year-round
2 miles, loop
Hiking time 1.5 hours
High point/elevation gain 60 feet, 100 feet
Accessible parking, restrooms, picnic area; White Pines Trail accessible

GETTING THERE
- From I-295 North take exit 20, Desert Road, Freeport.
- Travel 1.3 miles north on US 1 to L. L. Bean in Freeport.
- Turn right onto Bow Street.
- In 2.4 miles, turn right onto Wolf Neck Road, following a sign for Wolfe's Neck Woods State Park.
- Drive 2 miles to a driveway on the left that leads to the parking area for Wolfe's Neck Woods State Park.

■ In season, you'll pay a day-use fee at the gate house. Off season, if gates are closed, park off Wolf Neck Road and walk the 0.25 mile to the trailhead.

ON THE TRAIL

At Wolfe's Neck Woods, no waterfalls explode over cliffs, no panoramic views stretch over mountaintops to far horizons. This hike is not intended to bombard your senses; the rewards here are far more subtle. Watch spiders silently spinning webs, smell the salt on the ocean breeze, study the gulls swooping over Casco Bay and the pattern made by a cluster of trailside ferns. Kids will appreciate the numerous split-log bridges, the two encounters with water, and the abundance of knee-high natural treasures along the level trail. Adults will emerge from this preserve relaxed and refreshed.

From the southwestern side of the parking area, head into the woods and almost immediately bear right (west) onto the Harraseeket Trail. This level path wanders through thick woodlands and tracks across

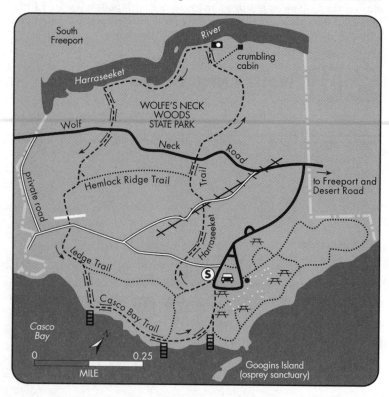

Casco Bay from the trail at Wolfe's Neck Woods State Park

several wet areas with adequate stepping stones. Kids will have to pick up their feet because rocks poke through the pine needle carpet and roots spread like a witch's fingers across the trail. At a junction with the Old Woods Road Trail, continue straight (north) on the Harraseeket Trail. Children can run ahead to the lengthy, split-log bridge at 0.2 mile that spans soggy terrain. Continue straight (northwest), following arrows as a cleared swath for powerlines cuts across the trail.

The trail sidesteps a tree whose roots cling desperately to a barren boulder. Who will be the first to spot a trailside spider's web? Do the kids know why spiders don't get caught in their own webs? (In addition to the sticky thread it produces, a spider incorporates strands of "nonsticky" thread in its web so that it is able to walk across without getting stuck.)

As the Hemlock Ridge Trail joins from the left, continue straight. After crossing another damp section on logs, walk across Wolf Neck Road and reenter the woods. Cross one more log bridge before dropping gently to the bank of the Harraseeket River, 0.7 mile from the start. The main trail descends to a ledge overlook of the river, 20 feet below. The trail turns left (east) to follow the riverbank, passing a chunk of ledge at 0.75 mile that broke away from the riverbank to form a steep, stark island. The trail winds above the river under a canopy of hemlocks and pines. As the slope to the water's edge lessens, the trail rolls in and out of wet gullies on split-log bridges. The trail angles east away from the river to wander over more streams. Kids will have fun navigating these crossings.

The trail cuts across Wolf Neck Road again, crosses another stream, switches back over a ledge outcropping on the left, and cuts back right. (This is a tricky section and the only spot on this hike where you're likely to get a little confused.) At 1.2 miles, you'll arrive at a trail junction with the Hemlock Ridge Trail. As the Hemlock Ridge Trail goes left (northeast), you bear right staying on the Harraseeket Trail, passing the Ledge Trail on the left, and heading southeast through varied woods. The path cuts through a stone wall to cross another woods road, still meandering generally southward. At the 1.4-mile mark, continue straight on the Harraseeket Trail to the Casco Bay Trail.

As the kids run across a lengthy stretch of split logs, they'll hear the sounds of breaking waves and feel the sea breezes sweeping inland. In the daytime, the cool air over the ocean rushes inland as the sea breeze. At night, when the ocean is warmer than the mainland, the cooler air gusts out to sea. The trail reaches the edge of Casco Bay and heads left (east) to follow the Casco Bay Trail along the rocky shoreline for 0.3 mile, crossing a number of streams on sturdy footbridges. The adults can relax on the trailside benches while the kids scamper down intermittent sets of wooden steps that provide better views of the bay. The final set of stairs along this route leads to a rocky shore. Just offshore on Googins Island, the kids may spot an osprey nest in a tall, broken pine. An osprey family often uses the same nest year after year, reinforcing it each spring. Look for other shorebirds here, too: sandpipers, terns, gulls, cormorants, loons.

From the rocky shore, return to the trail and head north at a four-way intersection. Cross a substantial footbridge over a tiny gorge, and shortly you'll reach the picnic area with tables and charcoal grills. At 0.1 mile from the bay, you arrive at the parking area close to the trail map sign and the start of the Harraseeket Trail.

Note: The park is open daily from 9:00 AM to sunset. Charcoal fires are permitted only in grill areas. Pets are allowed on a four-foot leash.

59 BURNT MEADOW MOUNTAIN

BEFORE YOU GO
Map USGS Brownfield
Current Conditions No contact agency

ABOUT THE HIKE
Day hike
Moderate for children
May–October
2.6 miles, round trip
Hiking time 2.5 hours
High point/elevation gain
1575 feet, 1200 feet

GETTING THERE
■ From the junction of US 302, ME-113, and ME-5 in Fryeburg, take ME-5 and ME-113 heading south.

- In 6.9 miles, at the junction with ME-160 in East Brownfield, turn right onto ME-160 South.
- In exactly 3 miles, as the road bends right, park on the right-hand shoulder.
- Alternatively, from the junction of ME-25 and ME-160 in Kezar Falls, travel northward on ME-160 for 8.7 miles to the parking area on the left.

ON THE TRAIL

Burnt Meadow Mountain, close to the New Hampshire border, comprises three similar summits. The well-marked (though somewhat overgrown) route described here scales the eastern spur of North Peak and offers grand views beginning just 0.15 mile from the start. The broad, grassy summit gives kids room to run and adults room to spread out a feast with the White Mountains as a backdrop. The climb is somewhat steep—count on carrying preschoolers part of the way.

The blue-blazed trail heads northwest into the woods, weaving upward on a moderate grade. At 0.15 mile, on exposed ledge, you'll enjoy your first long-range views to the southeast. Through the trees to the right (north), you'll catch a glimpse of Pleasant Mountain. The pitch levels through airy woodlands to an open ridge 0.35 mile from the start where far-reaching panoramas persist. Fire raced across this mountain in 1947; can the kids

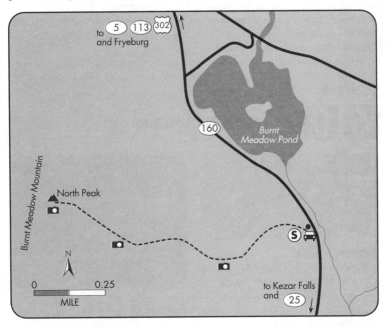

spot any signs of the devastating blaze? (Hug a tree; do your arms reach all the way around? This is a forest of young, slender trees.)

After nearly 0.5 mile of hiking, the trail crests a shoulder and drops into a boulder-strewn sag. Assign the youngest child to find the "grand-daddy" boulder off the trail to the left and assign the oldest one to point out the summit, looming ahead through the trees. After the col bottoms out in dense woods at 0.55 mile, the trail begins to wind uphill once more. Climbing westward, the path crosses more exposed granite with cairns and blazes marking the route. Quite a few bear dens have been found on the three mountains. Ask the children "If you were bears, where would you sleep?"

The grade steepens at 0.7 mile and levels on a second shoulder where Burnt Meadow Pond shimmers far below. The respite is brief, however, as the trail rises moderately to curl in and out of thin woods with ever-improving views from open baldface. Can the kids see the other peaks of Burnt Meadow Mountain to the southwest? Wildflowers fringe the trail on either side. Remember to encourage sniffing of these wildflowers, not picking.

At 1.15 miles, scramble over rock ledges and soon tackle a steep slide with precipitous cliffs approaching the trail from the left. Loose rocks make for slippery footing, so kids will need a hand. At 1.3 miles, you'll reach the broad, barren summit of North Peak. Here, grass softens the rocky terrain in contrast to the rugged trail you just climbed. The kids can run about, scouting for blueberries and mountain cranberries. Look northeast toward the Presidentials, south into a lush valley. To the northeast, Burnt Meadow Pond is a bluish puddle, reminding you of the 1200 feet you have just climbed.

After devouring a picnic lunch, head down the mountain the way you came, overlooking the two dominant shoulders you traversed on the way up.

60 SABATTUS MOUNTAIN

BEFORE YOU GO
Map USGS North Waterford
Current Conditions The Greater Lovell Land Trust (207) 925-1056

ABOUT THE HIKE
Day hike
Easy for children
May–October
1.4 miles, loop
Hiking time 1 hour
High point/elevation gain
1253 feet, 500 feet

GETTING THERE
■ From the junction of ME-5 and ME-93 in Lovell, travel north on ME-5 for 4.5 miles, passing Center Lovell General Store at 3.8 miles.

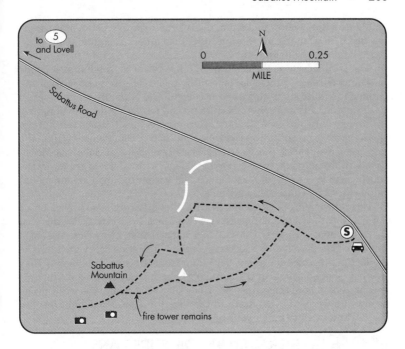

- Turn right onto Sabattus Road (also called Sabattus Mountain Road) and drive 1.4 miles to a fork.
- Bear right, still on Sabattus Road (now gravel).
- At 2.0 miles (0.6 mile beyond the fork), park in the lot on the right, marked with a Sabattus Mountain sign.

ON THE TRAIL

Sabattus Mountain, less than a 1-hour drive from the White Mountain National Forest (WMNF), is the baby of the Oxford Hills family. Amazingly, this hike up a gentle slope leads to dramatic views from the vertical cliff on the mountain's southwestern face. Bring a wildflower guidebook to enhance a midday hike or a flashlight for a walk at sunset.

Head behind the sign and begin an easy climb through logged woods. Logging is big business in Maine: Eighty-seven percent of the state is forested. How many things can the kids name that come from trees? In less than 0.1 mile reach a sign at the loop junction for the summit trail; bear right. Can the kids see any evidence of woodpeckers trying to root out insects living in the trunks of pine trees?

The pitch steepens after 0.25 mile of hiking, leading through a mixed hardwood forest. The grade gradually steepens to crest the north side of the mountain at 0.6 mile. If you are hiking in early summer, assign each child one wildflower to find along the trail: Starflower, aster, pipsissewa, wintergreen, Canada mayflower, Indian cucumber root, and trailing arbutus are all prevalent.

The trail sidesteps the remains of a fire tower on the left at 0.7 mile and quickly reaches the open summit ledges. (Be sure to have dogs and children in your sight and in your control; the cliffs are steep and can be dangerous.) The precipitous cliffs extend for 0.25 mile, providing tremendous views of Burnt Meadow Mountain (Hike 59) to the south; from the ledges above the cliffs, you'll be able to see Doublehead (Hike 48), and the Presidential Range to the west. The shape of Sabattus Mountain—mildly sloping on the northern side with a steep grade on the southern side—is called *stoss* and lee and is very common among mountains carved by continental glaciers.

After devouring a picnic lunch with this breathtaking panorama as a backdrop, follow the cliffs eastward and pick up a side trail indicated by yellow blazes. Shortly, this trail drifts northeast, away from the ridge and into the woods, also marked by yellow. The kids can watch for the peaked erratic boulder about 0.15 mile from the summit ridge. If they find egg-shaped pellets at the boulder's base or a quill or two, it probably means that a porcupine has recently called this home. The trail drops easily and winds its way down to the loop junction. Turn right back to the parking area to finish your hike.

61 BICKFORD BROOK SLIDES AND BLUEBERRY MOUNTAIN

BEFORE YOU GO
Maps USGS Wild River (New Hampshire) and Speckled Mountain (Maine)
Current Conditions White Mountain National Forest Evans Notch Information Center (207) 824-2134 or White Mountain National Forest Supervisor's Office (603) 528-8721
White Mountain National Forest Use Pass encouraged to support the forest

ABOUT THE HIKE
Day hike
Moderate for children
May–September
4.2 miles, round trip
Hiking time 3.5 hours
High point/elevation gain
1781 feet, 1400 feet

GETTING THERE
■ From the junction of US 2 and ME-113 in Gilead, head south on ME-113.

■ In 10.1 miles, turn left into a parking area for Brickett Place (operated by the Lexington, Massachusetts, Boy Scouts), guided by a hiking trail sign.

ON THE TRAIL

You'll have no trouble keeping kids motivated along this hiking route. Three major "kid" features—two water slides and a mountain summit—will keep them racing along the trail to find out what's next. At the Upper and Lower Bickford Slides, water streams down smooth rocks, collecting in pools that kids will find irresistible in warm weather. At the Blueberry Mountain summit, kids can munch on berries while the adults gaze at the view and try to name the distant peaks. A list of recommended items for the trip includes bathing suits or extra pairs of shoes for wading, long pants for protection through scratchy brush, containers for picking blueberries in season, bug repellent, and a camera to capture the picturesque water slides.

Look for the Bickford Brook Trail sign on the eastern side of the grassy Brickett Place parking area. The trail ascends moderately through mixed woods, joining a stone wall at 0.1 mile and a White Mountain National Forest (WMNF) access road at 0.3 mile. Here, turn right (southeast) onto the road, climbing gently. Turn right at 0.6 mile onto the yellow-blazed Blueberry Ridge Trail as it diverges from the woods road, dropping gently southward to the bank of the cascading Bickford Brook. The kids will have fun trying to determine if a leaf boat can beat a twig boat to the next bend. Turn right and follow the unmarked (though distinct) trail for 0.1 mile into the shallow ravine carved by Bickford Brook. Drop carefully down the steep embankment for a view of the brook's sliding falls, Lower Bickford Slide. The kids may want to wade or take a quick dip in one of the icy pools.

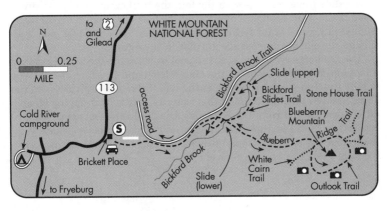

Retrace your steps 0.1 mile to the trail junction (keep your wading shoes on for now) and cross the brook on stepping stones to begin the ascent of Blueberry Mountain on the Blueberry Ridge Trail. (Now you can put your hiking boots back on!) Climb moderately through mixed hardwoods on stone steps. Are the kids hungry enough to stop for a sandwich or a piece of fruit? Talk about what forest creatures might be snacking on right now: Gray squirrels like acorns, fungi, seeds, and berries; porcupines prefer the inner bark of trees and sweet corn; deer munch on twigs, grass, bark, apples, and acorns.

At 1.2 miles, the trail travels over sections of ledge to approach the first exposed ridge 0.2 mile later. Following cairns now, the trail weaves in and out of scrub evergreen on a moderate ascent with fine western views to the Conway region of the White Mountains. True to its name, the mountain nourishes an abundance of low-bush blueberries that make a perfect snack for July hikers.

As the White Cairn Trail to Shell Pond joins from the right, continue on the Blueberry Ridge Trail, following signs to Speckled Mountain. In 100 yards, at 1.6 miles, the Outlook Trail splits right. Follow this trail marked by cairns and yellow blazes to circle the broad mass of Blueberry Mountain, with frequent views in all directions. At 1.85 miles, the trail has made a U-shaped sweep to rejoin the Blueberry Ridge Trail at a junction where the Stone House Trail heads right (east). Turn left here and, 2 miles from the start, you'll reach the Outlook Trail junction to complete the loop around the summit.

Return along the Blueberry Ridge Trail to Bickford Brook. Before recrossing the brook at the 3-mile mark, turn right (east) to follow the trail to the Upper Bickford Slide. The hard-packed trail climbs easily, guided by an occasional yellow blaze. After crossing a tributary at 3.15 miles, scale a muddy embankment and recross the tributary. As soon as the slide comes into view on the left, the trail swerves left and drops down to the wide, deep pool of water at the base of the slide. On a muggy August day, you'll want to linger poolside (bug repellent is a must), although the slides are most spectacular in springtime.

The trail crosses the base of the pool over adequate stepping stones and ascends a steep slope on the slide's left-hand (western) bank. Who will be the first to spot the cave to the left of the trail? At the top of the slide, another pool has formed that you can access by dropping steeply off the trail to the right. At 3.4 miles, the trail intersects the Bickford Brook Trail (still a woods road); turn left. The Blueberry Ridge Trail joins from the left in 0.2 mile; stay on the Bickford Brook Trail, and in 0.8 mile you'll be back at your vehicle.

EAST ROYCE MOUNTAIN

BEFORE YOU GO
Maps USGS Wild River (New Hampshire) and Speckled Mountain (Maine)
Current Conditions White Mountain National Forest Evans Notch Information Center (207) 824-2134 or White Mountain National Forest Supervisor's Office (603) 528-8721
White Mountain National Forest Use Pass required

ABOUT THE HIKE
Day hike
Challenging for children
May–September
3.2 miles, round trip
Hiking time 3 hours
High point/elevation gain
3114 feet, 1750 feet

GETTING THERE
- From the junction of US 2 and ME-113 in Gilead, head south on ME-113.
- In 7.3 miles, turn right into a large parking area for East Royce Trail.

ON THE TRAIL
Even though you'll travel along the same trail both up and down this mountain, you'll be amazed at how different the route seems. On the way up, the steep grade focuses attention on your goal, the summit; on the way down, you'll be more concerned with your footing, leading to a greater awareness of your immediate surroundings. With a lot of

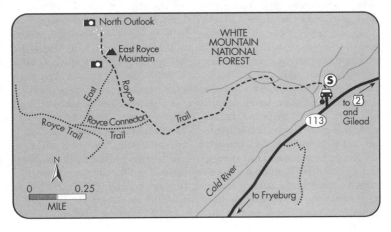

Signs point the way to North Outlook and Royce Mountain.

streams to cross on stepping stones and a number of challenging climbs, kids will be too busy to bicker or grumble. This is a demanding hike, best suited for older children with previous hiking experience.

The yellow-blazed East Royce Trail leaves the western side of the parking area on a moderate, northward climb, soon curling left to head westward. In 0.15 mile, you'll cross a rock slab spanning a hurrying stream. It's always tempting for kids to conduct a few water experiments: Does a twig swim faster than a leaf? Do acorns float? How about mushrooms?

Curling westward, the trail weaves more steeply to cross another branch of the stream at 0.25 mile. Leading hikers in a northerly direction through hemlocks and birches, the trail soon swings westward on a moderate pitch. Two more stream crossings just before the 0.5-mile mark will continue to pique the kids' interest. Are any frogs poised on the bank, ready to belly flop into the water? Ask the children if they have ever seen frogs hopping about in the wintertime. No? Actually, most frogs bury themselves in a pond's muddy bottom until spring.

As the trail continues to snake up the relatively steep slope, watch for the impressive white birches lining the trail at 0.75 mile. Here the trail becomes steeper and rockier before arching left (southwest) on a more gradual grade. Let the kids count moss-covered stones. Why does moss seem to grow so well here? Moss is one of the few plants that can survive these shady, acidic conditions. It began as a sea plant and still requires constant moisture. In fact, it needs water to reproduce.

At 0.8 mile, the trail continues to twist and climb, briefly mounting natural stone steps before the pitch eases at 1 mile. Soon, at a junction, the Royce Connector Trail diverges left (west), leading to Royce Trail and West Royce. Remain on the East Royce Trail, heading northwest to cross another small stream trickling through a gully. The path zigzags up a moderate-to-steep slope as granite slab sweeps underfoot at 1.1 miles. A mossy ledge looms on the left. At 1.2 miles, look behind you for a fine easterly view that promises even more expansive vistas shortly.

Soon the trail opens onto exposed granite and begins bounding over steep ledge, testing the kids' agility and stamina. At 1.3 miles, the trail scales a grooved stretch of rock slab, swerving left partway up, following yellow arrows. Just under 1.5 miles from the start, a sign points to the right (north) toward the East Royce Summit (200 yards away) and toward North Outlook (400 yards away). Here, you'll have commanding views east, south, and west over the foothills of southern Maine and some substantial mountains in the Conway region of New Hampshire.

Drop briefly through a spruce forest, still guided by yellow blazes. Remind the kids that Olympian Carl Lewis can cover 200 yards in 20 seconds! Assign someone to time your group's 200-yard hike along a level ridge to the enclosed summit, marked by a rock with a yellow X. From here, drop gently to North Outlook. You'll have one of the finest views of New Hampshire that Maine has to offer, with the Presidentials dominating the western horizon. Can the kids point to Mount Washington? (Tell them to look for its characteristic cloud halo.) The uniquely shaped Carter Dome lies to the northwest.

On the return trip, you'll be able to take in superb easterly views from the exposed ridge. Head back to your vehicle along the familiar East Royce Trail.

 THE ROOST

BEFORE YOU GO
Map USGS Speckled Mountain
Current Conditions White Mountain National Forest Evans Notch Information Center (207) 824-2134 or White Mountain National Forest Supervisor's Office (603) 528-8721
White Mountain National Forest Use Pass required

ABOUT THE HIKE
Day hike
Easy to moderate for children
May–October
1.3 miles, round trip
Hiking time 1 hour
High point/elevation gain
1374 feet, 650 feet

GETTING THERE
■ From the junction of US 2 and ME-113 in Gilead, head south on ME-113 for 2.9 miles.
■ The Roost Trail is on the left.
■ Drive an additional 100 yards across a bridge and park in the trailhead parking area.

ON THE TRAIL

You don't have to do a lot of advance planning to take on The Roost, a family favorite in the Evans Notch region of the White Mountain National Forest (WMNF). It's a short, easy climb to the top of this hill, perfect for the little guys. Afraid the older ones will be bored? Let them race along the well-defined path to the summit sign for The Roost (there are no trail junctions to confuse anyone). As with so many other hikes included in this guide, a minimum effort reaps maximum rewards. The views to the north, south, and west over the Wild River Valley and Evans Brook Valley are delightful.

Walk to the trailhead. The yellow-blazed Roost Trail heads east and settles into a moderate ascent. At 0.25 mile, the path leads through a stand of birches, then crosses a trickling stream 0.1 mile later. Do any frogs hop into the water as you pass by? Ask the kids how they distinguish frogs from toads. They probably use their sense of touch: Toads are dry and bumpy while frogs are smooth and slick. Observant little naturalists may have noticed that most frogs have teeth; most toads don't.

The trail levels at the 0.5-mile mark on exposed baldface fringed with hemlocks, spruces, and pines. A sign at the height of the land welcomes hikers to The Roost, where the grand views will delight you. Following signs to another scenic view, bear right onto a side trail as the main trail continues straight. The path then drops more gently through an evergreen forest, heading southwest. While adults anticipate the panoramas, the kids are probably more curious about the treasures closer at hand. Encourage them to locate a hole at the base of a tree. If there aren't any cobwebs covering the opening, if the leaves in front of the hole are matted down, and if there are bits of fur nearby, it is probably the home of a woodland creature.

The trail opens onto the overlook 0.65 mile from the start. Spread out your picnic lunch and

Toad or frog? Can your kids tell?

take in the expansive views over the Wild River Valley, southwest to East Royce Mountain (Hike 62), and west to the more prominent peaks of the White Mountains.

Return to your vehicle by retracing your steps.

64 STEP FALLS PRESERVE

BEFORE YOU GO
Map USGS Puzzle Mountain
Current Conditions The Nature Conservancy in Maine (207) 729-5181 or Bethel Area Chamber of Commerce (207) 824-2282

ABOUT THE HIKE
Day hike
Easy for children
May–October
1.5 miles, round trip
Hiking time 1.5 hours
High point/elevation gain 1250 feet, 400 feet

GETTING THERE
- From where ME-26 departs US 2 and ME-5 in North Bethel, drive north on ME-26 for 7.7 miles.
- Just before metal guardrails that border each side of the road, turn right onto a gravel road and drive to a grassy parking area. (You've gone too far on ME-26 if you cross the Grafton town line, 0.45 mile north of the gravel road turnoff.)

ON THE TRAIL

There's no doubt that this waterfall was created with kids in mind. Dropping 200 feet along Wight Brook in a series of cascades, Step Falls beckons little hikers to scale granite rocks alongside the tumbling water and to plunge into the deep, icy pools. (Don't forget bathing suits!) But this waterfall won't just appeal to the children—the gentle, unremitting roar will soothe and relax adults stretched out near the wading pools. If you're determined to interest the kids in family hiking, start with this one—it's a winner. And if you're a veteran hiker who enjoyed the hikes to Georgiana and Harvard Falls (Hike 39), Bickford Brook Slides (Hike 61), and Hamilton Falls (Hike 4), this, too, will make your list of favorites.

The well-traveled trail (initially unmarked but soon white blazed) leaves the northern side of the parking area and ducks into the woods, passing a Nature Conservancy sign. You'll hear the whispers of Wight

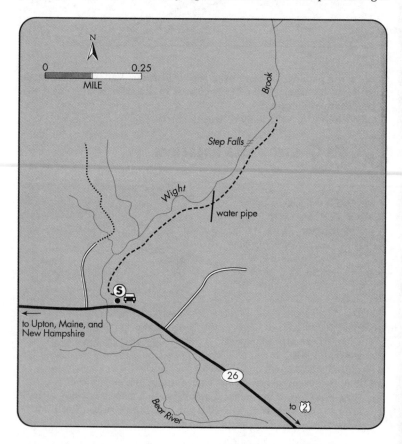

Water slips down Step Falls.

Brook to the left as the rocky trail leads through groves of spruce, fir, and hemlock. Can the kids tell these evergreens apart? The fir has flat needles and cones growing upright on its branches; the hemlock also has flat needles, but cones hang from the ends of its branches; and the spruce has sharp, square needles and dangling cones.

At 0.1 mile, the sound of cascading water intensifies and a side trail branches left to approach the bank of the Bear River. Continue straight on the white-blazed trail, rising gently and avoiding the water until the 0.25-mile mark. Here, the side trail and the main trail converge along the right (northeast) bank of Wight Brook. At 15 feet below, the water splashes and spills into a series of chilly pools. See if the kids can identify some of the trailside wildflowers and ground covers: partridgeberry, Indian cucumber, goldthread, Canada mayflower, trillium, and bunchberry.

At 0.35 mile, the trail and the river bend to the right (southeast) and again the white-blazed trail veers away from the brook to travel along an elevated ridge while an unmarked trail continues along the bank. The white trail marches through a stand of fine white birches at 0.45 mile that seems to illuminate the shaded path. Beech and sugar maple trees also dot these woods. Kids, find a maple tree to examine. Are the leaves on a given tree all the same size and shape? (No! Their size and shape vary with their age and position on the tree.) Can you guess what we make with the sap from the sugar maple tree? (Maple syrup!)

The trail begins a gradual-to-moderate ascent with the tumbling brook drowning out all other wilderness sounds. At 0.5 mile, the trail has resumed its northeasterly course. After crossing over a 10-inch water pipe, the trail emerges onto the bald rock slab that carries the dramatic falls. (Warn the kids that the wet rocks may be slippery.) Enjoy the concert of rock and water as you scale the riverside boulders or climb along the wooded trail. Near the top of the cascading falls, waterside rock slabs overlook several wide, deep pools. Stop here for a relaxing picnic lunch. The largest pool offers cautious bathers a partially submerged rock to ease themselves into the icy waters. While the "polar bears" take a dip, the others can crest the top of the falls, just 0.1 mile farther up the granite brook bed.

Return the way you came.

Note: Day use only; no fires.

CREATING THE PRESERVE

Step Falls Preserve was the first preserve of the Maine chapter of The Nature Conservancy. It was acquired in 1961, following a fund-raising drive to protect the area.

 TABLE ROCK

BEFORE YOU GO
Map USGS Old Speck Mountain
Current Conditions Grafton Notch State Park (207) 824-2912
Small fee

ABOUT THE HIKE
Day hike
Challenging for children
May–October
2.4 miles, loop
Hiking time 2.5 hours
High point/elevation gain
2405 feet, 1000 feet

GETTING THERE
■ From the junction of US 2, ME-5, and ME-26 in Bethel, drive north on ME-26 for 12 miles to a large off-road parking area on the left (for Old Speck Mountain).

ON THE TRAIL
Kids are always excited about the initial leg of any hike: the challenging ascents, the anticipation of a waterfall or summit or wilderness lake up ahead, the sense of working toward a worthwhile goal. But what about

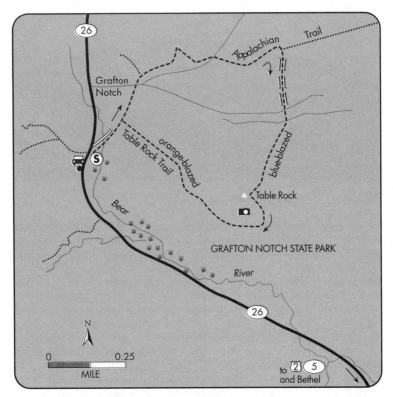

the return trip, usually summed up as "Retrace your steps"? Ho-hum, right? Not on this hike! The trip to Table Rock along the Appalachian and Table Rock Trails is as gratifying as any ascent, but the return trip through a maze of boulders dotted with dark caves and mysterious tunnels is far from anticlimactic. In fact, it is so demanding we recommend that groups with less experienced hikers turn back after exploring the first set of caves and, yes, "Retrace your steps." (Even though this increases the total hiking distance to 3.5 miles, the hike will be downgraded to a rating of moderate.) The one guarantee we'll make to those of you who forge ahead: No one in your group will complain about the dull descent!

From the northern side of the parking lot, pass the wooden trail map and plunge into the woods on the white-blazed Appalachian Trail (AT). Quickly, the blazes lead across ME-26. Reenter the woods on the AT at a sign showing a hiker with a walking stick. Pass through thick woodlands and cross several halved-log bridges over wet areas and a trickling stream. In 0.15 mile, an orange-blazed trail splits right on its

Table Rock, as seen from Route 26

way to Table Rock; you follow the left-going AT. (You will be returning along the orange-blazed Table Rock Trail.) If any little hikers begin to complain, remind them that many others who have walked along this very trail did so on their way from Springer Mountain in Georgia to Katahdin in Maine, a distance of more than 2000 miles. Suddenly a 2.4-mile hike won't seem so long after all!

The trail ascends briefly but levels to cross a stream at 0.35 mile. Follow the white blazes and rise on a moderate grade. At 0.5 mile from the start, the trail travels beside a stream that races raucously down the mountainside. How far will a stick tumble before a stone or fallen branch halts its reckless journey?

After the trail crosses the stream, it flattens and soon reaches a marker where it turns right (southeast) and begins climbing moderately. The wide, rugged trail narrows to cross a wet area on two split logs at 0.8 mile. Soon, the AT departs left (east) as you turn right (south) on the blue-blazed trail at a sign for Table Rock. Climb moderately and then more steeply for 0.5 mile to Table Rock, traversing damp sections and streams on halved logs.

You won't quibble with the name of this rock plateau, perched 1.4 miles from the start. The large, flat tabletop of rough granite 30 feet long and equally wide juts out over its supporting base. On a clear day, the views of Sunday River, Old Speck, and Puzzle Mountain are delightful, although you may spend more time watching the children than the horizon (the drop-off is dangerous).

To continue along the orange trail, begin at the northeastern corner of the rock and drop into the woods. In 50 feet, turn right (southeast) into a gully. At 0.1 mile from the rock, the path curls northeast to pass below the ledges supporting Table Rock. The trail crawls along the base of the ledges for 0.2 mile, winding through a rock labyrinth of slab caves and tunnels guaranteed to thrill every young hiker (and most old ones).

This expansive rock chaos will slow you down, but the kids will enjoy every minute, although you may need to carry their packs here. The ancient Romans believed that nymphs and sibyls lived in caves like these. The kids can probably make some more accurate guesses as to what kinds of creatures call these caves home. The trail turns left (west) away from the ledges to tumble down the rocky hillside for 0.3 mile. As the descent slackens, the path winds through a hodgepodge of rocks that makes footing difficult for another 0.2 mile. Beyond the rocky area, the path plummets for 0.1 mile before easing to drop gently toward the AT, joining it 1.3 miles from Table Rock. Turn left and retrace the initial route back to your vehicle.

LITTLE ABOL FALLS

BEFORE YOU GO
Map USGS Abol Pond
Current Conditions Baxter State Park (207) 723-5140
Moderate fee for out-of-state visitors; fee for camping

ABOUT THE HIKE
Day hike
Easy for children
May–October
1.6 miles, round trip
Hiking time 1.5 hours
High point/elevation gain 1560 feet, 350 feet

GETTING THERE

- To reach the southern entrance of Baxter State Park: Take ME-157 west through Millinocket. At a sign for Baxter State Park, turn right and continue to follow signs for 18 miles to the Togue Pond Gatehouse. To reach the Matagamon Gatehouse: From Patten, travel 26 miles on ME-159 and Shin Pond Road, following signs to Baxter State Park.
- From the Togue Pond Gatehouse, follow Park Tote Road 5.7 miles to Abol Campground.
- Park in the day-use lot across from the campground.

ON THE TRAIL

Although Baxter State Park is probably best known as home to Mount Katahdin—Maine's highest mountain and the northernmost stop on the Appalachian Trail—it also offers over 200 miles of hiking trails, bound to suit everyone's hiking interests and abilities. A trip to Baxter State Park requires some planning and travel time, but it is definitely worth the effort. Per the insightful stipulations and vision of former Governor Percival Baxter, who gifted the park to the State of Maine, most of Baxter

State Park has been maintained as a wildlife sanctuary and kept in its natural state as much as possible. Because of this, hikers will be treated to pristine surroundings in which wildlife abounds. Waterfalls, mountain peaks, streams, meadows, and ponds are all there to enjoy. Make reservations for camping ahead of time and plan to stay more than a day to take advantage of all Baxter State Park has to offer. Be sure to sign in and out before and after each hike and practice Leave No Trace ethics on the trails, in campgrounds, and throughout the park. Several commercially produced maps of the park, as well as information brochures, are available for sale at park headquarters, the Togue Pond Visitor Center, and some of the park campgrounds.

This is a terrific hike for younger children or those looking for reward without a huge amount of effort. Although the trail is uphill on the way to the waterfall, the ascent is fairly gradual. You will reach the falls in less than a mile, and the trip back will be virtually all downhill. You may never even hear the questions "Are we there yet?" and "How much

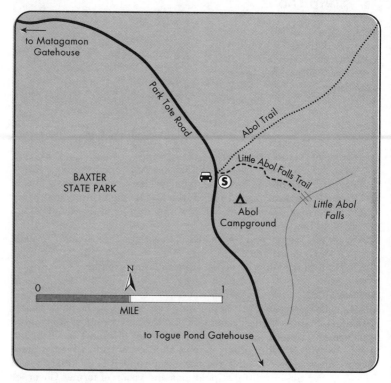

Opposite: Little Abol Falls

farther?" (Or at least you won't hear them for long.) Near the falls is a perfect spot to sit and have a snack before heading back down the trail.

Register for your hike at the ranger station at Abol Campground. To begin, follow the blue blazes through the campground. Just past the signs for the Abol Trail look for signs directing you to the Little Abol Falls Trail. Head out on this trail, and immediately cross the stream over rocks and logs. You may have to carry little ones across, as the crossing can be a little slippery. Enter the woods and have the kids do some tree identification. Can they point out the birch trees? How about pine or maple? Also have them listen carefully. Can they hear the sounds of the stream off to their left?

The trail curves right and climbs slightly before leveling out at a little over 0.3 mile. Are there more deciduous or coniferous trees here? Who knows the difference? Around 0.5 mile the trail curves left and gets rockier. Have the types of trees changed at all? At 0.8 mile, you will be greeted by the sights and sounds of Little Abol Falls. Take pictures, have a snack, and relax before returning the way you came. Remember to stop at the ranger station to enter your time of return.

GRASSY POND LOOP TRAIL

BEFORE YOU GO
Map USGS Doubletop Mountain
Current Conditions Baxter State Park (207) 723-5140
Moderate fee for out-of-state visitors; fee for camping

ABOUT THE HIKE
Day hike
Moderate for children
May–October
1.8 miles, round trip
Hiking time 2 hours
High point/elevation gain
1150 feet, 240 feet

GETTING THERE
- To reach the southern entrance of Baxter State Park: Take ME-157 west through Millinocket. At a sign for Baxter State Park, turn right and continue to follow signs for 18 miles to the Togue Pond Gatehouse. To reach the Matagamon Gatehouse: From Patten, travel 26 miles on ME-159 and Shin Pond Road, following signs to Baxter State Park.
- The day-use parking area for Grassy Pond is located off Park Tote Road between the Katahdin Stream Campground and Foster Field, approximately 8.5 miles north of the Togue Pond Gatehouse and 32.5 miles south of the Matagamon Gatehouse.
- Park in the designated area on the side of the road.

ON THE TRAIL

Three ponds in under 2 miles—what could be better? You can also add a fourth pond by extending the hike. There are different ways to reach Grassy Pond; you also can get there from Daicey Pond. This route takes you from Park Tote Road and heads south on the Appalachian Trail (AT) for a shorter trip. As you pass different trail junction signs, you will realize how interconnected many of the trails are, which makes various options available to you. This area offers prime wildlife watching, so keep your eyes and ears peeled. If you get a key ahead of time from the Daicey Pond Ranger Station, you can add a canoe trip to your hike with canoes available at both the inlet and outlet of Grassy Pond.

From the parking area turn left and head north on Park Tote Road a short distance to pick up the southbound AT. Almost immediately, you will be above the water of Tracy Pond—who can spot it through the trees? Use caution as you cross two log bridges over water—past the first bridge is a slight climb uphill over roots followed by a rocky scramble downhill to the second footbridge. The trail skirts Elbow Pond to your right, where you will have excellent views. In 0.2 mile from the Elbow Pond outlet, reach a junction and sign in. Here, leave the AT by turning left on the blue-blazed Grassy Pond Loop Trail. (Staying straight on the AT would take you to Daicey Pond in 0.9 mile.)

Follow the Grassy Pond Loop Trail uphill and along a ridge where you can see mountains through the trees—can anyone pick out Mount OJI or Doubletop Mountain? Soon, the trail crests the hill as you wind through big boulders, before turning and descending to Grassy Pond, approximately 0.5 mile from the junction. As the trail skirts the edge, you can see the pond to your left before it veers left and deposits you at the inlet to Grassy Pond. If you have the canoe key, head out on the water to enjoy the views from a different vantage point. Return the way

View of the mountains over the pond

you came. (If you are in the mood for a longer hike, you have some choices here. You can remain on the Grassy Pond Loop Trail and turn right (north) on the AT and head back to your vehicle, or you can add a loop around Daicey Pond for a total trip of 3.5 miles. (This is where a good map comes in handy.)

WALK ON THE WILD SIDE

Do your part to keep wildlife "wild." Never approach, follow, or feed animals. If you spot wildlife, be sure to observe quietly from a distance and move away from and discourage any animal that tries to follow you. Moose, although exciting to see, can present dangers to you as they are very protective of their territory.

  LITTLE AND BIG NIAGARA FALLS

BEFORE YOU GO
Map USGS Rainbow Lake East
Current Conditions Baxter State Park (207) 723-5140
Moderate fee for out-of-state visitors; fee for camping

ABOUT THE HIKE
Day hike
Moderate for children
May–October
2.4 miles, round trip
Hiking time 2 hours
High point/elevation gain 1100 feet, 180 feet

GETTING THERE

■ To reach the southern entrance of Baxter State Park:
Take ME-157 west through Millinocket. At a sign for Baxter State Park, turn right and continue to follow signs for 18 miles to the Togue Pond Gatehouse. To reach the Matagamon Gatehouse: From Patten, travel 26 miles on ME-159 and Shin Pond Road, following signs to Baxter State Park.
■ From the Togue Pond Gatehouse, drive a little over 10 miles to the sign pointing to Daicey Pond.
■ Turn left on this road and drive another 1.5 miles.
■ Park in the day-use parking area on the right-hand side.

ON THE TRAIL
You will be treated to not one but two waterfalls on this hike along a section of the Appalachian Trail (AT). Your children will enjoy exploring on the rocks near the falls—under your close supervision, of course. The

Getting a close-up look of a tree growing on a rock.

water gushing over the rocky ledges of Big Niagara Falls is sure to be awe-inspiring for the whole family.

After signing in, immediately cross a footbridge over a stream and begin winding your way south between rocks and over roots, following the white blazes of the AT. This is also a section of the Daicey Pond Nature Trail, which circles the pond. In 0.1 mile, you will reach a trail junction. Here, the Daicey Pond Nature Trail heads left. Stay to the right on the AT to head toward the falls. Be sure to peek to your right to see glimpses of mountains through the trees. Can anyone hear the gurgling of a stream? In approximately 0.3 mile, the trail curves to the left and a side trail on your right heads down to a picturesque view of the stream set against a spectacular mountainous backdrop.

Right around the 0.5-mile mark, have your kids look for some of the many trees spreading their roots over the tops of boulders. Although tempting to climb, remind your children of the importance of not trampling on fragile forest plants. At the sign for Toll Dam, turn right. At 0.9

mile, another side trail leads right to Little Niagara Falls. After taking in the sights, tell your kids that it is not much farther to Big Niagara Falls and head back to the AT.

For the final stretch, descend slightly on a rocky section before following a ridge up slightly for a short distance. Upon hearing the sounds of rushing water, you will come to a sign pointing to Big Niagara Falls in 0.1 mile. Here the trail gets a little steeper and rockier, so be sure to use caution with younger children. The powerful and awesome rush of water will make any tired kids forget the effort it took to get there. A snack or picnic on the rocks beside the falls will refresh everyone. Hike back the way you came.

DAICEY POND NATURE TRAIL

BEFORE YOU GO
Map USGS Doubletop Mountain
Current Conditions Baxter State Park (207) 723-5140
Moderate fee for out-of-state visitors; fee for camping

ABOUT THE HIKE
Day hike
Easy for children
May–October
1.8 mile, loop
Hiking time 1.5 hours
High point/elevation gain 1120 feet, 40 feet

GETTING THERE

- To reach the southern entrance of Baxter State Park: Take ME-157 west through Millinocket. At a sign for Baxter State Park, turn right and continue to follow signs for 18 miles to the Togue Pond Gatehouse. To reach the Matagamon Gatehouse: From Patten, travel 26 miles on ME-159 and Shin Pond Road, following signs to Baxter State Park.
- From the Togue Pond Gatehouse, drive a little over 10 miles to the sign pointing to Daicey Pond.
- Turn left on this road and drive another 1.5 miles.
- Park in the day-use parking area on the right.

ON THE TRAIL
Because of the variety of habitats on this hike, wildlife is plentiful. This relatively flat trail encircles a pond through forest and edge habitat. You and your children can have fun looking for plants and berries and figuring out what kinds of animals make their home here. If you can, pick up a guide ahead of time from the rangers to help with identification. You can

make games out of trying to search for different flora and fauna along the way.

From the day-use parking area, find the sign-in for the Daicey Pond Nature Trail. You will be starting along the Appalachian Trail (AT), heading left to follow the AT's white blazes. The trail begins in a mixed forest—who can find and name a spruce, a pine, a fir, a birch, and a maple? In 0.2 mile, you will start to get views of the water as the trail begins its circumnavigation of the pond and drops down to the water's edge. Around the 0.5-mile mark the Daicey Pond Nature Trail splits from the AT. Stay straight on the blue-blazed Daicey Pond Nature Trail as the AT heads right.

After traveling another 0.2 mile around the pond, you will reach a junction with the Grassy Pond Trail. Head slightly uphill to a trail sign and follow the Daicey Pond Nature Trail to the right. In 0.3 mile, another trail junction with the Lost Pond Trail presents itself on your left. (Getting some idea of just how many hiking opportunities there are at Baxter? Taking that trail would lead you to Lost Pond in 1.0 mile.) Once again, remain on the Daicey Pond Nature Trail; you will be treated to views of Daicey Pond and mountains. Who sees Katahdin? Some of the other mountains you can see are Barren, Owl, Doubletop, and OJI.

Your last 0.5 mile will take you through shrubs—hungry hikers may

Ssshh . . . If you're quiet, you may spot wildlife.

be able to munch on blueberries or huckleberries in season—and back into a predominantly evergreen forest. You will pass behind some cabins before reaching another trail junction with the trail to Little and Big Niagara Falls on the left. Heading straight or right will take you to the road where you will turn left to reach the parking area.

WATCH FOR WEASELS

If you're lucky, you may spot a mink. A member of the weasel family, minks like the moist areas around Daicey Pond. The pine marten is another member of the weasel family that lives in the area. All pine martens are nocturnal, but you may chance across one in the early morning or on overcast days.

 SOUTH BRANCH FALLS

BEFORE YOU GO
Map USGS Wassataquoik Lake
Current Conditions Baxter State Park (207) 723-5140
Moderate fee for out-of-state visitors; fee for camping

ABOUT THE HIKE
Day hike
Easy for children
May–October
1.0 mile, round trip
Hiking time 1 hour
High point/elevation gain 1100 feet, 100 feet

GETTING THERE

■ To reach the southern entrance of Baxter State Park:
Take ME-157 west through Millinocket. At a sign for Baxter State Park, turn right and continue to follow signs for 18 miles to the Togue Pond Gatehouse. To reach the Matagamon Gatehouse: From Patten, travel 26 miles on ME-159 and Shin Pond Road, following signs to Baxter State Park.

■ From Park Tote Road, reach Trout Brook Crossing either by traveling 33.8 miles north from the Togue Pond Gatehouse or 7.3 miles south from the Matagamon Gatehouse.

■ Turn onto South Branch Pond Road and drive a little over 1 mile to the South Branch Falls parking area on your right.

ON THE TRAIL
You will be walking along, surrounded by a thick forest on all sides, when abruptly everything opens up and there before you are open

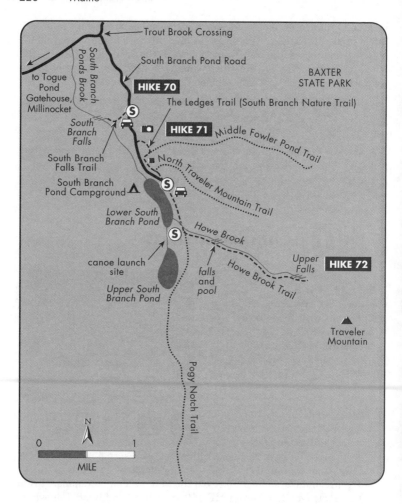

ledges, a rushing river, and beautiful waterfalls. This hike is a younger child's dream: short and sweet with a huge watery reward.

From the parking area, head southwest on the South Branch Falls Trail through a thick mixed forest. After a very brief initial ascent, the trail descends slightly as you head through the trees. Have your kids look for signs of animals. You may come across scat on the trail. You can tell what kinds of animals live in the area from what they leave behind. Fruits, nuts, or berries in the scat can tell you what the animal's diet consists of and can provide clues to identifying the animals that make their homes here.

In approximately 0.3 mile the sound of water will greet your ears. In 0.4 mile the trail curves right to parallel South Branch Ponds Brook. The trail then heads over a rocky ledge overlooking the water before heading more steeply down to the falls. You will find some safe, flat areas to observe the cascades and look for butterflies before heading back the way you came.

 SOUTH BRANCH NATURE TRAIL, THE LEDGES

BEFORE YOU GO
Map USGS Wassataquoik Lake
Current Conditions Baxter State Park (207) 723-5140
Moderate fee for out-of-state visitors; fee for camping

ABOUT THE HIKE
Day hike
Easy for children
May–October
1.4 miles, loop
Hiking time 1 hour
High point/elevation gain 1210 feet, 200 feet

GETTING THERE

- To reach the southern entrance of Baxter State Park: Take ME-157 west through Millinocket. At a sign for Baxter State Park, turn right and continue to follow signs for 18 miles to the Togue Pond Gatehouse. To reach the Matagamon Gatehouse: From Patten, travel 26 miles on ME-159 and Shin Pond Road, following signs to Baxter State Park.
- From Park Tote Road, reach Trout Brook Crossing either by traveling 33.8 miles north from the Togue Pond Gatehouse or 7.3 miles south from the Matagamon Gatehouse.
- Turn onto South Branch Pond Road and drive a little over 2 miles to the day-use parking area on your left.

ON THE TRAIL
Have your cameras ready for this one. A moderately steep, but fun, rocky climb will reward you with dramatic views of Upper and Lower South Branch Ponds and the surrounding mountains. You and your children can snap pictures while looking for people canoeing on the water far below.

The trail begins near the South Branch Pond Campground. Register at the sign-in near the ranger station and follow the main road north away from the campground. Shortly after the day-use parking area, you will see a sign for The Ledges Trail on your right. Although you can start the loop here, your views will be more dramatic if you continue on the road another 0.2 mile to the next junction with The Ledges Trail on your right. When you reach the second sign for The Ledges Trail, turn right off the road and follow the blue blazes and cairns of the trail.

Almost immediately after beginning a rocky scramble, you will have views of the mountains to your right. You are traveling over volcanic bedrock; be sure to follow the blazes so as not to damage the fragile lichen and vegetation. In 0.2 mile from the road, reach The Ledges viewpoint with vistas and astounding views all around. Can you hear or see any broad-winged hawks soaring?

Follow the trail past The Ledges and begin your descent through aspen, birch, and maple trees. Look for rows of holes in the tree trunks of the bigger trees. Who can guess what those are? Whoever said woodpeckers is correct. Two species common to the area are the hairy woodpecker and the yellow-bellied sapsucker. Approximately 0.3 mile from the viewpoint is the intersection with the Middle Fowler Pond Trail. Stay straight on The Ledges Trail another 0.3 mile and turn left on the road back toward the campground.

A family makes its way up to The Ledges viewpoint.

7 2 HOWE BROOK TRAIL

BEFORE YOU GO
Map USGS Wassataquoik Lake
Current Conditions Baxter State Park (207) 723-5140
Moderate fee for out-of-state visitors; fee for camping

ABOUT THE HIKE
Day hike
Easy to moderate for children
May–October
4.0 miles, round trip from canoe launch site;
6.0 miles, round trip from South Branch Pond Campground
Hiking time 3 hours from canoe launch site, 4 hours from campground
High point/elevation gain 1760 feet, 700 feet

GETTING THERE

- To reach the southern entrance of Baxter State Park: Take ME-157 west through Millinocket. At a sign for Baxter State Park, turn right and continue to follow signs for 18 miles to the Togue Pond Gatehouse. To reach the Matagamon Gatehouse: From Patten, travel 26 miles on ME-159 and Shin Pond Road, following signs to Baxter State Park.
- From Park Tote Road, reach Trout Brook Crossing either by traveling 33.8 miles north from the Togue Pond Gatehouse or 7.3 miles south from the Matagamon Gatehouse.
- Turn onto South Branch Pond Road and drive a little over 2 miles to the day-use parking area on your left.

ON THE TRAIL

You can complete this whole hike or just a fragment, and it will still be a worthy outing. In fact, you may not get far at all once you reach the brook. There's something about rocks and water that lends itself to easy entertainment for children. Once distracted by throwing rocks in the water or playing along the water's edge, it may be difficult to get kids to move on. So prepare to take this one slowly, and be happy with whatever ground you cover.

There are two ways to reach the trailhead. You can hike to the start, or for a small fee and a little more adventure you can rent a canoe and paddle south across Lower South Branch Pond to the canoe launch site and trailhead. The launch site is very obvious and marked by signs. To hike to the landing, find the Pogy Notch Trail, which starts behind campsite 18 of the South Branch Pond Campground. Follow this trail south alongside the pond over a series of footbridges 0.9 mile to the

Canoeing to the Howe Brook trailhead

canoe launch site. However you get there, be sure to listen for loons and frogs when you arrive.

From the canoe launch site turn right for 0.1 mile to the junction with the Howe Brook Trail. At the junction in 0.1 mile, stay straight on the Howe Brook Trail, where a sign indicates that the falls and pool are 0.2 mile away and Upper Falls is 2 miles from this point. Immediately beyond here the trail curves left by a rocky streambed and parallels the brook. Kids will want to stop constantly to climb on the rocks, throw sticks in the water to watch them float downstream, and look at the mini-waterfalls cascading over rocks and logs. Remind them of the importance of treading lightly so as not to damage any fragile plants. At 0.2 mile from the last trail junction, you reach a small set of falls and pool, which may or may not be a good turnaround point depending on your energy levels.

If you decide to continue beyond here, head along the gently climbing trail as it stays its course alongside the brook. Around 0.8 mile, the trail heads into the woods for a short stretch before dropping back to the water's edge. In places, the trail is eroded, so use caution and hold younger children's hands if necessary. In a little over a mile, a side stream comes down and you will be walking with water on both sides for a spell. If you still have the energy, follow the trail slightly uphill to a large waterfall in the side of Traveler Mountain at 2 miles. Return to the trailhead the way you came.

TROUT BROOK MOUNTAIN

BEFORE YOU GO
Map USGS Trout Brook Mountain
Current Conditions Baxter State Park (207) 723-5140
Moderate fee for out-of-state visitors; fee for camping

ABOUT THE HIKE
Day hike
Challenging for children
May–October
3 miles, loop
Hiking time 4 hours
High point/elevation gain
1767 feet, 1102 feet

GETTING THERE

- To reach the southern entrance of Baxter State Park: Take ME-157 west through Millinocket. At a sign for Baxter State Park, turn right and continue to follow signs for 18 miles to the Togue Pond Gatehouse. To reach the Matagamon Gatehouse: From Patten, travel 26 miles on ME-159 and Shin Pond Road, following signs to Baxter State Park.
- Travel 38.5 miles from the Togue Pond Gatehouse or 2.5 miles from the Matagamon Gatehouse to the Trout Brook Farm Campground.
- Park in the day-use area across from the campground.

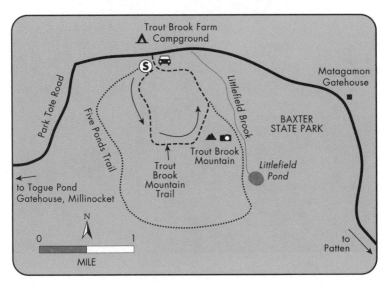

ON THE TRAIL

It may not be Katahdin, but children will nonetheless be proud to reach the peak of Trout Brook Mountain, as they should be. Even though this is one of the easier peaks to climb in the park, it is still challenging and a great deal of energy and determination are required to reach the summit. It's worth it if you and your family have the stamina. At an elevation of 1767 feet, Trout Brook Mountain rewards you with outstanding 360-degree views of Baxter State Park.

After signing the register, begin climbing the trail leading to the top of Trout Brook Mountain. As you climb through a mixed forest following the blue blazes, have your kids look for wild strawberries and other tiny plants. The trail is rooty and rocky—sturdy shoes are a must. Be sure your children pay attention to the rock over which they are traveling. Much of it was left by glaciers, and it is glacial drift (a platey type of rock carried by glaciers) or ground moraine (different-size material that dropped from the ice).

Higher up, you can see rock that was formed by volcanoes. Close to the 0.5-mile mark, the trail becomes more of a rocky scramble with some loose scree and stones. At 0.7 mile, you will reach your first set of ledges and be energized by the gorgeous views and the fact that you are over halfway to the summit. This is a great place to stop for a snack and water break, as the ledges offer many flat areas and rocks for sitting.

Past this point, the trail curves left and enters the woods. You will have some short level sections between climbs with some views along the

Summit of Trout Brook Mountain

way to keep you going. At 1.3 miles, you will reach the summit, marked by a sign indicating you have made it. Congratulate each other and take in the views of Matagamon Lake, Horse Mountain, Bald Mountain, and the Traveler Range interspersed with many kettle-hole ponds.

To descend, return the way you came for a total distance of 2.6 miles or continue around the east side of the mountain for some fantastic views and to complete the loop.

If you continue ahead from the summit sign, head left for another mile, following the arrow toward Littlefield Pond. Look for cairns and blue blazes to mark your way. As you take in the scenery, use extreme caution—the trail becomes steep, rocky, and more exposed before entering the woods. The views here, however, are incomparable. Soon after entering the woods, you will encounter a bog filled with grasses and lush ferns. As you descend, you will encounter some steep sections before the trail levels out a bit at 0.8 mile from the summit. One mile from the summit, at a junction with the Five Ponds Trail, turn left toward Trout Brook Farm Campground. In about another half mile, the fairly level trail turns sharply left above Littlefield Gorge. Follow the Five Ponds Trail another 0.2 mile through the evergreen forest back to the parking area.

KETTLE-HOLE PONDS

Kettle-hole ponds were formed from large blocks of ice left by glaciers. The chunks of ice were partially buried by sediment—when the ice melted, it left depressions, which filled with the meltwater and groundwater to create these ponds.

  MOUNT BATTIE

BEFORE YOU GO
Map USGS Camden
Current Conditions
Camden Hills State Park (207) 236-3109 or (207) 236-0849 off season
Small fee

ABOUT THE HIKE
Day hike
Moderate for children
May–November
1 mile, round trip
Hiking time 1 hour
High point/elevation gain
800 feet, 600 feet

GETTING THERE
■ From the junction of US 1 and ME-52 in Camden, drive north on ME-52 for about 100 yards.

- Turn right onto Megunticook Street.
- Drive 0.4 mile to the end of this residential road.
- Park at the gravel turnout on the left.

ON THE TRAIL

The Camden Hills, rising over Penobscot Bay's northern shore, compete with the peaks of Mount Desert Island for the title of "Finest Coastal Hiking Area in the Northeast." The summit of Mount Battie is the most popular destination for folks hiking around Camden and has long been a favorite with families. The steep climb leads in just 0.5 mile to the summit where, from ground level or atop the stone tower, kids can see boats bobbing in the bay and imagine the far-off ocean liners and battleships cutting through the open waters of the Atlantic. A map near the tower points out nearby and distant islands, peninsulas, and mountain peaks, making this a terrific first hike in the Camden area.

Locate the sign marking the Mount Battie trailhead on the northern

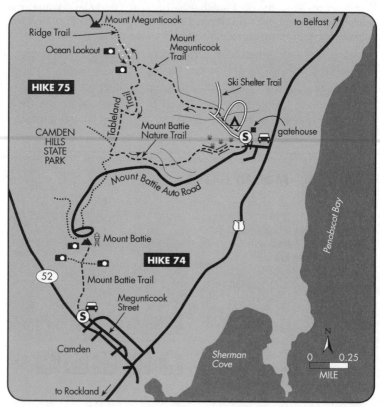

View of Camden and the harbor from the stone tower on Mount Battie

side of the parking area. The blue-blazed trail heads north over rocky, wooded terrain, then quickly swings eastward on a moderate ascent to leave behind the bustling neighborhood and the small-town traffic. In 0.1 mile, as the trail switches from right to left, heading due west, the ledge outcrops form natural steps to aid hikers on a stiff climb. Can the kids find any signs of the red squirrels so common in northern climates? Look for a squirrel midden, a pile of scales from pine and spruce cones, near a tree stump or a log. Squirrels scrape off the scales to get at the cone's small inner seeds, a mainstay of their diet. Another sign of red squirrel activity is mushrooms drying in the crotch of a tree or spread across a tree branch.

At 0.2 mile, the trail squeezes between two outcroppings and crests a shoulder before climbing steeply once again. As the trail scales a set of 15-foot cliffs, children will have to drop to all fours to make it to the top. Here, the trail opens onto the barren ledge that it will follow for the remainder of the ascent. Look over your shoulder for expanding views of Camden and Penobscot Bay. The trail continues steeply until, at 0.35 mile, the grade eases to approach the summit on a gentle ascent. Enjoy the peaceful views from the side trails that split left and right 0.1

mile before the summit because you'll be sharing the panoramas on the mountaintop with all those folks who drove up the auto road. Tell the kids to look for wild blueberries in season.

At the summit, kids can climb the stone tower built as a war memorial in 1921. Imagine what it must have been like to visit the hotel that sat grandly upon this spot at the turn of the century! Everyone should study the placard showing such land features of Penobscot Bay as Owl's Head, Dead Man's Point, Curtis Island, Northeast Point, Sherman Cove, Mount Desert Island, and Seven Hundred Acre Island. You'll see many of these same places from the other Camden hikes (Hikes 75, 76, and 77).

If you are hiking in fall, you may be fortunate enough to witness the hawk migration. Can the kids figure out how birds know when it is time to migrate? Because birds time their departures so precisely, ornithologists believe that birds use the length of the day to influence the start of their journey. As the days get shorter with the approach of winter, birds sense that it is time to begin the trip south. Many birds could withstand the frigid temperatures in the Northeast; it is the lack of food during winter that makes migration necessary.

Return to your vehicle the way you came.

75 OCEAN LOOKOUT ON MOUNT MEGUNTICOOK

BEFORE YOU GO
Maps USGS Camden and Lincolnville
Current Conditions Camden Hills State Park (207) 236-3109 or (207) 236-0849 off season
Small hiking/parking fee; fees for campground and auto road

ABOUT THE HIKE
Day hike or overnight
Moderate for children
May–October; campground and auto road May 15–October 1
3 miles, loop
Hiking time 3 hours
High point/elevation gain 1350 feet, 1150 feet

GETTING THERE

- From the junction of US 1 and ME-52 in Camden, drive 1.5 miles north on US 1 to signs for Camden Hills State Park and the Mount Battie Auto Road.
- Turn left there and park in the area before the gatehouse.
- Alternatively, a second parking area has been added where the Nature Trail intersects with the Mount Battie Auto Road. Hikers for the Megunticook Trail can also access that trail from the parking area.

ON THE TRAIL

From Ocean Lookout on a ridge of Mount Megunticook, the kids can scan Camden Harbor for windjammers and the coastal hillsides for church steeples. This hike, within the limits of most young hikers, will also challenge those with more experience since the first mile climbs the eastern side of the mountain on a steady grade with no relief. If you hike in the afternoon, you will return just in time for a picnic supper and an overnight stay at the Camden Hills State Park campground (reservations accepted but not required).

Head westward on the paved park road, passing the gatehouse and the Mount Battie Auto Road. Walk into the campground and, 0.1 mile from your vehicle, a sign marks the start of the Mount Megunticook Trail, initially a gravel woods road through mixed hardwoods. Do the kids hear any rustling in the forest? Have them guess what animal might be making the noises: raccoons, perhaps, or a toad, or maybe a red squirrel. Red squirrels might scold you for invading their territory, but they also might climb into your pack for a closer look!

Shortly, as the pitch steepens, you'll reach a junction; stay left on the wide Mount Megunticook Trail. At another junction 0.2 mile from

View of Penobscot Bay from Ocean Lookout

the start, continue straight on the Mount Megunticook Trail as the Ski Shelter Trail goes right. Immediately cross a footbridge over a brisk stream. Put the youngest hiker in charge of finding the first blue blaze, indicating that this is part of the blue-blaze trail system that criss-crosses the Camden Hills area.

After briefly hugging the stream bank, the trail curls westward on a moderate ascent, winding through the woods on a root-choked path. Don't be surprised if a garter, milk, or ring-necked snake (all nonpoison-ous varieties) slithers across the trail. It may look to kids as if snakes have no bones at all, but in fact as many as 145 pairs of ribs are at-tached to a snake's sectioned backbone.

At 0.5 mile from the start, as a brook approaches from the left, the pitch steepens and hikers climb up convenient stone steps. Shortly, the brook departs and the trail levels to cut northeastward across the slope on rockier terrain. At 0.65 mile, a boulder slide tumbles to-ward the trail from the left. Who smells the spruce trees ahead? After the trail turns northwestward to meet a swift stream at 0.85 mile, it climbs on stone steps then continues to curl west/southwest toward Ocean Lookout through more evergreens.

At a junction with the Tableland Trail 1.2 miles from the gatehouse, keep kids close as you drink in the splendid easterly views over Maine's largest bay, Penobscot, dotted with dozens of islands. Can the kids see the windjammers gliding gracefully across the bay? The steeples and rooftops of charming Camden lie to the south, while to the southwest you'll see dwarfed Mount Battie (Hike 74). Continue northwest along the Ocean Lookout ledges to explore or find an ideal picnic spot before returning to the trail junction. (The true Megunticook summit—at 1385 feet, the second highest on the northeast coast—is 0.4 mile far-ther to the northwest along the Ridge Trail. Its views are limited by denser woods.)

To return to your vehicle, follow the Tableland Trail southward to-ward Mount Battie for a 0.3-mile moderate descent across exposed ledges and through mixed woods. Over the next 0.2 mile, the trail drops easily on rolling terrain into the saddle between Megunticook and Bat-tie, arriving at a junction with a carriage road 0.5 mile from Ocean Lookout. Continue straight. In another 0.1 mile, after dipping through a soggy area on rock steps, turn left (east) at an intersection with the Mount Battie Nature Trail to continue the modest descent, now paral-leling the Mount Battie Auto Road. As the evergreen woods give way to more deciduous trees, cross two narrow streams. After hiking along the Mount Battie Nature Trail for 0.7 mile, cross a series of log bridges over trickling streams and wet areas. When you emerge onto the Mount Battie Auto Road, turn left and in less than 0.1 mile you will arrive at your vehicle.

BALD ROCK MOUNTAIN

BEFORE YOU GO
Map USGS Lincolnville
Current Conditions
Camden Hills State Park (207)
236-3109 or (207) 236-0849
off season
Small fee

ABOUT THE HIKE
Day hike or overnight
Easy for children
April–October
3.4 miles, round trip
Hiking time 2.5 hours
High point/elevation gain
1110 feet, 700 feet

GETTING THERE
- From the junction of ME-173 and US 1 in Lincolnville, drive west on ME-173 for 2.2 miles.
- Turn left at Stevens Corner onto Youngtown Road.
- Immediately on your left is the gravel Multi-Use Trail, suitable for horse, bicycle, and foot traffic.
- Park in the parking area near the trailhead.

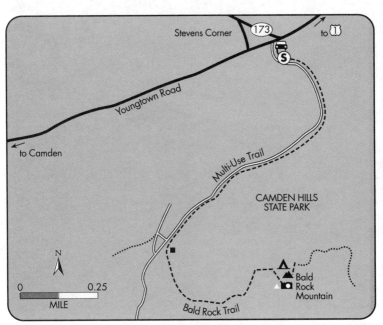

ON THE TRAIL

On the hike to Bald Rock Mountain, the end more than justifies the means. Although the initial mile or so along the gravel road may become monotonous for the little guys, the foot trail engages hikers on its final 0.5-mile climb to the summit with splendid views and—TA-DAH!—a rustic shelter for overnight camping. Because the climb to the mountaintop is not too arduous, this makes a perfect first campout for younger kids.

Follow the rugged Multi-Use Trail through mixed woods. It may take some effort to maintain the kids' enthusiasm along this lengthy and rather uneventful stretch of road. They can lumber like elephants, leap like frogs, stalk like tigers, or dash like gazelles. Play Name that Tune: Take turns singing the first few notes of familiar melodies while the others guess the title. For the first 0.5 mile, the road journeys south; then it gently curls westward.

At 1.2 miles, soon after the woods road crosses a stream on a camouflaged wooden bridge, the Bald Rock Trail splits left (south) over a cleared knoll. At this junction you'll notice an overgrown woods road joining the trail from the right (north). Following the Bald Rock Trail,

Camping shelter on Bald Rock summit

cut diagonally right across the knoll where you'll pass the cement footings of an old picnic shelter, or perhaps a picnic shelter itself if it is rebuilt. Shortly, a sign continues to guide you on the Bald Rock Trail; from here, it becomes an old logging road leading you to the summit in 0.5 mile.

After an initial gradual climb through an evergreen forest, rock steps facilitate the ascent up a moderate slope through mixed woods. Test the kids' abilities to identify different types of trees by feeling the bark (eyes closed, of course). At 0.35 mile from the Multi-Use Trail, the Bald Rock Trail leads over exposed granite and ledge outcrops. Look for Indian pipe, a thick, white plant with one flower that hangs from the top as if permanently wilted.

A final rise through spruce and fir trees leads to the expansive, level summit of Bald Rock Mountain. Adults admiring the commanding view across Penobscot Bay need not worry about their curious kids because the ledges drop off gradually in tiers. Looking eastward, you'll see Cadillac Mountain (Hike 81) and the other distant peaks of Mount Desert Island reaching for the ocean. To the south, over the left shoulder of Mount Megunticook, is the quaint sea village of Camden.

Heading northward from the summit through sparse woods, you'll come upon a lean-to capable of sleeping about six people, a hearth for a fire, and an outhouse. There are plenty of level spots here to pitch a tent, too. Imagine watching the evening sun illuminate Penobscot Bay before you slide into your sleeping bags! If you're not planning an overnight stay, how about building a fire and toasting some marshmallows? Afterward, retrace your steps to your vehicle.

MAIDEN CLIFF

BEFORE YOU GO
Maps USGS Camden and Lincolnville
Current Conditions Town of Camden Department of Parks and Recreation (207) 236-3438

ABOUT THE HIKE
Day hike
Moderate for children
May–October
2.5 miles, round trip
Hiking time 2 hours
High point/elevation gain
925 feet, 750 feet

GETTING THERE
- From US 1 and ME-52 in Camden, travel north on ME-52.

- In 2.7 miles, a driveway on the right leads uphill to a parking area.

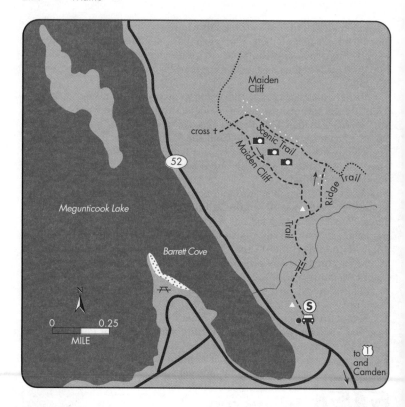

ON THE TRAIL

In our high-tech world chock full of special effects, we forget that kids are still interested in simple things such as a wooden bridge over a fast-moving stream, glacial boulders perched beside the trail, a hollowed-out shell of a tree, and panoramas over a sprawling lake. The hike to Maiden Cliff offers all these, plus the potential for a swim and picnic at Barrett Cove after the hike. Your destination is the lofty cross that perches on the edge of the cliff, erected in memory of twelve-year-old Eleanora French. On May 7, 1864, this farmer's daughter fell to her death as she chased her windblown hat. (Let that be a warning.)

Follow the blue blazes of the Maiden Cliff Trail from the north side of the parking area up a moderate grade. The wide path continues northward, rising modestly through mostly deciduous woods. The kids can run ahead to the impressive glacial erratic, 0.1 mile from the start on

Opposite: Hikers visit the cross that marks Maiden Cliff. Megunticook Lake dominates the view.

the left. Who will be the first one to hear the bustling brook? At 0.2 mile, the trail approaches the narrow stream from the right. As the ribbon of water cascades through a gorge, kids can toss in leaf and stick boats and witness the inevitable shipwrecks. Two wooden bridges span the stream at 0.25 mile, and the trail begins a rocky, moderate ascent. Can anyone hear the rapid tapping of woodpeckers?

About a half mile from the start, the Maiden Cliff Trail meets the Ridge Trail and heads left (north). You follow the Ridge Trail right (east) on a modest ascent. After flirting briefly with the swift stream, the rocky path curls left (north) and embarks on a brisk climb. Kids will find that the ascent is easier than it looks; the rocks provide solid footing. Soon, you'll see glimpses of Megunticook Lake as the trail sweeps right (east) and snakes steeply up ledges to arrive on open baldface high over the lake and the rolling hills.

The trail intersects the Scenic Trail 0.3 mile from the Maiden Cliff Trail/Ridge Trail junction. As the Ridge Trail veers right (east), follow the Scenic Trail left (northwest) toward Maiden Cliff, 0.8 mile farther. A gradual ascent through sparse woods leads in 0.1 mile to open ledges, where the Scenic Trail earns its name. As you hike along this exposed area for 0.3 mile, guided by cairns and blue blazes, the dizzying views to Bald and Ragged Mountains, Camden Harbor, and the Atlantic are postcard perfect. Let the kids act as photographers—you can't miss with this view. If you look left (south) to the tip of Megunticook Lake, you'll see Barrett Cove with its sandy beach and picnic area.

Along this sloping baldface the kids should be kept in sight and cautioned to step carefully. If you become confused here, remember that the trail follows the western edge of the ledges. Before the ledges end, the blue blazes curl left (west) to drop off the ledges and begin a moderate-to-steep descent through the woods. The trail levels shortly before a three-way intersection with the Maiden Cliff Trail (continue straight) and then dips to the top of Maiden Cliff and the cross. Kids can safely visit the cross but

should be warned that just below the cross is an abrupt drop-off. Keep your eyes peeled for bald eagles and turkey vultures that inhabit the area.

After admiring more spectacular views across Megunticook Lake, return to the Maiden Cliff Trail and Scenic Trail junction and turn right (southeast) on the Maiden Cliff Trail. Let the youngest member lead the group for 0.1 mile to a large tree with a hollowed trunk on the right, just the right size for a little person to step inside. At 0.2 mile from the cross, the trail tumbles back down the hillside into the ravine. As the terrain levels, you'll see a large boulder marking the intersection with the Ridge Trail. Bear right, still on the Maiden Cliff Trail, and hike the 0.5 mile back to your vehicle.

Note: When the hike is done in reverse (following only the Maiden Cliff Trail), you can reach Maiden Cliff in 30 to 45 minutes. This is a good option if you just want to hike to Maiden Cliff and back.

7 8 BEECH CLIFF AND BEECH MOUNTAIN

BEFORE YOU GO
Map USGS Southwest Harbor
Current Conditions Acadia
National Park (207) 288-3338
Moderate entrance fee

ABOUT THE HIKE
Day hike
Challenging for children
April–October
**4.1 miles, round trip with
one parked vehicle**
Hiking time 3.5 hours
High point/elevation gain
830 feet, 700 feet
Visitor center accessible;
guidebook available on
accessible services and facilities

GETTING THERE

- From the junction of ME-3, ME-102, and ME-198 (just beyond the causeway leading to Mount Desert Island), take ME-102 and ME-198 south toward Southwest Harbor.
- In 4.2 miles, as ME-198 goes left (south), continue straight on ME-102.
- In 8.8 miles from the causeway, turn right into the Echo Lake entrance of Acadia National Park.
- In 0.4 mile, the road ends at a parking area.

Directions for your second vehicle:
- From the Echo Lake entrance of Acadia National Park, drive north on ME-102 for 2.5 miles.
- Turn left onto Beech Hill Cross Road.
- In 0.9 mile, turn left onto Beech Hill Road.
- Drive 2.2 miles to the Beech Mountain parking area.

ON THE TRAIL

Two and a half million people visit Acadia National Park each year, making it one of the country's most popular national parks. Its 47,000 acres and 120 miles of trails encompass rocky peaks and shorelines, lush bogs, and lakes buried within deep valleys. The park occupies about half of Mount Desert Island and also includes the Schoodic Peninsula, Isle au Haut, and some small, nearby islands.

The visitor center should be your first stop. There you can watch an introductory film, examine a large relief map of the area, and browse through maps and other publications pertaining to Acadia.

About 350 million years ago, the peaks of Mount Desert Island were as high as the Rockies. Since then, the glaciers, water, wind, and freezing cycles have eroded thousands of feet from these rock giants. But even at their relatively minute stature, some of the island's mountains and cliffs present quite a challenge for today's adventurous families. Within the first 0.5 mile of this hike to Beech Cliff and Beech Mountain, a series of fixed iron ladders, steel cables, and handholds assist hikers in the steep climb along precipitous cliffs—too demanding for most inexperienced young hikers. In fact, we recommend that you leave a second vehicle at the Beech Mountain parking area because it would be difficult to guide even veteran young hikers down the sheer cliffs on the return trip.

Head down the flight of stairs at the northeastern end of the parking lot that leads to Echo Lake Beach; partway down, take the Canada Ridge Trail as it splits left at a sign for Beech Cliff and Beech Mountain. The trail quickly curls around the back side of the parking area, passing a chalet-style structure and a second sign, which appropriately warns hikers that the trail is steep with exposed cliffs and fixed iron rungs to aid hikers in the climb. (Though the signs do not mention Canada Cliff, the trail scales this set of cliffs before arriving at Beech Cliff.)

Continue on a gradual ascent through the deciduous forest, dotted with birches and spruce. Do the kids know the difference between deciduous trees such as oak, maple, and beech and conifers such as spruce

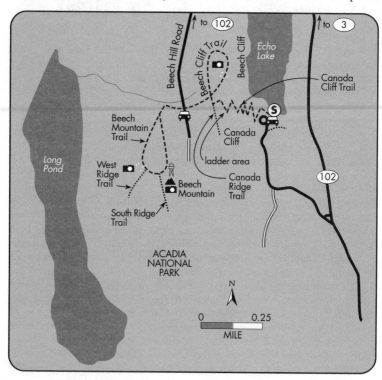

Looking from Beech Cliff to Acadia Mountain

and hemlock? (Deciduous trees lose their leaves in autumn, and coniferous trees have cones and always retain some of their needles.) As Canada Cliff looms ahead on the left, who can see Echo Lake on the right?

At 0.15 mile, the trail cuts left and begins a series of switchbacks leading eventually to the top of Canada Cliff. Frequent stone steps assist in the ascent. At 0.3 mile, a side trail straight (north) leads quickly to an overlook of the lake. Back on the main trail, the stiff ascent continues; hikers are aided by more steps and a handrail. Soon, overhanging ledges shelter the rugged trail. As the switchbacks tighten and the trail steepens, kids will need help and frequent words of encouragement. Handrails provide welcome assistance as the trail threads its way along the base of Canada Cliff with steep drop-offs at the trail's edge.

Soon, hikers begin the assault up segments of the sheer cliffs on iron ladders imbedded in the mountainside. After climbing a ten-rung ladder, you'll follow the trail as it snakes along the base of the next section of the cliff and switches right, now traveling precariously close to the edge to eventually reach an eighteen-rung ladder. Above this ladder, a steel cable aids hikers up the continued steep ascent. Finally, fourteen- and fifteen-rung ladders bring you to a high plateau at the crest of Canada Cliff and to a junction with the Canada Ridge Trail, 0.5 mile from the start. While the kids take a well-deserved breather, adults can enjoy the impressive view of Acadia's eastern mountains, notably Norumbega and Cadillac (Hike 81).

As the Canada Ridge Trail heads left (south), you head right (north) to the conclusion of the Canada Ridge Trail 100 yards farther at a four-way junction. Turn right onto the Beech Cliff Trail to begin the loop that circles the top of Beech Cliff. The views from the baldface over Echo Lake are among the best Acadia has to offer. As the trail winds in and out of sparse woods over the next 0.2 mile, kids can take turns listing the sounds they hear: noises from the highway, a woodpecker tapping for insects, squirrels scampering along the ground. After the trail loops back to the south, it arrives at the height of the land where far-reaching views unfold to the south over Southwest Harbor and the Atlantic Ocean. Shortly, you'll complete the loop and return to the four-way intersection.

Follow the right-hand trail for 0.6 mile to the Beech Mountain parking area; so far, you have hiked a spectacular 1.4 miles. (Even if you have opted to park a second vehicle here, the Beech Mountain summit is just 0.6 mile from the parking area and well worth the trip.) At the northern edge of the parking lot, head back into the woods on the Beech Mountain Trail. Can the kids find any signs of the white-tailed deer that live here? In spring, they can look for tracks in the mud; in fall, they can try to find marks on slender trees where bucks have rubbed the protective covering off their mature antlers.

After a short descent, head left at an intersection where a stream rushes past on the right. (This section of the loop leads more quickly—and steeply—to the summit.) The familiar pattern of passing through spruce woods to arrive on exposed rock continues. As you crest the summit across a massive expanse of baldface, have the kids look for the fire tower to the south. The Beech Mountain summit is the high point on the ridge that separates Long Pond from Echo Lake on the more remote western side of Mount Desert Island, and the panoramas from the tower are every bit as splendid as you would expect. If you're hiking in spring or early fall, have the kids watch through their binoculars for hawks on the hunt.

Locate the Beech Mountain Trail just north of the tower and follow the left-hand branch to continue the loop, guided by signs to the West Ridge Trail and the Beech Mountain parking area, 0.7 mile away. Just beyond an outhouse, the trail emerges onto open ledge with delightful western views of Long Pond. Here, at a junction, the West Ridge Trail splits left. You remain on the Beech Mountain Trail, descending gradually on a wide path with frequent overlooks. At 0.6 mile from the summit, the two ends of the Beech Mountain Trail loop converge. Continue straight for the 0.1 mile to your second vehicle or retrace your steps over Beech Cliff and Canada Cliff to enjoy freshwater swimming at Echo Lake (with lifeguard supervision) at the end of the hike.

NATIONAL PARK STATUS

Preserved land on Mount Desert Island was designated as a national park in 1919. This made it the first national park to be established east of the Mississippi River.

 WONDERLAND

BEFORE YOU GO
Map USGS Bass Harbor
Current Conditions Acadia National Park (207) 288-3338
Moderate entrance fee

ABOUT THE HIKE
Day hike
Easy for children
Year-round
1.3 miles, round trip
Hiking time 1 hour
High point/elevation gain
35 feet, 60 feet
Trail accessible, though assistance may be needed in places

GETTING THERE
- From the junction of ME-3, ME-102, and ME-198 (just beyond the causeway leading to Mount Desert Island), head south on ME-102 and ME-198 to Southwest Harbor.
- In 4.2 miles, as ME-198 bears left (south), continue straight on ME-102.
- In another 7.4 miles in Southwest Harbor, turn left (south) onto ME-102A.
- Drive 4 miles and park off the road on the left.

ON THE TRAIL
Even folks confined to wheelchairs or youngsters exploring from strollers will be able to enjoy all that Wonderland has to offer because the

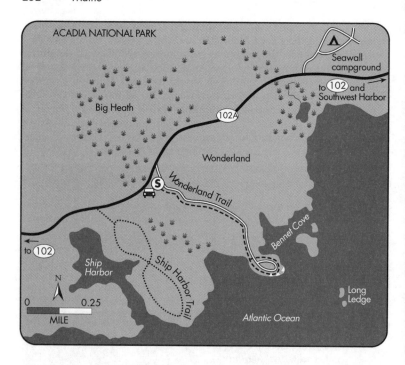

hiking route follows an old gravel road (not open to vehicles). The road winds through a spruce forest punctuated with bogs to arrive at a rocky coastline. Bikinis and beach volleyball have no place here; this is a true Maine seashore. The kids will delight in scaling the massive flattened chunks of ledge that line the beach. You may decide to extend the hike to join the Ship Harbor Trail farther along the beach.

A footpath leads from the southeastern side of the parking area and, in 20 yards, turns right as a gravel road merges from the left. The road is dusty and dry, but in the forest to each side are lush, spongy peat bogs. The trail winds easily, generally southward, through the bog areas and spruce forest. Spruce trees are common on Mount Desert Island because the meager soil adequately serves their shallow root systems. Can the kids find any spiderwebs hanging from the spruces' barren lower branches? Webs are especially easy to find after a rain shower or in the early morning when they are covered with dew.

Who will be the first to see the ocean? At 0.4 mile, the road splits at the bottom of its loop. You will return via the left-hand path; for now, go straight to arrive quickly at a rocky point that juts into the Atlantic Ocean, sheltering Bennet Cove to the northeast. Stop for a snack or to drink in the sights of the seashore, settling among the giant slabs of wave-worn rocks. Watch for shorebirds feeding when the tide is out and, on misty days, listen for the distant moan of foghorns.

In the tide pools—miniature oceans, in a sense—kids can look for tiny fish. Hungry gulls, rainstorms that dilute the pool water's salt concentration, and the harsh sun that often overheats the shallow water combine to make life difficult for these tide-pool dwellers. Remind the kids that if they pick up a sea creature to get a closer look, they should return it to the exact spot where they found it after inspection. Why isn't there a sandy beach here? For a sandy beach to occur, there must be a shoreline that does not rise too steeply, a source of sand to cover the beach, and something (like waves) to move the sand onto the shore. Wonderland's rocky shoreline obviously does not meet all these criteria.

To complete the 1.3-mile hike, finish the loop around the peninsula, keeping Bennet Cove on your right. At the trail junction, turn right and return to your vehicle the way you came. (To extend the hike, follow the shore in a westerly direction and in 0.6 mile you will arrive at the trail that winds along Ship Harbor and soon returns you to ME-102A. Turn right on 102A and walk 0.25 mile to your vehicle for a 3-mile total hike.)

Resting on rocks that border the shore at Wonderland

SOUTH BUBBLE

ABOUT THE HIKE
Day hike
Moderate for children
April–October
2 miles, loop
Hiking time 1.5 hours
High point/elevation gain
768 feet, 700 feet
Some accessible parking in
north lower lot of Jordan Pond
area

GETTING THERE

- From the Acadia National Park Visitor Center in Hulls Cove off ME-3, head south on Park Loop Road (a vehicle fee is required or you may opt to take a park bus).
- In 3 miles, continue straight at an intersection following a sign to Cadillac Mountain.
- In another 3 miles, turn right into a parking area for Bubble Rock.
- This parking area is 2.5 miles beyond the Cadillac Mountain Auto Road and about 1 mile beyond the parking area for Bubble Pond.

ON THE TRAIL

A hike to South Bubble, one of the two rounded hills of pink granite that rise over the northern end of Jordan Pond, is a relatively short, easy hike offering several points of interest for kids. They'll love circling the elephant-size glacial boulder that rests on the eastern slope of the Bubble, and they'll enjoy descending the steep rock slide to the edge of Jordan Pond. The older folks will appreciate the minimal effort required to reach this centrally located summit. Its commanding views of the surrounding peaks rival the vistas from any Acadia mountaintop.

On the western side of the parking lot, you'll find the trailhead at a sign for the paths to the North and South Bubbles, each 0.5 mile away. Head into the deciduous forest on a gradual ascent to an intersection with a wide woods road. Bear right and soon join a carriage road where a trail sign indicates that Bubble Mountain is 0.3 mile straight ahead. Go straight (northwest) on the carriage road as the woods road continues to the right. At 0.15 mile, the trail turns left (west) to climb moderately on terraced log and stone steps.

At an intersection 0.25 mile from the start, continue straight (west) on a significant grade to an intersection with the North Bubble Trail, 0.1 mile later. Here, turn left (southeast) toward South Bubble, following infrequent blue blazes. Can the kids find six erratic trailside boulders along this stretch? To the west you'll see the sheer Jordan Cliffs on Penobscot Mountain.

After sweeping over a section of baldface, the trail reaches the 768-foot summit of South Bubble, marked by a large stone cairn. From here, the kids can identify North Bubble, Eagle Lake, Jordan Pond, Penobscot and Cadillac Mountains, the Cranberry Isles, and the Atlantic Ocean. They can also try to spot a bald eagle, looking for its characteristic dark body, white head and tail, and yellow beak. Early colonists named this bird the bald eagle because *bald* originally meant "marked with white" and referred to the bird's white head.

Turning left at the cairn, descend eastward on a side trail to the dramatic Bubble Rock, precariously perched on the edge of the precipitous ridge. (Kids can examine the rock up close but should exercise caution on the ledges below the rock.) A glacier deposited this erratic boulder on South Bubble's eastern side 10,000 to 15,000 years ago. Kids, how do geologists know that this boulder was brought here by a glacier? (They discovered that its crystals differ in size and makeup from the solid rock underlying all the loose soil on the island.)

Return to the cairn and follow the exposed eastern ridge of South Bubble along blue blazes, heading south on a gradual descent. As the trail drops sharply, stay to the left (east) to avoid straying off the route.

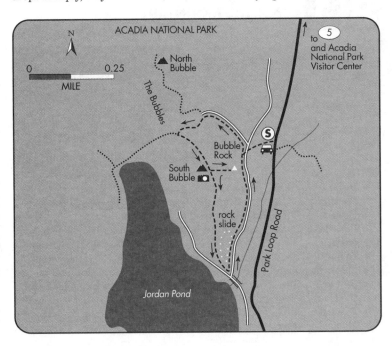

Magnificent panoramas of Jordan Pond, the Gulf of Maine, and the Atlantic Ocean rise to meet you. The trail winds down steeply over ledge with several challenging spots where kids will need a hand. Now heading south toward Jordan Pond, the blazes guide hikers down a massive (stable) rock slide into a young birch and evergreen forest to the edge of Jordan Pond. Here, 0.4 mile from the South Bubble summit, turn left onto a carriage road. As you follow along the water's edge, the kids may be able to hear some of Acadia's more common frogs, which are most vocal in early summer: Listen for the high-pitched whistle of the spring peeper, the deep rumbling of the bullfrog, or the low, snoring sounds of the pickerel frog.

Continue in an easterly direction, guided by the trail marker for the Bubbles parking area and Eagle Lake. At the pond's northeastern corner, as a bridge stretches over a brook to the right, you turn left (north) on an old carriage road on a gradual ascent, curling around the base of South Bubble. Along this wide path are more large glacial erratics for the kids to count. In 0.2 mile, ignore the right-hand side trail to the Bubbles parking lot and continue straight on the carriage road following the sign to Eagle Lake. In another 0.2 mile, at an intersection with another carriage road, turn right, then quickly left to arrive shortly at your vehicle.

 CADILLAC MOUNTAIN

BEFORE YOU GO
Maps USGS Seal Harbor and Southwest Harbor
Current Conditions Acadia National Park (207) 288-3338
Moderate entrance fee

ABOUT THE HIKE
Day hike
Moderate for children
April–November
4.4 miles, round trip
Hiking time 3 hours
High point/elevation gain
1530 feet, 1450 feet

GETTING THERE

- From the Acadia National Park Visitor Center in Hulls Cove off ME-3, head south on Park Loop Road (a vehicle fee is required or you may opt to take a park bus).
- In 3 miles, turn left onto the one-way section of Park Loop Road following a sign to Sand Beach. (Ignore the sign to Cadillac Mountain that points straight ahead at this intersection; this leads to the Cadillac Mountain Auto Road.)
- Drive 0.6 mile to find shoulder parking on the left. Parking is also allowed in the right-hand lane.

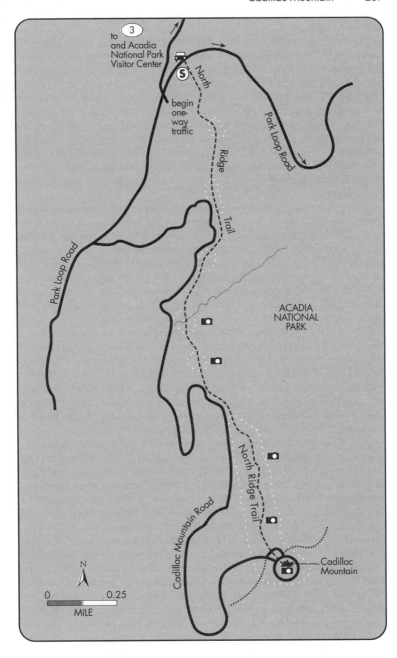

ON THE TRAIL

No monotonous woods-walking for the kids on this hike! Dramatic views over Bar Harbor will demand everyone's attention as you follow the North Ridge Trail on its gradual climb up Cadillac's nearly barren northern side. At the summit, the splendid 360-degree view of the island is a real-life version of the view you had at the visitor center when you examined the expansive relief map. Because an auto road also travels to the top, the summit is geared to tourists (in season), with a gift shop and restrooms. Take on Mount Desert's highest peak after lunch, with the sun over your shoulder, to maximize the view across Bar Harbor to the Atlantic. Or visit as the sun rises: Cadillac Mountain is said to be the first place on the eastern seaboard to greet the morning sun between October 6 and March 7.

A log post marks the North Ridge trailhead on the right-hand side of Park Loop Road. According to the sign, the Cadillac summit is 2.2 miles away. The trail, marked with blue blazes and cairns, reveals its true character from the start as it steadily works its way toward the mountaintop with long stretches along exposed granite baldface punctuated by short trips through pockets of birch and spruce trees. See whether the kids can tell a red spruce from a white one. (The red spruce has needles that are dark green; the needles of the white spruce are light green and have a skunky smell when they are crushed.)

Though the trail offers little to shelter hikers from the elements, it also offers little to block impressive panoramas toward Bar Harbor. At 0.2 mile, as the trail plateaus, look to the right (west) for a good view of Eagle Lake and straight ahead for your first view of the Cadillac Mountain summit. At 0.2 mile farther, you will have distant views to the open Atlantic Ocean. The trail passes to the left of and below the auto road at the 0.5-mile mark and weaves through a sweet-smelling spruce forest at 0.8 mile, shortly before a sag and a small stream crossing.

At 1 mile, the trail climbs granite steps through a young birch forest toward an exposed section. Tell the kids to look back to see where the trail and roadway almost met. At the 1.3- and 1.7-mile marks, the trail again flirts with the auto road. Soon the trail sweeps across a large expanse of baldface with cairns to guide the way. Kids can plod like an elephant from the first cairn to the second, gallop like a horse from the second to the third, and so on. As the trail works its way southward, you will proceed through more frequent clusters of spruce and regain your westerly views.

The trail merges with the auto road at 2 miles, turns left, and follows this road another 0.2 mile to the summit along a stone sidewalk. It's hard to believe that the views from the peak could surpass those from the trail, but you'll have to agree they do. Glass-encased maps point to interesting landmarks and offer historical information. When you are done surveying the island, Frenchman Bay, and the Atlantic from 1530 feet, return the way you came.

82 GORHAM MOUNTAIN

BEFORE YOU GO
Map USGS Seal Harbor
Current Conditions Acadia
National Park (207) 288-3338
Moderate entrance fee

ABOUT THE HIKE
Day hike
Moderate for children
April–October
4 miles, loop
Hiking time 3.5 hours
High point/elevation gain
525 feet, 750 feet

GETTING THERE

- From the Acadia National Park Visitor Center in Hulls Cove off ME-3, drive south on Park Loop Road (a vehicle fee is required or you may opt to take a park bus).
- In 3 miles, turn left onto the one-way section of Park Loop Road and follow a sign to Sand Beach.
- In another 6 miles (0.3 mile past the toll booth), continue past the turnoff into the parking areas for Sand Beach and the Ocean Trail.
- Drive another 1 mile on Park Loop Road (Ocean Drive).
- Turn right into the parking area for the Gorham Mountain Trail.

ON THE TRAIL

An ancient sea cave and overhanging cliffs, dramatic views, a peaceful pond. . . . This delightful hike, well marked with frequent signs, is best suited for kids with endurance and some hiking experience. Younger children can hike to the turnaround point and back, taking in the rock tunnel, cliffs, and sea cave, for a total hike of 1 mile. The bulk of Acadia's visitors converge on the island in July and August (and this hike is a popular one), so if you want to have the woods to yourself, come in early summer or fall.

At the southern end of the parking area, look for the Gorham Mountain trailhead, announced on a log signpost. Head over exposed granite to an intersection at 0.1 mile; bear right as an unused trail continues straight. Follow the path as it curves northward through an area crowded with pitch pines. Point out to children the relatively young age of this forest. Much of the area was burned in the 1947 fire that raged for nine days on the island, destroying hundreds of palatial summer homes and the vegetation on 17,000 acres. By studying patterns of plant growth here after the fire, biologists were able to learn about the positive consequences of such a blaze. Today, carefully managed fires are used to enhance the environment by, for example, perpetuating open meadows and encouraging the propagation of species that flourish in fire-scarred soil.

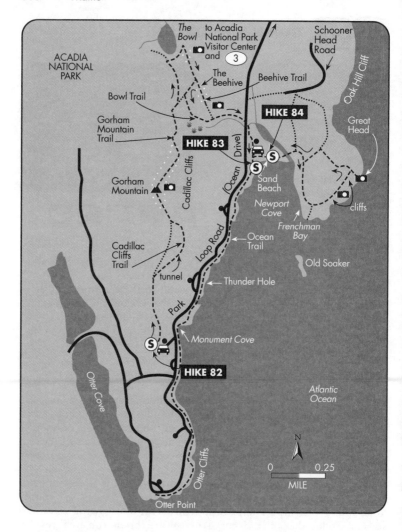

As the Gorham Mountain Trail and the Cadillac Cliffs Trail intersect 0.3 mile from the start, turn right onto the Cadillac Cliffs Trail. The path, rising gradually, leads hikers through a rock "squeezer" to snake along the base of the massive, overhanging Cadillac Cliffs. Soon, the kids will lead the way through a 10-foot-long tunnel created when a portion of the overhanging ledges broke off. Send the kids ahead to find the formidable cave on the left, 0.5 mile from the start. Although adults must enter and exit through the cave's large mouth, little hikers will be able to exit 15 feet up the trail (north) through a small hole. Can any of the children find the smooth boulder at the back of the cave that was worn by long-ago waves? Kids will be amazed to learn that this cave—now 200 feet above sea level, thanks to the work of glaciers—once sat at the edge of the ocean.

The trail continues to the end of the cliffs where a steel bar handhold assists hikers on a steep ascent. At 0.7 mile, as the Cadillac Cliffs Trail rejoins the Gorham Mountain Trail, turn right. The Gorham Mountain Trail ascends moderately for another 0.1 mile to an exposed mountain ridge where the views are almost as extensive as those from the summit of Cadillac Mountain (Hike 81), the island's highest peak.

Just over 1 mile from the start, kids can look for the short, wooden cross that marks the Gorham summit at 525 feet. Continue due north over the mountain, following cairns on the generally exposed baldface. At 1.3 miles, the trail winds down off the eastern side of the baldface, then dives into deciduous woods, reaching a damp sag, then tracking over rolling terrain for the next 0.25 mile. A stake marks a junction at 1.7 miles. (To the right, Park Loop Road is 0.6 mile away.) Continue straight (northwest) on a moderate ascent for another 0.2 mile to The Bowl, a pristine pond sheltered by the surrounding high hills. Turn right and follow along the southeastern bank of The Bowl, heading toward The Beehive.

Soon after the trail turns eastward over ledge on a moderate ascent, it arrives on open baldface with fine views of Champlain Mountain to the north, Gorham Mountain to the south, and the Atlantic Ocean to the southeast. At the crest, the trail turns left, dips into a sag, and meets a trail coming in from the right. Continue straight to the top of The Beehive's high ledges for more dramatic island views. After the kids grab a snack to maintain their energy, return to the trail junction in the sag and begin a moderate descent on the Bowl Trail. In 0.2 mile, the trail reaches another sag and trail junction. Turn left toward Park Loop Road, 0.5 mile away, on a rocky trail through a young birch forest.

Although many of Acadia's creatures are primarily nocturnal, the gray and red squirrels that are common to the area are active during the day. See if the kids can catch sight of a squirrel or a squirrel's home. These animals live in hollow trees or haphazard nests at least 30 feet above the ground. At a trail junction 2.8 miles from the start (where the Beehive Trail heads left), continue straight, crossing a boulder field, to reach Park Loop Road in 0.1 mile. Turn right and cross the road. In 100 yards, you'll arrive at the parking area for Sand Beach and the Ocean Trail. Hike the final mile along the Ocean Trail back to your vehicle.

If you had to pick an Acadia favorite, wouldn't this be it?

83 OCEAN TRAIL

BEFORE YOU GO
Map USGS Seal Harbor
Current Conditions Acadia
National Park (207) 288-3338
Moderate entrance fee

ABOUT THE HIKE
- Day hike
Easy for children
Year-round
3.6 miles, round trip
Hiking time 3 hours
High point/elevation gain
60 feet, 100 feet
Accessible restrooms and ramp
near Thunder Hole

GETTING THERE

- From the Acadia National Park Visitor Center in Hulls Cove off ME-3, drive south on Park Loop Road (a vehicle fee is required or you may opt to take a park bus).
- In 3 miles, turn left onto the one-way section of Park Loop Road (Ocean Drive) following a sign to Sand Beach.
- In another 6 miles (0.3 mile past the toll booth), turn left into the parking areas for Sand Beach and the Ocean Trail.
- The Ocean Trail parking area is to the right and above the Sand Beach parking area.

ON THE TRAIL

Ocean Trail, a level path that snakes along the coastline beside Park Loop Road, is Maine's version of the Cliff Walk of Newport, Rhode Island. Instead of Newport's architectural masterpieces, however, Mother Nature's handiwork is on display here. Your camera will capture the rock climbers at Otter Cliffs and the bold gulls that settle within arm's reach, but only a tape recorder will do at Thunder Hole, where the ferocious booms in the chasm mingle with the distant clang of bell buoys. All members of the family will enjoy this close-up look at the dramatic boundary between the ocean and the land.

The hike on the Ocean Trail (also called the Shore Trail) begins on a wide path at the southern end of the parking area where a log signpost lists the distances to points of interest: Thunder Hole, 0.6 mile; Otter Cliffs, 1.5 miles; Otter Point, 1.8 miles. With only a few diversions, the trail travels beside Park Loop Road for its entire distance, providing hikers with lovely ocean views from a considerable height. The kids can watch lobster boats chugging through the fields of brightly colored buoys. At 0.2 mile, a side trail on the left leads to an overlook of Newport Cove and Great Head (Hike 84). Walk another 0.4 mile to a flight of stairs on the left that ends abruptly at Thunder Hole, a long, deep

Safe behind a sturdy fence, visitors peer into Thunder Hole.

chasm well guarded by a sturdy fence. Incoming waves crash into the back of the cavern, compressing pockets of trapped air to cause a deep boom that sounds like thunder. For the most dramatic sound effects, visit at midtide rising.

Beyond Thunder Hole, the trail veers left away from the road under a canopy of spruce, then quickly rejoins the auto road. Staghorn sumac borders the path; have the kids identify it by feeling its fuzzy branches. Poison ivy also grows nearby—teach the kids to identify that by sight, not touch! Ask your young companions to describe how the plant life along this trail differs from that along the inland trails. Explain that the thin soil combined with the ceaseless ocean winds and salt spray discourages the growth of all but the hardiest of plants. Those that survive hover close to the ground and have thicker, more durable surfaces and leaves.

Soon, you will catch a glimpse of Monument Cove on the left with its spectacular boulder beach. How and why does this beach differ from its neighbor, Sand Beach? As you pass through a spruce forest at 1.2 miles, point out the old man's beard, the lichen that hangs like Spanish moss from the branches. Numerous side trails split off to the left at the 1.5-mile mark leading to the Otter Cliffs. Rock climbers often scale these sheer walls, dangling up to 50 feet above the churning ocean with belayers at the top to protect them. Can the kids see any ducks or cormorants diving into the water for small fish?

The trail continues to its conclusion at Otter Point, 0.3 mile later, where the shore is more accessible. Children can explore the shallow tide pools, examining the varieties of seaweed that cling to the rocks. Does seaweed have roots? No, it has something called a *holdfast* that helps it adhere to rocks or shells. Look for dulse, a coarse, reddish brown plant that is edible. Lay some on the rocks to dry and then take a bite! Maybe you'll find some colander, a brown, wide-bladed plant dotted with holes. (Why do you think it is called "colander"?) Kelp, another common seaweed found here, has a long, flat blade with a tail-like stem that can be up to 25 feet long!

When you're ready, return along Ocean Trail the way you came.

84 GREAT HEAD

BEFORE YOU GO
Map USGS Seal Harbor
Current Conditions Acadia National Park (207) 288-3338
Moderate entrance fee

ABOUT THE HIKE
Day hike
Easy for children
April–October
1.5 mile, loop
Hiking time 1.5 hours
High point/elevation gain
160 feet, 200 feet

GETTING THERE

■ From the Acadia National Park Visitor Center in Hulls Cove off ME-3, drive south on Park Loop Road (a vehicle fee is required or you may opt to take a park bus).

■ In 3 miles, turn left onto the one-way section of Park Loop Road following a sign to Sand Beach.

- In another 6 miles (0.3 mile past the toll booth), turn left into the parking areas for Sand Beach and the Ocean Trail. Continue past the Ocean Trail parking area and park in the Sand Beach parking area.

ON THE TRAIL

Great Head epitomizes what most Acadia fans love about this park; here, the mountains reach out to meet the ocean. The cliffs that rise over the rocky shoreline provide a unique look at some of the best scenery Acadia has to offer. Kids will delight in the distant rumbling of Thunder Hole and the short-range views of the nearby beach (Acadia's only sandy beach and one of the few sandy beaches on this section of the Maine coast). This relatively easy and tremendously rewarding walk will appeal to kids of all ages and ability levels. Summer visitors can enjoy a posthike swim with lifeguard supervision at Sand Beach.

From the parking area, descend to Sand Beach by way of the stairs and cross the beach to its easternmost point with Newport Cove on your right. If the kids brought a magnifying glass, have them examine the range of colors in a handful of sand: They'll see tiny pieces of blue mussel shells, green bits of the sea urchin's shell (called a *test*), and pink potassium feldspar crystals. Cross the lagoon behind Sand Beach and have the kids find the log post marking the Great Head trailhead. Head into a spruce forest up a flight of rocky steps. At the top of the slope, turn right onto a grassy trail following blue blazing. Soon, the trail becomes hard-packed and then rocky as it sweeps along the top of the ridge through a deciduous forest. Who can imitate the sound of the waves exploding on the rocks below? The trail switches back left over rock ledge to arrive at the height of the land and then marches southward.

Shortly, at a junction 0.3 mile from the start, a trail splits to the left (east) as you continue straight. You will complete a loop and rejoin the trail here. Look west to see beyond Newport Cove and Sand Beach to The Beehive and Champlain Mountain. The path continues on a gradual descent along the ridge rising 100 feet above Frenchman Bay. From the southern tip of the Great Head peninsula, look for Old Soaker, a rocky island (or shatter zone) where the schooner *Tay* was destroyed in 1911. Today, the wind and waves sometimes expose pieces of the wrecked ship on Sand Beach. As the trail swings along Great Head's southern point, brave and surefooted children can carefully scramble closer to the water's edge.

The path curls north and sweeps across exposed rock guided by cairns with precipitous cliffs on the right. After descending into a wet sag, it arrives on another section of open baldface—the summit of Great Head—with splendid views. Here, at 0.7 mile, the cliffs plummet 100 feet to the choppy surf below. To the north, you can see Champlain Mountain. Look to the northwest for The Beehive, east across Frenchman Bay to the

A hiker pauses to look over Frenchman Bay from the sheer cliffs of Great Head.

Schoodic Peninsula (can you see Egg Rock Lighthouse?), southwest for the Otter Cliffs. Point out to the kids that the pine trees are *wind-flagged,* that is, the branches appear to grow on just one side of the trunk because of the action of the wind. Watch carefully for the cairns and paint blazes that will guide you left (northwest) back into the woods. At 1 mile, turn left (west) at a trail junction, following the sign to Sand Beach as the right-hand (northern) trail heads for Schooner Head Road.

The return trip begins on a rocky, gradual ascent where the trail quickly curls south on blue blazes, reaching a crest on exposed baldface with more dramatic ocean views. After following the level ridge top for 0.1 mile, the trail turns right (west) and shortly intersects with the section of trail traveled earlier, just above the switchbacks. Turn right and return to your vehicle.

BAR ISLAND

BEFORE YOU GO
Map USGS Bar Harbor
Current Conditions Acadia National Park (207) 288-3338
Moderate entrance fee

ABOUT THE HIKE
Day hike
Easy for children
Year-round
2 miles, round trip
Hiking time 1.5 hours
High point/elevation gain 100 feet, 150 feet

GETTING THERE

- From the junction of ME-233 and ME-3 in Bar Harbor, drive 0.1 mile on ME-3 West.
- Turn right onto Cottage Street following signs to the waterfront.
- In 0.3 mile, turn left onto Main Street.
- Travel another 0.1 mile to the intersection with West Street.
- Turn left and park along West Street.

ON THE TRAIL

The hike to Bar Island, a satisfying short hike in a less crowded area of Acadia, will bring out the adventurous spirit in every member of the family. Hikers cross over to the island along a sandbar at low tide, head to the eastern tip of the island for an oceanside picnic, and return before the rising water has covered the sandbar (at high tide, to a depth of 6 to 8 feet!). Put an older child (with adult supervision) in charge of keeping track of the time and tide schedule. If you would like more time to explore, plan a private, extended stay on Bar Island between twice-daily low tides.

Check the tide schedule (at the Acadia National Park Visitor Center or the Bar Harbor Chamber of Commerce information station) to confirm that the sandbar is exposed and the tide is receding. Walk down Main Street to the tidal bar and head across toward the island. Distances are often deceiving: Can the kids guess the distance from the mainland to the island? (0.4 mile.) Though the sandbar (technically, a *tombolo*: a sand or gravel bar connecting an island with the mainland or another island) may be spongy in places, it won't be hard for the kids to avoid wet feet. Bare feet won't do because in places the sandbar is coated with sharp pieces of shells, due in large part to the gulls. Watch as they fly up and drop mussels or other creatures onto the hard surface below in attempts to shatter the shells. The kids will be tempted to comb the sand for beach treasures now, but urge them to wait until the return trip when parents will feel less anxious about the impending high tide. Kids may want to poke a stick into the ground at water's edge to see how high the tide will rise while they are hiking.

Once you have reached the island, head through a gate and into the woods, where you'll begin a gradual climb on a wide gravel road. In 0.15 mile (all mileages are from the start of the island walk), the road passes along the right side of a meadow fringed by deciduous, pine, and spruce trees. Here, point out to the kids the cropped view of Mount Desert Island's higher peaks. In 0.25 mile, the gravel road continues straight at a sign indicating a private residence. You turn left onto a grassy foot trail

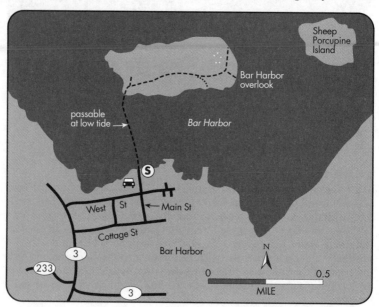

to Bar Harbor Overlook. Watch for an old foundation off the trail to the right. Remind the kids that where there is a cellar hole, there is often an old well nearby that may no longer be covered.

At 0.4 mile, a side trail swings right to an overlook where hikers can survey tranquil Bar Harbor. Back on the main trail, the path curls left, sidestepping a high ledge and a rock slide on the left. As you approach the island's eastern shore, the path ends in disarray at the rocky beach bordered by a thin ribbon of evergreens. Pick a resting spot from among the large flat boulders rimming the shore. Enjoy a snack or picnic lunch. With one eye on your watch, reverse direction and hike back to your vehicle. (As you cross the tombolo, look for driftwood, gull feathers, and such varieties of common shells as periwinkle, whelk, clam, and mussel.)

Note: No camping or fires allowed on Bar Island.

IMPORTANT ADDRESSES AND PHONE NUMBERS

GENERAL
Appalachian Mountain Club
5 Joy Street
Boston, MA 02108
Phone: (617) 523-0636
Fax: (617) 523-0722
Email: info@amcinfo.org
Website: *www.outdoors.org*
Publishes *AMC White Mountain Guide, AMC Guide to Mount Desert Island and Acadia National Park, AMC Guide to Mount Washington and the Presidential Range,* and *AMC Maine Mountain Guide.* Develops and maintains trails and facilities, sponsors outings.

Appalachian Trail Conference
P.O. Box 807
Harpers Ferry, WV 25425
Phone: (304) 535-6331
Fax: (304) 535-2667
Email: info@atconf.org
Website: *www.appalachiantrail.org*
Publishes *Guide to the Appalachian Trail in New Hampshire and Vermont.* Coordinates those who maintain the Appalachian Trail.

DeLorme Mapping
2 DeLorme Drive
P.O. Box 298
Yarmouth, ME 04096
Phone: (207) 846-7000
Website: *www.delorme.com*
Publishes an *Atlas & Gazetteer* for Vermont, New Hampshire, and Maine with state information and detailed local maps.

Leave No Trace Center for Outdoor Ethics
P.O. Box 997
Boulder, CO 80306
Phone: (800) 332-4100 or (303) 442-8222
Website: *www.lnt.org*
Provides information and training on Leave No Trace practices and principles, as well as relevant newsletters, publications, and mail-order items.

New England Trail Conference
33 Knollwood Drive
East Longmeadow, MA 01028
Website: *www.wapack.org / netrails*
Publishes *Hiking Trails of New England*. Provides information about trail and shelter conditions throughout New England.

U.S. Geological Survey Distribution Branch
Box 25286
Federal Center, Building 810
Denver, CO 80225
Phone: (888) ASK-USGS
Website: *www.usgs.gov*
Distributes USGS maps.

VERMONT

Ascutney Trails Association/Upper Valley Trails Alliance
1 Day Street
Windsor, VT 05089
Phone: (802) 674-9509
Email: twogirouxs@adelphia.net
Website: *www.uvtrails.org*
Publishes *Guide to the Trails of Ascutney Mountain*. Maintains the mountain's trails and shelters.

City of South Burlington Recreation Department
575 Dorset Street
South Burlington, VT 05403
Phone: (802) 846-4108
Fax: (802) 846-4101
Website: *www.south-burlington.com / recdept*

Green Mountain Club, Inc.
4711 Waterbury–Stowe Road
Waterbury Center, VT 05677
Phone: (802) 244-7037
Fax: (802) 244-5867
Email: gmc@greenmountainclub.org
Website: *www.greenmountainclub.org*
Publishes *Day Hiker's Guide to Vermont* and *Guide Book of the Long Trail*.

Green Mountain National Forest

Forest Supervisor
231 North Main Street
Rutland, VT 05701
Phone: (802) 747-6700
Website: *www.fs.fed.us/r9/gmfl/green_mountain/index.htm*
Publishes maps and guides of the national forest. Maintains trails,
recreational areas, and campgrounds.

Green Mountain National Forest, Manchester Ranger Station

2538 Depot Street
Manchester Center, VT 05255
Phone: (802) 362-2307

Green Mountain National Forest, Middlebury Ranger Station

1007 Route 7 South
Middlebury, VT 05753
Phone: (802) 388-4362

Green Mountain National Forest, Rochester Ranger Station

99 Ranger Road
Rochester, VT 05767
Phone: (802) 767-4261

Merck Forest and Farmland Center

P.O. Box 86, Route 315 Rupert Mountain Road
Rupert, VT 05768
Phone: (802) 394-7836
Website: *www.merckforest.org*

Mount Equinox, the Mountain

Phone: (802) 362-1114 or (802) 362-1115
Website: *www.equinoxmountain.com*

The Nature Conservancy of Vermont

27 State Street
Montpelier, VT 05602
Phone: (802) 229-4425
Fax: (802) 229-1347
Website: *www.nature.org/wherewework/northamerica/states/vermont*

Vermont Department of Forests, Parks, and Recreation

103 South Main Street
Waterbury, VT 05671
Phone: (802) 241-3655
Fax: (802) 244-1481
Website: *www.vtstateparks.com*
Publishes free trail maps, *Vermont State Parks and Forest Recreation Areas,* and *Vermont Guide to Primitive Camping on State Lands.* Maintains trails, campgrounds, and recreational areas in state parks and forests.

Vermont Travel Division

National Life Building, 6th Floor, Drawer 20
Montpelier, VT 05620
Phone: (802) 828-3676 or (800) VERMONT
Website: *www.travel-vermont.com*
Will send a copy of the *Vermont Official State Map and Touring Guide* upon request. This lists most of the state's public and private campgrounds.

Westmore Association Trail Committee

RFD 2
Orleans, VT 05860
Publishes free maps and guides of Lake Willoughby region trails. Maintains area trails.

Williams Outing Club

Williams College
Williamstown, MA 01267
Publishes trail guide and map of area trails. Maintains trails in northwestern Massachusetts and southwestern Vermont.

Woodstock Chamber of Commerce

P.O. Box 486
Woodstock, VT 05091
Phone: (802) 457-3555 or (888) 496-6378
Website: *www.woodstockvt.com*

NEW HAMPSHIRE

Appalachian Mountain Club

Pinkham Notch Visitor Center
P.O. Box 298, Route 16
Gorham, NH 03581
Phone: (603) 466-2727
Fax: (603) 466-2822
Website: *www.outdoors.org*
Provides general hiking information for the White Mountains region.

Appalachian Mountain Club Highland Center at Crawford Notch
Route 302
Bretton Woods, NH 03575
Phone: (603) 278-4453
Fax: (603) 278-4444
Website: *www.outdoors.org*

Beaver Brook Association
117 Ridge Road
Hollis, NH 03049
Phone: (603) 465-7787
Fax: (603) 465-9546
Website: *www.beaverbrook.org*

National Weather Service
Concord, NH 03302
Phone: (603) 225-5191
Broadcasts forecast for White Mountains region each morning.

Newfound Audubon Center, Paradise Point Nature Center and Wildlife Sanctuary
North Shore Road, P.O. Box 142
East Hebron, NH 03241
Phone: (603) 744-3516 or (603) 224-9909

New Hampshire Audubon Society
3 Silk Farm Road
Concord, NH 03301
Phone: (603) 224-9909
Fax: (603) 226-0902
Website: *www.nhaudubon.org*

New Hampshire Division of Forests and Lands
P.O. Box 1856
172 Pembroke Road
Concord, NH 03302-1856
Phone: (603) 271-2217
Website: *www.nhdfl.org*

New Hampshire Division of Parks and Recreation
P.O. Box 1856
172 Pembroke Road
Concord, NH 03302-1856
Phone: (603) 271-3556
Fax: (603) 271-2629
Website: *www.nhstateparks.org*

New Hampshire Division of Travel and Tourism
P.O. Box 1856
172 Pembroke Road
Concord, NH 03302-1856
Phone: (603) 271-2665
Fax: (603) 271-6784
Email: vistnh@dred.state.nh.us
Website: *www.visitnh.gov*
Provides information on state parks and park campgrounds.

Seacoast Science Center
570 Ocean Boulevard
Rye, NH 03870
Phone: (603) 436-8043
Fax: (603) 433-2235
Website: *www.seacoastsciencecenter.org*

Society for the Protection of New Hampshire Forests
54 Portsmouth Street
Concord, NH 03301
Phone: (603) 224-9945
Fax: (603) 228-0423
Email: info@spnhf.org
Website: *www.forestsociety.org*
Publishes *Trees and Shrubs of Northern New England.* Protects mountains, forests, and wetlands of the state and promotes conservation and wise forestry practices. Manages several properties including land on Mount Monadnock and in Kinsman Notch.

Squam Lakes Association
P.O. Box 204
Holderness, NH 03245
Phone: (603) 968-7336
Fax: (603) 968-7444
Website: *www.squamlakes.org*
Protects the Squam Lakes watershed and maintains over 50 miles of trails.

Town of Plymouth Chamber of Commerce
P.O. Box 65
Plymouth, NH 03264
Phone: (603) 536-1001
Fax: (603) 536-4017
Website: *www.plymouthnh.org*

White Mountain National Forest
Supervisor's Office
719 North Main Street
Laconia, NH 03246
Phone: (603) 528-8721
Fax: (603) 528-8722
Website: *www.fs.fed.us / r9 / forests / white_mountain*

White Mountain National Forest
Androscoggin Ranger District, Gorham Office
300 Glen Road
Gorham, NH 03581
Phone: (603) 466-2713

White Mountain National Forest
Evans Notch Information Center
18 Mayville Road
Bethel, ME 04217
Phone: (207) 824-2134

White Mountain National Forest
Pemigewasset Ranger District, Plymouth Office
1171 NH Route 175
Holderness, NH 03245
Phone: (603) 536-1315

White Mountain National Forest
Saco Ranger District
33 Kancamagus Highway
Conway, NH 03818
Phone: (603) 447-5448

MAINE
Acadia National Park
P.O. Box 177
Bar Harbor, ME 04609
Phone: (207) 288-3338
Fax: (207) 288-8813
Website: *www.nps.gov / acad*

Baxter State Park
64 Balsam Drive
Millinocket, ME 04462
Phone: (207) 723-5140
Website: *www.baxterstateparkauthority.com*

The Greater Lovell Land Trust
Box 181, 208 Main Street
Center Lovell, Maine 04016
Phone: (207) 925-1056
Website: *www.gllt.org*

Maine Appalachian Trail Club
P.O. Box 283
Augusta, ME 04332
Website: *www.matc.org*
Publishes *Guide to the Appalachian Trail in Maine.*

Maine Audubon Society
20 Gilsland Farm Road
Falmouth, ME 04105
Phone: (207) 781-2330
Fax: (207) 781-0974
Website: *www.maineaudubon.org*

Maine Bureau of Parks and Lands
22 State House Station
18 Elkins Lane
Augusta, ME 04333
Phone: (207) 287-3821
Fax: (207) 287-8111
Website: *www.maine.gov/doc/parks*

Maine Coast Heritage Trust
Bowdoin Mill, 1 Main Street, Suite 201
Topsham, ME 04086
Phone: (207) 729-7366
Fax: (207) 729-6863
Website: *www.mcht.org*
Statewide conservation organization.

Natural Resources Council of Maine
3 Wade Street
Augusta, ME 04330-6351
Phone: (800) 287-2345
Fax: (207) 622-4343
Website: *www.maineenvironment.org*
Nonprofit environmental group that protects and preserves Maine's
environment.

The Nature Conservancy
Fort Andross
14 Maine Street, Suite 401
Brunswick, ME 04011
Phone: (207) 729-5181
Website: *www.nature.org / wherewework / northamerica / states / maine / contact*
Protects lands in Maine and provides information to the preserves.

Wells National Estuarine Research Reserve at Laudholm Farm
342 Laudholm Farm Road
Wells, ME 04090
Phone: (207) 646-1555
Fax: (207) 646-2930
Website: *www.wellsreserve.org*

York Parks and Recreation Department
186 York Street
York, ME 03909
Phone: (207) 363-1040
Fax: (207) 351-2967
Website: *www.yorkmaine.org*
Provides information on Mount Agamenticus.

INDEX

ABOUT THE AUTHOR

Emily Kerr grew up hiking, camping, canoeing, and cross-country skiing with her family. She now shares her love of the outdoors with her husband, two sons, and her dog—her favorite and most reliable hiking buddies. A full-time mom and freelance writer, she lives with her family in Exeter, New Hampshire.

THE MOUNTAINEERS, founded in 1906, is a nonprofit outdoor activity and conservation club, whose mission is "to explore, study, preserve, and enjoy the natural beauty of the outdoors. . . ." Based in Seattle, Washington, the club is now the third-largest such organization in the United States, with seven branches throughout Washington State.

The Mountaineers sponsors both classes and year-round outdoor activities in the Pacific Northwest, which include hiking, mountain climbing, ski-touring, snowshoeing, bicycling, camping, kayaking, nature study, sailing, and adventure travel. The club's conservation division supports environmental causes through educational activities, sponsoring legislation, and presenting informational programs.

All club activities are led by skilled, experienced instructors, who are dedicated to promoting safe and responsible enjoyment and preservation of the outdoors.

If you would like to participate in these organized outdoor activities or the club's programs, consider a membership in The Mountaineers. For information and an application, write or call The Mountaineers, Club Headquarters, 300 Third Avenue West, Seattle, WA 98119; 206-284-6310. You can also visit the club's website at www.mountaineers.org or contact The Mountaineers via email at clubmail@mountaineers.org.

The Mountaineers Books, an active, nonprofit publishing program of the club, produces guidebooks, instructional texts, historical works, natural history guides, and works on environmental conservation. All books produced by The Mountaineers Books fulfill the club's mission.

Send or call for our catalog of more than 500 outdoor titles:

The Mountaineers Books
1001 SW Klickitat Way, Suite 201
Seattle, WA 98134
800-553-4453
mbooks@mountaineersbooks.org
www.mountaineersbooks.org

The Mountaineers Books is proud to be a corporate sponsor of The Leave No Trace Center for Outdoor Ethics, whose mission is to promote and inspire responsible outdoor recreation through education, research, and partnerships. The Leave No Trace program is focused specifically on human-powered (nonmotorized) recreation.

Leave No Trace strives to educate visitors about the nature of their recreational impacts, as well as offer techniques to prevent and minimize such impacts. Leave No Trace is best understood as an educational and ethical program, not as a set of rules and regulations.

For more information, visit *www.LNT.org,* or call 800-332-4100.

OTHER TITLES YOU MIGHT ENJOY FROM THE MOUNTAINEERS BOOKS

Best Hikes with Kids:
Connecticut, Massachusetts, & Rhode Island
Cynthia Copeland, Thomas Lewis, and Emily Kerr
More fun for little feet

Best Hikes with Dogs:
New Hampshire and Vermont
Lisa Densmore
Where to hike with Fido—all
trails recommended as dog safe and dog fun!

Loop Hikes:
New Hampshire's White
Mountains to the Maine Coast
Jeff Romano
It's new scenery every step of the way with
the only guide dedicated to loop hikes in New
Hampshire and Maine

Tent and Car Camper's Handbook
Advice for Families & First-Timers
Buck Tilton, Kristin Hostetter
The lowdown on car and tent camping—no
experience necessary

The Don't Die Out There Deck
Christopher Van Tilburg, M.D.
A playing card deck that puts survival
tips in the palm of your hands

Outdoors Online: The Internet Guide
to Everything Wild & Green
Erika Dillman
Everything you wanted to know about the
outdoors but couldn't find it on the web

The Mountaineers Books has more than
500 outdoor recreation titles in print.
Receive a free catalog at
www.mountaineersbooks.org.